Charity and Condescension

Charity & Condescension

Victorian Literature and the Dilemmas of Philanthropy

DANIEL SIEGEL

Ohio University Press • Athens

Ohio University Press, Athens, Ohio 45701
ohioswallow.com

Printed in the United States of America
Ohio University Press books are printed on acid-free paper ∞ ™

First paperback printing in 2022
Paperback ISBN: 978-0-8214-2519-0

Library of Congress Cataloging-in-Publication Data available upon request.
Siegel, Daniel, 1972-
Charity and condescension : Victorian literature and the dilemmas of philanthropy / Daniel Siegel.
p. cm.
Includes bibliographical references and index.
ISBN 978-0-8214-1991-5 (hc : alk. paper) -- ISBN 978-0-8214-4407-8 (electronic)
1. English fiction--19th century--History and criticism. 2. Charity in literature. 3. Social values in literature.
4. Literature and society--England--History--19th century. I. Title.
PR830.C475S53 2012
820.9'355--dc23

2011053349

for my parents

Contents

Acknowledgments

For her invaluable help with this book, my first and warmest thanks go to Karen Chase, my friend and advisor at the University of Virginia. Though the most incisive of readers, Karen has affirmed me automatically, even unreasonably, whenever my confidence was in short supply; she has liked my work when I have not. I also want to express my deep gratitude to Stephen Arata, Alison Booth, Michael Levenson, and Herbert Tucker, who illuminated the Victorians for me with bright lights of differing hues, and all of whom assisted this writing profoundly.

It is a pleasure to acknowledge my debt to the friends, colleagues, and students at the University of Virginia and the University of Alabama at Birmingham who have helped me bring this book to completion. I have said it before: no one has friends as smart as mine. I owe particular thanks to Rebecca Bach, Peter Bellis, Corey Brady, Flowers Braswell, Alison Chapman, Scott Cohen, Jenny Geer, Randa Graves, Kyle Grimes, Ann Hoff, Justin Humphreys, Michael Kightley, Sue Kim, Marilyn Kurata, Bruce McComiskey, Ana Mitric, Derek Nystrom, Ken Parille, John Picker, Kent Puckett, Pat Rippetoe, Cynthia Ryan, Raphael Shargel, Gale Temple, and Jacquie Wood—people who have wonderfully supported me by reading these pages, offering professional guidance, and challenging my ideas about Victorian life and literature.

At Ohio University Press, Joe McLaughlin has been generous with his advice and enthusiasm, and I thank him for both. I am grateful to Kevin Haworth for steering me so efficiently through the publication process and to Nancy Basmajian and Sally Bennett for their incredibly careful and attentive editing. I would also like to thank the two external readers, whose comments greatly helped me strengthen the book where it was weakest.

Parts of this book have appeared previously in print. Chapter 1 was published as "Help Wanting: The Exhaustion of a Dickensian Ideal," *Dickens Studies Annual* 32 (2002): 195–232, copyright ©2002 by AMS Press, Inc., all rights reserved. A version of chapter 2 was published as "Preacher's Vigil, Landlord's Watch: Charity by the Clock in *Adam Bede*," *Novel* 39 (2005): 48–74, copyright ©2005 by Novel, Inc., reprinted by permission of the publisher, Duke University Press. Part of the introduction was published as "The Failure of Condescension," *Victorian Literature and Culture* 33, no. 2 (2005): 395–414, copyright ©2005 by Cambridge University Press. I thank AMS Press, Duke University Press, and Cambridge University Press for allowing me to reproduce these articles.

I thank my parents and brother for their amazing, unqualified support for my work, going all the way back. Thanks, too, to the Skillen family for their ready interest and good humor. For endless pleasure and diversion, I thank my dear son, Nathaniel, who loves everything that moves and grows, and who could not care less about this book. To Jeanene Skillen, who can repair any sentence, I am indebted for whatever good sense or clear expression has made its way into these pages. Jeanene has parsed my thoughts with much more care than they merit; she has been my greatest companion in this book as in all other things.

Introduction

Charity and Condescension

She stands before us: scattering tracts, ordering the children about, peering into cupboards, tripping over the furniture, crowing lines of scripture, blocking the exit. She marshals the forces of sound doctrine, domestic economy, and hygienic science against whatever comforts the poor might have been able to salvage amid their penury and squalor. She condescends.

It is this last offense we blame her for most. The lady visitor, along with her close associate the mincing curate, is a familiar figure of horror—a stock character in the Victorian charity gothic—and we are appalled by her unbearable condescension. This is not to say that there is any consensus on Victorian charity.

Generations of critics have debated whether Victorian philanthropy achieved its stated aims, whether those aims masked other political or social agendas, and whether the donors and recipients of charity were working in concert or at cross-purposes. Scholars ask how charity fit into the bigger picture, by which they alternately refer to the management of a new class of industrial urban poor, the creation of a liberal public sector, the emergence of the welfare state, the professionalization of social work, the public ambitions of middle-class women, or the distinctive cultural practices and survival strategies of working-class communities. Still, alongside the broader social questions, the image of the lady visitor retains its vividness and evokes a divided response. To some critics she represents everything that was wrong with Victorian charity; to others she is a phantom, a decoy, constructed to deny the reality of a different kind of figure: a charity worker who was genuinely responsive to the needs of her neighbors.[1] Our disagreements over the big picture sometimes cover a more visceral feeling about Victorian charity, a feeling that has much to do with this particular portrait of the condescending lady visitor. Some take it as axiomatic that Victorian philanthropists, despite their equivocal virtues, were fundamentally condescending.[2] Others would have it that Victorian philanthropists, despite their inevitable faults, were driven by a sense of the dignity of the less fortunate and that when we assume otherwise, it is we who condescend.[3]

Given the economic and political complexities of Victorian charity, it may seem pointless to ask whether or not philanthropists were condescending. Such a question seems to confuse cause and effect, examining personalities rather than the deeper structural realities that stand behind them. But I am going to argue that it is a good question. More than we realize, it is a question the Victorians asked themselves. The charge of condescension has been freely leveled against Victorian missionaries, essayists, mistresses, husbands, clergymen, and social workers; nevertheless, we inherit our distaste for condescension from them, a distaste that appears especially acute when we notice that, just decades before, condescension had been considered a great social virtue. Condescension became a problem in the Victorian period, not because the Victorians were more or less condescending than those who came before but because the meaning of condescension was changing.

The meaning of condescension itself is what changed, not the meaning of the word, which signifies today what it always has: lowering oneself to the level of one's inferiors. Yet the aroma around condescension is utterly different from what it once was. Condescension is for us a sign of arrogance, of pettiness, of a narcissistic insensibility to the real feelings of others—so that when Joseph

Addison praises Ulysses for the "condescension which never dwells but in truly great minds," or when Fanny Burney's Lord Orville pays tribute to the sweet condescension of his beloved, we feel we are in the presence of something archaic.[4] Whenever we come across the word in works by Samuel Richardson, Fanny Burney, or Maria Edgeworth, we have to make a quick adjustment; we remind ourselves that we are looking at a world where condescending gestures and tones of voice solved problems rather than causing them.

No history of condescension has been written, but we can imagine the outlines of such a history. Condescension originally denoted an act whereby an authority figure temporarily abdicated the privileges of his or her position for the benefit of a dependent. In this way, condescension was traditionally used as an argument for paternalism, a model of government in which the legitimacy of empowered groups rested on the ability and disposition of those groups to provide for the less fortunate. When over the course of the nineteenth century paternalist views were eroded and marginalized by the growth of liberalism, condescension came to seem dissonant. It cut against the core liberal principle of contractual relation, which supposes a nominal equality between free social agents. In a society built on the contractual model, even relations of authority are ostensibly entered into voluntarily by two parties for their mutual benefit.[5] Furthermore, it is important to the idea of the contract not only that both parties benefit but also that each party benefit through the active pursuit of his or her own interests. This is why condescension cannot operate constructively within a liberal framework—because, even though the condescension scene confers a benefit upon the subordinate, the subordinate has not acquired that benefit through his or her own agency or insistence.

The liberal emphasis on self-determination was felt in a number of traditionally paternalistic contexts where condescension would once have served: in labor (with the emergence of the Labour Movement), marriage (with the Married Women's Property Acts and the doctrine of separate spheres), electoral politics (with the expansions of the franchise), and education (with the cheap press, the Working Men's Institutes, and the growth of popular education), among others. An extreme example of the displacement of paternalism by liberal self-determination was the Workhouse Test, a scheme that, by requiring the poor to decide for themselves whether they were desperate enough to reach out for relief on the most uncongenial terms, reconfigured the very scene of public provision as a solitary affair in which the sufferer must have it out with his or her own conscience.

Condescension loses its power to reconcile within a liberal framework. It requires a setting in which authority is not the outcome of a negotiation but the intractable expression of intrinsic differences between people. When one condescends in an environment governed by contracts, it must seem as though one attempts to naturalize a social difference that ought to have been treated as provisional and voluntary. Condescension therefore became, in the nineteenth century, a sign of an outmoded ideology; it represented the grasping determination of a ruling elite to maintain status distinctions and to stifle reform. This loss of faith in condescending behavior was accompanied by a major shift in the normal connotations of the word. To condescend was no longer to renounce but to make a show of renunciation; it was no longer to help others but to demean them for one's own gain. Victorian writers paraded condescension's failures. From literary works to the treatises and memoirs of philanthropic innovators, the condescension scene became an emblem of the limitations of charity, a ritual in which fantasies of help degenerated into visions of social collapse.

The assault against the social utility of condescension was partly accomplished through a transformation in the literary uses of the condescension scene. While the literature of the eighteenth and early nineteenth centuries—crystallized in writers such as Sir Walter Scott, Jane Austen, and Maria Edgeworth—displays the ability of condescension to negotiate and validate social authority, the great Victorian novelists saw condescension as an obstacle to conciliation. Victorian scenes of condescension are frequently catastrophic, creating new narrative problems and calling for new solutions. Victorian fiction is full of condescension scenes; among the most famous are Edward Rochester's marriage proposal to Jane Eyre, Mrs. Jellyby's efforts for the natives of Borrioboola-gha (*Bleak House*), Miss Havisham's invitations to Pip (*Great Expectations*), and Edward Casaubon's patronage of Will Ladislaw (*Middlemarch*). All of these episodes backfire. Rochester's marrying days are behind him; Mrs. Jellyby's domestic problems disqualify her from any charity more distant; Miss Havisham's uses for Pip are narcissistic and fleeting; and Casaubon's payments to Will are a self-imposed blackmail, motivated by the haunting consciousness of a family wrong. The best-intentioned acts of condescension are thwarted: in *A Tale of Two Cities*, Dr. Manette, though a hero of the Bastille, can do nothing for his son-in-law; in *Middlemarch*, when Mr. Brooke tries to comfort the farmer Dagley, he is reviled; and in *Framley Parsonage*, Fanny and Lucy Robarts are rejected and humiliated while on a charitable mission to the Crawley family. The blame in these cases is shared between the high and the low, the powerful and the disaffected. While the causes are multiple, the problem is the same: condescension is consistently invoked as a plausible means of reconciling people, and it is consistently rejected as a poor solution. Victorian fiction stages countless scenes where acts of goodwill fail, due sometimes to the insensibility of those who have and sometimes to the viciousness of those who want.

In the nineteenth century, the most severe attacks against philanthropic condescension often came from philanthropists themselves, many of whom write about visitors not unlike Dickens's Mrs. Pardiggle.[6] The literature of philanthropy is fully alive to the dangers of condescension and cautions visitors against doing anything that could seem intrusive or presumptuous.[7] This worry almost amounts to an obsession. Louisa Twining, one of the greatest promoters of charitable visitation, puts it bluntly: "To our own feelings nothing can be more repugnant than the practice urged by many good people of intruding upon the poor at all hours and seasons for the purpose of the reading the Bible to them in the midst of their daily toil and household work, when we ourselves should consider such an intrusion as unwarrantable, and the proposition to receive it both out of time and place. If the feelings of the poor are not respected, but, on the contrary, a patronizing, condescending tone adopted, we have no hesitation in saying that such visits do more harm than good."[8]

Twining was not unusual in seeing style or manner as even more important than substance; while modern historians of Victorian philanthropy have tended to emphasize the "content" of charitable aid (and its balancing of spiritual and economic imperatives),[9] many Victorian writers shared Twining's belief that the visitor's manners were paramount, perhaps more important even than her compassion or sense of purpose. The advice books focus on the visitor's physical bearing and basic protocol. One advises the visitor, "Enter their cottages in your daily walk,—not as a dictator, not as a mere giver of alms,—not as a spy upon their household arrangements: go as their equal. Carry with you no sense of superiority, but that which a more elevated tone of piety and a more enlightened intellect may claim" (an admittedly equivocal prescription). The author continues in some detail: "A call upon a family in humble life should always be made at seasonable hours; it should be preceded by a tap at the door, and the visitor should instantly withdraw with an apology, if he discovers them to be at meals, or otherwise busily engaged."[10] Charles Kingsley makes the point more forcefully: "You must regulate your conduct to them, and in their houses, even to the most minute particulars, by the very same rules which apply to persons of your own class."[11] Not only should the visitor refrain from taking liberties, but she should refuse even to allow her host to treat her with distinction: "Piety, earnestness, affectionateness, eloquence,—all may be nullified and stultified by simply keeping a poor woman standing in her own cottage while you sit, or entering her house, even at her own request, while she is at meals. She may decline to sit; she may beg you to come in: all the more reason for refusing to obey her, because it shows that that very inward gulf between you and her still exists in her mind, which it is the object of your visit to bridge over" (63). This is a strange image—the visitor who, out of respect for the poor woman, refuses that woman's courtesy—but Kingsley clearly thinks such radical measures are necessary as a way of deprogramming both the rich and the poor woman, disrupting the cycle of condescension and gratitude.[12]

To drive home their warning against condescension, these philanthropic authorities paint an unflattering portrait of the visitor as exactly the type of person who would condescend: a sheltered young lady seeking a kind of moral satisfaction. "We know," explains Twining, "that the office of district visitor is often undertaken by those who, in the midst of a life of weary and unsatisfying gaiety, long for something real (even though it be a painful reality) on which to expend their energies and a portion of their time."[13] Twining finds such feelings sympathetic but rarely conducive to productive charity work. Kingsley goes further, delving into the lady visitor's unconscious motives:

> It seems so much easier to women to do something for the poor, than for their own ladies' maids, and housemaids, and cooks. And why? Because they can treat the poor as *things*: but they *must* treat their servants as persons. . . . [A woman] is afraid of beginning a good work with [her servants], because, if she does, she will be forced to carry it out; and it cannot be cold, dry, perfunctory, official; it must be hearty, living, loving, personal. She must make them her friends; and perhaps she is afraid of doing that, for fear they should take liberties . . . and so she is tempted, when she wishes to do good, to fall back on the poor people in the cottages outside, who, as she fancies, know nothing about her, and will never find out whether or not she acts up to the rules which she lays down. (53–54)

Kingsley portrays the charity worker as a woman not just neglecting her household but specifically dodging her servants. Servants, actual dependents, are dangerous; they have legitimate claims on their mistress's resources, and they may have her "a little in their power."[14] Safer is perfunctory charity, which can be taken up and left off as is convenient. Kingsley's criticism often assumes the worst of the visitor. He is quick to demean her, as if in retribution for the way that she is likely to have demeaned the visited poor: "A lady can go into a poor cottage, lay down the law to the inhabitants, reprove them for sins to which she has never been tempted; tell them how to set things right, which, if she had the doing of them, I fear she would do even more confusedly and slovenly than they" (53); "Why not encourage [the poor woman], praise her, cheer her on her weary way by loving words, and keep your reproofs for yourself—even your advice; for she does get on her way, after all, where *you* could not travel a step forward" (62). Kingsley, Twining, and other observers (including, a decade later, the leadership of the Charity Organisation Society) lay the success or failure of philanthropy at the feet of the visitor. Perhaps paradoxically, writers such as these, even as they remind would-be volunteers that the poor are self-determining moral agents, tend to think that the "failure" of a charitable visit is most often due to a mistake on the visitor's part. As early as 1836, one writer asserts that "if to the poor of a different order [i.e., not given to vice] the attentions of a superior are ever unwelcome, it must be the fault of the visitor himself."[15]

Were the visitors worried about their own condescension? If we were to judge only by their accounts, it would not seem so; despite what essayists and directing clergymen advised, the visitors tend not to turn much scrutiny upon themselves. Rather, they focus on the internal struggle of the visited. For any reader looking for signs of philanthropic self-assurance, there is plenty here to be found. Fishers of men, the visitors reel the sinners in, and they suggest that their own task is mainly to get an early start and keep a steady hand. In a typical story of a cottager's education and conversion, the visitor's role can be quite muted: "A young female in a deep decline . . . was not only ignorant of, but reckless of, that future state upon the very brink of which her poor benighted soul was hovering. And very heavily and very slowly she received those blessed truths on the belief of which depended the eternal welfare of her immortal spirit. She languished in much bodily suffering for a few months and through the grace of God became by degrees sensible of her state as a miserable sinner and of the all sufficiency of her Saviour's redeeming love."[16] This account, with others like it, shows little self-consciousness; neither boastful nor self-doubting, it simply is not concerned with the visitor's own merits or shortcomings. The crisis belongs to the young woman in decline, and the triumph is hers as well—hers and God's. The visitor essentially watches a drama that is not her own. She may help set the stage, and she may look on with prayer and encouragement, but the story is not about her. This is not to say that a visitor never expresses doubts, but when she does, she does not worry about the rightness of her calling or the appropriateness of her methods; she worries that her message will fall on deaf ears: "I know not whether my fellow brother and sister visitors experience, as I do, much faintness of heart and weariness of spirit, while passing over and over again from house to house—from family to family—imparting the glad tidings of great joy which we bear in hand and in heart—received with so much apathy and so little concern."[17]

Notwithstanding the confidence of their accounts, it seems that, in reality, some visitors felt uncertain as to the propriety of their visits. The visitors' accounts, as sincere and self-revealing as many of them are, still bear the marks of an official discourse; confidence was the lingua franca of the business, and the lack of discouragement was itself a measure of success. But the boundary-crossing that visiting entailed was an equivocal act, and many books and articles attempt to encourage the visitor in the face of her own uneasiness and despondency. One, for instance, acknowledges the popular conception that "the poor dislike such interference in their concerns" but cites testimonies from several cities showing that it is not so.[18] J. L. Davies, in a lecture printed alongside Kingsley's half-harangue (quoted above), tries to buoy the would-be visitor: "The most delicate, that is, the most womanly, women shrink from forcing themselves upon the acquaintance of others just because they are poorer. They are afraid that this reluctance of theirs may have its counterpart in the disgust with which an intrusive visit would be met by those who have not lost all sensitiveness and self-respect."[19] Davies reassures such women that their reluctance is an effect of their own sense of guilt and inadequacy, not a response to any actual disgust on the part of the visited poor. "It is a matter of fact, for which we have cause to thank God," Davies promises, "that any lady, behaving like a lady, and coming to the poor in an avowed religious character, is sure to be well received" (124). Davies's lecture works both against and in tandem with Kingsley's: while Kingsley chastises lady visitors for their inevitable propensity to condescend, Davies urges them not to be paralyzed by the fear of condescension.

Together, the two lectures encapsulate the philanthropist's dilemma. Charity was in its glory. The need was great, the opportunities were boundless, and every pulpit and newspaper broadcasted a call to storm the barricades between rich and poor. At the same time, all agreed—philanthropists more than anyone—that attempts to do good could well cause harm and that condescension, once a method of breaking down walls, had since become responsible for building them up. It is the contest between these two forces—the confidence but also the anxiety that charity's effects could no longer be reliably squared with its intentions—that was the real "Time-Spirit" of Victorian charity.[20] And by this light we are left with a new image: a Mrs. Pardiggle who hears the brickmaker's protests and wonders, with Esther Summerson, what precisely is to be done.

All of this would suggest that when we argue about whether philanthropists were condescending, we are actually participating in the Victorian Time-Spirit rather than flouting it. It is no coincidence that the value of condescension was shifting exactly during the decades when the institutions of English philanthropy and poor relief were struggling to rewrite their charter. The movement to discard the old methods of poor relief was, at every point, plagued by an uncertainty as to alternatives. To many, the welfare state was the great evil to be avoided; on the other hand, the seeming callousness of the campaign against pauperism (and against public charity) struck some Victorians as forfeiting the compassion that characterized other aspects of social reform. Throughout the debates over philanthropy and relief, what was at issue was always what could be preserved from the old forms of middle-class provision (before the 1834 Poor Law amendment) and what must be abolished. In these debates the question of condescension took on a great many inflections. For some, the relation that charity established between rich and poor must had to be maintained even if relief itself were abandoned, while for others, it was exactly this relation that needed to be altered. Condescension had long been seen as the anchor of English charity, and in some ways as its very object. The Victorians' concerns about condescension, then, represented a much greater concern about how, in a liberal society, charity could be secured, its value guaranteed.

Condescension in Literature

In its traditional sense, the word *condescension* designated an act of exceptional generosity, an act that fell beyond the scope of expectation and almost automatically provoked responses of gratitude and even wonder. It was a talisman of the encounter between the noble and the common, or indeed, between the divine and the human. Twice, for instance, John Milton's Adam thanks the angel Raphael for condescending to reveal to him the divine plan of history. In the eighteenth century, condescension lost some of its aura of exceptionalism and came to mark a more ordinary but still commendable generosity of spirit. In eighteenth-century prose, it is therefore common to find the word *condescension* qualified by adjectives such as *generous, good, kind, humble,* and particularly *affable.* This last word shows that condescension had become an index not only of ethical practice but also of personality. To condescend demonstrated an easy-going flexibility of temperament, a willingness to compromise. In *Clarissa,* Mrs. Howe chides Anna for being unwilling to forgo her pride and condescend however slightly to Hickman ("You know not what it is to condescend"); elsewhere, Anna agrees that Clarissa's condescension, whereby she has consented to exchange letters secretly with Lovelace, "has no doubt hitherto prevented great mischiefs."[21] Eighteenth-century condescension thus connoted a whole range of practices spanning from extreme renunciation to polite deference.

Like the other canonical virtues, condescension was often exposed by eighteenth-century writers as a mask for vice. "False" condescension was therefore—and frequently—seen as a tool for dissimulation and hypocrisy, in a manner that affirmed, rather than denied, the value of "true" condescension. But while the idea of a pernicious condescension was quite common in the eighteenth century, in the nineteenth century true and false condescension became hard to distinguish. The condescension act came to be thought of as double by nature, comprising generosity and self-interest at the same time. Austen's *Emma* expresses it precisely this way: "Emma did not repent her condescension in going to the Coles. She must have delighted the Coles—worthy people, who deserved to be made happy!—and left a name behind her that would not soon die away."[22] As Emma sees it, the establishment of her reputation does not compromise the condescension act; it validates it. For Emma, condescension is a sign of good character, and it is only fitting that charity should reap its benefits in renown. When Mr. Elton, for instance, meets Emma and Harriet on a charitable errand, Emma decides that the mutual satisfaction attached to the act of charity may well bring about a declaration of love between the others. Yet the novel itself, less sanguine about the uses of reputation and pride, suggests that the complacency brought about by Emma's charity has its defects. The doubleness of condescension is elaborated even more explicitly in *Guy Mannering:* "The Baronet received his visitor with that condescending parade which was meant at once to assert his own vast superiority, and to show the generosity and courtesy with which he could waive it, and descend to the level of ordinary conversation with ordinary men."[23] Scott goes a step further than Austen: whereas Emma sees her reputation to be a fortuitous effect of her condescension, the baronet makes reputation his deliberate rationale.

In the Victorian period, the belief in a constructive condescension largely fell away, and the word itself (with exceptions) was given over to its negative connotations. Condescension came primarily to signify self-promotion at another's cost; to condescend was to assert one's own superiority in a way that degraded others. Like Emma Woodhouse, Martin Chuzzlewit finds his own condescension "inexpressibly delicious to him" (231). Mr. Dombey cannot imagine that anyone would not wish to be distinguished by his condescension (594). Frequently the self-promotion of condescension is accidental, emphasizing even further the insensibility of the superior. Thus, in *Scenes of Clerical Life*, the well-intentioned "Miss Assher's smiling condescensions were torture to Caterina";[24] thus, too, in Dickens's *Little Dorrit*, does the disaffected Miss Wade remark of her conciliatory schoolmates, "They were always forgiving me, in their vanity and condescension. Little images of grown people!" (663). Just as the condescension that exalts the self is reviled, its absence is often praised. "There are many girls," observes the narrator of *Can You Forgive Her?* "who could submit themselves at a moment to the kindness of such a woman as Lady Glencora . . . for of all such women in the world, Lady Glencora was the least inclined to patronize or be condescending in her kindnesses."[25] Shirley Keeldar gladly observes that "[Sir Philip Nunnely] did not *condescend* to their society—he seemed *glad* of it."[26] In these cases, the exaltation of the superior has become incompatible with the dignity of the subordinate, and a condescension that achieves the former must necessarily default on the latter.

Another equally negative—and equally common—Victorian connotation of the word takes exactly the opposite view: condescension is seen not as promoting but as degrading the one who condescends. In such cases, the object of condescension is thought to be unworthy; consequently, to condescend is to be compromised. Scott can serve here as our locus classicus: "[T]he high rank of the marshals of the lists would have been held degraded, had they condescended to superintend the sports of the yeomanry."[27] Some decades later, Trollope uses the word almost exclusively to imply degradation. For instance, in *The Warden*, Mr. Harding will not condescend to tell a lie. In *Orley Farm*, Sir Peregrine implores Lady Mason not to condescend to notice Mr. Dockwrath's legal action against her, roughly equating condescension with subscription to blackmail. And in *Can You Forgive Her?* George Vavasor, making a typical Trollopian calculation, concludes that "whether or no he cared to marry his cousin . . . it was necessary for his honour that he should have that for which he condescended to ask."[28] In these examples, condescension is a threat not to the subordinate but to the superior, who, by lowering him- or herself to the level of the common, risks losing dignity or authority.

The failure of Victorian condescension, then, takes multiple shapes, and while many of the examples above show condescension to be a locus of bitter contention, it can also take on the nostalgia, pathos, and ridiculousness of a faded ideal. Thus it is in the last number of *Bleak House*, in which Dickens describes the efforts of Volumnia Dedlock, "a young lady (of sixty)" (390), to recover her former glory on the rare occasion of a public ball:

> Then, indeed, does she captivate all hearts by her condescension, by her girlish vivacity, and by her skipping about as in the days when the hideous old general with the mouth too full of teeth, had not cut one of them at two guineas each. Then does she twirl and twine, a pastoral nymph of good family, through the mazes of the dance. Then do the swains appear with tea, with lemonade, with sandwiches, with homage. Then is she kind and cruel, stately and unassuming, various, beautifully wilful. Then is there a singular kind of parallel between her and the little glass chandeliers of another age, embellishing that assembly-room; which, with their meagre stems, their spare little drops, their disappointing knobs where no drops are, their bare little stalks from which knobs and drops have both departed, and their little feeble prismatic twinkling, all seem Volumnias. (875)

Here condescension is celebrated as in the pre-Victorian days, but the celebration is itself a relic, a kind of carnival reenactment of a scene that might have made sense in Volumnia's childhood, a scene that can no longer do what Volumnia needs it to do. In her desire to captivate and conquer, in the ritualized mystification of the dance, and in the aristocratic voraciousness that ingests homage with its lemonade and sandwiches, Volumnia is the figure for a vitiated condescension. The doubleness (self-interest and generosity) of an earlier condescension persists in Volumnia's kindness and cruelty, her stately and unassuming manner—as if a show of vivacity might palliate the encroaching demands of a world beneath her.

In some cases, even during and after the tectonic shift we have been examining, the word *condescension* retains its earlier hopefulness. The novels of Elizabeth Gaskell are interesting in this regard; charting the nuances of status and authority in industrial towns and country villages, Gaskell's writings provide an index to the malleability of condescension at midcentury. In many of her works, the word is caught between inflections, at times seeming ironic or fruitless in the modern sense, at other times seeming more traditionally to suggest a behavior that is laudable or benign. It is surprisingly benign in *Mary Barton,* a novel otherwise charged with class resentment. The word occurs only twice: once in a comical vein and once in a nostalgic one, as Mary recalls Jem's condescension when, in their childhood, he pretended to be interested in her trifles.[29] Rather than invoke condescension as a figure for the class conflict that fills the novel, Gaskell chooses to reserve it as an idyllic sort of relation, one that might exist between an older and younger child of the same class. Curiously, in *Cranford,* the less inflamed setting of ordinary country life seems to activate the more aggressive edge of condescension. The term is applied mockingly to the behavior of the imperious Mrs. Jamieson and her servant Mr. Mulliner, and concernedly to Miss Matty at the point that she considers degrading herself (in the narrator's eyes) by entering into trade.[30] In *North and South,* the word remains a site of discomfort. Mrs. Thornton suggests with displeasure that Margaret might condescend "to be curious as to the manufactures of Milton"; later, Mr. Bell suggests that Thornton and the other Milton men "condescend to send up your to-day's difficulty to Oxford." In both cases, the request for condescension is actually a reprimand: Margaret is being put in her place for her ignorance of the Milton works, and Thornton is teased for his careless dismissal of what happens at Oxford.[31]

In Gaskell's last work, *Wives and Daughters,* condescension is frequently mentioned, but without the anxiety seen in *Cranford* and *North and South;* the author seems to have come to terms with this mode of relation. It generally suggests the lightest hint of irony, as when Lady Cumnor is praised for responding to the "obeisance" of the townspeople with condescending thoughtfulness; though there is something a little crass about Lady Cumnor's sense of importance, her kindness within the town is genuine and well-received.[32] Her daughter Lady Harriet is condescending as well, so much so that when Molly hears that her family has had a "condescending" visitor in her absence, she instantly knows that the visitor was Lady Harriet (205). But here, too, Gaskell applies a light touch. While the novel does not precisely condone Lady Harriet's attitudes, it forgives her for them, and Molly gently corrects her condescension when, for instance, she asks Lady Harriet not to refer to the Browning sisters as Pecksy and Flapsy (199). At its worst, then, the condescension in *Wives and Daughters* is careless and correctable; at its best, it represents a yearning for community, for contact. Still, while Gaskell and later writers (well into the twentieth century) were able to use the word *condescension* to invoke utopian yearnings, they did so conspicuously. In other words, these later appeals to the ideal of condescension must be felt as revivals, or perhaps as salvage operations.

The shift in the word's connotations tracks an equally significant shift in the representation of the condescension act. A couple of literary scenes, written at different points in the century, can illustrate the evolution of the condescension act from a constructive measure to a harmful or futile one. The first, taken from Scott's *The Antiquary* (1816), justifiably brought tears to the eyes of Virginia Woolf's Mr. Ramsay. Steenie Mucklebackit, a fisherman's son, has drowned, and the grieving family is visited by Oldbuck, the laird of Monkbarns. The scene is not concerned with the drowning itself so much as with the problem of consolation. The mourners cannot be comforted. The fisherman is entirely possessed by his grief, and he can neither look at his son's coffin nor look away from it. The narrator explains that the fisherman's "family had not yet dared to address to him a word, either of sympathy or consolation."[33] Similarly, we read that the mother's friends are "endeavouring to stun the grief which they could not console" (286). The grandmother has fallen into a state of incomprehension and defies approach. When the clergyman enters the hut, his consolations are initially ignored and then come to meet a worse fate from the grandmother: "She drew up her head and body, shook her head in a manner that showed at least impatience, if not scorn, of his counsel, and waved her hand slightly, but with a gesture so expressive as to indicate to all who witnessed it a marked and disdainful rejection of the ghostly consolation proffered to her" (289).

The family's paralysis can be broken down only by an extreme act of condescension on the part of Oldbuck. The coffin is about to be interred, and the onlookers remind the family of the custom that the father should support the head of the coffin, a duty that he is reluctant to assume. At this point, the narrator explains, "Oldbuck interfered between the distressed father and his well-meaning tormentors, and informed them that he himself, as landlord and master to the deceased, 'would carry his head to the grave'" (290). The results of this proposal follow:

> In spite of the sorrowful occasion, the hearts of the relatives swelled within them at so marked a distinction on the part of the laird; and old Alison Breck, who was present among other fish-women, swore almost aloud, 'His honour Monkbarns should never want sax warp of oysters in the season (of which fish he was understood to be fond), if she should gang to sea and dredge for them hersell, in the foulest wind that ever blew.' And such is the

> temper of the Scottish common people that, by this instance of compliance with their customs, and respect for their persons, Mr. Oldbuck gained more popularity than by all the sums which he had yearly distributed in the parish for purposes of private or general charity. (290)

Even at the moment of intensest grief, the father can be swelled by the laird's distinction. We see that condescension is far from a mere public exchange of formalities; it is a probing act of recognition that can unlock the most private sorrow. Even so, Oldbuck's most personal consolations cycle back to him in the form of a sort of universal fealty. Here again is the doubleness we saw earlier, as the laird's largesse so instantly profits him.

There are other hints as well of the difficulty condescension would face in the coming decades. In the previous quotation, for instance, we see that Oldbuck gains popularity for his compliance with custom; as the scene develops, the necessity of compliance becomes pronounced, and Oldbuck's popularity is shown to be tenuous. For instance, although he objects to the mourners' decision to wear crape on their caps, he must keep still: "Monkbarns would probably have remonstrated against this superfluous expense, had he been consulted; but, in doing so, he would have given more offence than he gained popularity by condescending to perform the office of chief mourner" (290). A departure from popular custom would expose Oldbuck's superiority as callous and removed. More disturbing than this is an earlier moment when, at the laird's entrance, the distracted grandmother offers an ominous toast: "Wishing a' your healths, sirs, and often may we hae such merry meetings!" (287). The woman's grief has caused her to forget her grandson's death, and her statement receives a response of "shuddering horror" from all who are present. But her very mistake correctly exposes the fact that the condescension of superiors necessarily trades on the distress of subordinates. In a sense, the success of condescension is only as great as the distress that makes it possible. The grandmother's celebratory pledge is really, then, another form of the gratitude of the whole family toward the laird, a gratitude that entails a momentary abandonment of the drowned boy. By the same token, the boy's specter—and in general, the consciousness of distress—provides an undertow that pulls against the success of condescension.

By May 1852, which saw the publication of the third number of *Bleak House,* everything had changed. In Dickens's episode of the brickmaker's cottage, the condescension of the rich is not a mixed blessing but a failing cause. The keynote of this failure is struck by Mrs. Pardiggle, whose "forcible composure" seems to Esther "calculated . . . to increase [the brickmaker's] antagonism" (107). Perhaps Pardiggle's most telling characteristic is her complacency, her sense that the protests of the cottagers affirm her purpose: "I enjoy hard work; and the harder you make mine, the better I like it" (107).[34] Pardiggle's self-congratulation belies a condescension meant to reward the philanthropist, and this time the reward is not incidental to the interests of the needy but explicitly in conflict with them. Dickens voices a critique that was common at the time and would become even more so in the 1860s and '70s, an attack against the philanthropic establishment for seeking its own glory above all. Pardiggle's self-absorption leads her to hear all the brickmaker's objections as routine gestures, and the force of his claims eludes her.

The force of Pardiggle's claims, by contrast, does not elude the brickmaker; out of them he creates a personal drama of assault and justification to rival those of Miss Flite and Richard Carstone in the shadow of the Lord Chancellor. The brickmaker perceives Pardiggle's condescension to be an assertion of her dominance, and he struggles to control the situation by preempting her interrogation: "Now you're a-going to poll-pry and question according to custom—I know what you're a-going to be up to. Well! You haven't got no occasion to be up to it. I'll save you the trouble" (107). Yet by way of denying her the "occasion," the brickmaker subjects himself to a battery of charges, charges that are only partially undermined through his reappropriation. Against some of these charges the brickmaker disdains to defend himself: "How have I been conducting of myself? Why, I've been drunk for three days; and I'd a been drunk four, if I'd a had the money. . . . And how did my wife get that black eye? Why, I giv' it her; and if she says I didn't, she's a Lie!" (107). But mixed in with his disdain is an eagerness to mount a defense: "Have I read the little book wot you left? No, I an't read the little book wot you left. There an't nobody here as knows how to read it; and if there wos, it wouldn't be suitable to me. It's a book fit for a babby, and I'm not a babby. If you was to leave me a doll, I shouldn't nuss it" (107). By making his case, the brickmaker inadvertently empowers Mrs. Pardiggle, betraying a persistent, though attenuated, faith in the condescension gesture. The philanthropist's intrusion is both an outrage and an opportunity; like the aggrieved Chancery suitor Gridley, the brickmaker compulsively petitions his oppressor for a reprieve. The condescension of the rich thus means as much to the poor of *Bleak House* as it does to the poor of *The Antiquary*, and yet it means something quite different. Whereas Lord Oldbuck's solicitude for the fisherman's family and, particularly, his attention to local custom mark him as part of the organic life of the community, Mrs.

Pardiggle's visits confirm the poor in their demoralized suspicion of a ruling class that offers a great deal but has nothing to give.

Dickens's episode seems at first, therefore, to have given up on condescension and to contend that the problems of the poor can only be understood and addressed by the poor themselves. Esther and Ada, who accompany Mrs. Pardiggle, both feel "painfully sensible that between us and these people there was an iron barrier, which could not be removed by our new friend. By whom, or how, it could be removed, we did not know; but we knew that" (108). Their inability to help becomes emphatically clear when, as Ada touches the face of the poor couple's newborn infant, the child dies. This incident revises the scene from *The Antiquary*, in which Oldbuck supports the head of the dead child to the grave; Ada has become an angel of death. But while Esther and Ada's capacity to help is undermined, they still carry authority in the cottage, a class authority that the novel goes on to validate. The two return to the brickmaker in the evening, with the intention of comforting the mother of the dead child. The mother is asleep, but the sister of the dead infant "was standing laughing and talking, with some other young women . . . but she seemed ashamed, and turned away as we went by" (110). Meanwhile, the woman attending to the mother is "a-watching for my master. . . . If he was to catch me away from home, he'd pretty near murder me" (110). Ada and Esther are duly impressed by the woman's devotion: "'May Heaven reward you!' we said to her. 'You are a good woman'" (110). The two girls still have no help to offer, but they activate both the shame and the honor of the poor in a way that signifies their unflinching concern. It is as if Esther and Ada have become the compassionate but firm judges that the brickmaker fruitlessly sought in Mrs. Pardiggle. In this manner the episode still bears the traces of a constructive condescension, showing the power of this model and the difficulty that a mid-century writer would encounter in his or her attempts to change course.

The Logic of Condescension

Condescension, as described in this historical outline, is not really an idea or a structure of feeling but a transactional protocol, a social and literary convention. In particular, it is a convention associated with charity and giving. This gives us a clue as to why condescension has not been investigated before. There is a long tradition of talking about charity as a necessarily spontaneous and unregulated expression of feeling. This tradition was challenged, around the middle of the nineteenth century, by a movement to replace spontaneous charity with a highly organized institutional philanthropy. In the ensuing debates, which of course persist to this day, the subjective impulse was clearly distinguished from the institutional form, and scenes of giving were held to demonstrate either one or the other. Little thought has been given to the structural patterns in which the subjective impulse takes shape, the conventions through which particular acts of charity are realized. Condescension is just such a convention. The pages that follow investigate nineteenth-century condescension as a conventional form, a form that, even as it participated in the broader movements of social and literary history, had its own particular logic.

Theories of convention tend to run in two channels. The first holds convention to be a product (and agent) of materialist determination; because convention has a social mandate, every aspect of a convention can be correlated to its ideological function.[35] Alternatively, conventions can be seen as ritualized performances that, over time, become autonomous from the practical needs that generated them.[36] We can reconcile these views by way of Stuart Hall's discussion of ideology, following Antonio Gramsci. For Hall, an ideological conception is not the spontaneous articulation of a class interest or a political force, but the battleground on which opposed classes and forces contend. If so, then it is precisely because a convention has developed its own rationale—because its grammar has been fixed—that it can become an effective site of contestation. A convention can function in the service of variable social agendas only because it has, in the popular imagination, turned its back upon its moment of origin. In other words, it is because conventions are not reducible to particular structures of feeling that they can be a vehicle for articulating these structures. Therefore, if we want to understand the variable aspects of a convention, the places where ideology becomes visible, we must first understand its autonomous symbolic language.[37]

Condescension is a word, like *belligerence*, *amnesty*, or *degeneration*, that can be used to characterize any number of social interactions. It is extraordinary that the valence of such a word can change across so many contexts at once—that condescension can come to seem a problem as it operates between teachers and students, pastors and parishioners, wives and husbands, employers and laborers, nurses and patients, the indigent and relief-workers. The word's thematic capaciousness suggests that it may be no more than a nexus of multiple ideas sedimented together, with no unifying logic, no semantic code. And yet the failure of condescension, so sudden and so definitive, seems to call for a structural exposition.[38] Georg Simmel sets the strongest sociological precedent for studying social forms in this way: "We do find that the same form of interaction obtains among individuals in societal groups that are the most unlike imaginable in purpose and significance. Superiority, subordination, competition, division of labor, formation of parties, representation, inner solidarity coupled with exclusiveness toward the outside, and innumerable similar features are found in the state as well as in a religious community, in a band of conspirators as in an economic association, in an art school as in a family."[39] Following Simmel, I believe it is possible to develop a structural model that applies to every condescension act but can also be used to illuminate the workings of condescension at the most local level. This allows us both to identify the logic that governs condescension as a signifying system and to examine what is at stake in condescension from an experiential or perceptual point of view.

When social historians have sought an abstract language for the ideology of Victorian philanthropy, they have sometimes referred to Marcel Mauss's description of the gift—and although Mauss's analysis of gift giving emerged from his observation of noncapitalist societies (and did not precisely include almsgiving), there is an important resonance between the gift as Mauss describes it and the ideal forms of charity that the Victorians pursued.[40] Victorian charity, like Mauss's gift, was in constant retreat from the material. Particularly in the wake of the New Poor Law, Victorians tried to imagine forms of charity that would forgo the economic, that would involve no donations. Most often, when material goods were given, it was in the context of a mission that was primarily spiritual; thus, Ellen Ranyard's Bible and Domestic Mission distributed blankets and Bibles on the same system, and General Booth's Salvation Army manifesto argued that one must save bodies to save souls. But apart from delivering material or even spiritual assistance, the declared objective of most charitable institutions (from the church-directed district visitors to the secular Charity Organisation Society) was to enable a new kind of relationship between rich and poor. Philanthropists argued that any help they offered, spiritual or temporal, could have value only in the context of a personal, reciprocal relationship between themselves and those in need; as a result, Victorian charity became more and more explicitly focused on its interpersonal content. In this light, charity looks a lot like Mauss's gift, which resists commodification and enshrines the event of its own giving. Condescension makes visible exactly this relational component that Mauss claims to be the essence of the gift and Victorian philanthropists claimed to be the essence of charity. When we celebrate or denounce the condescension of philanthropists, we are bracketing questions of material transaction and foregrounding the way rich and poor relate to each other. The condescension act has no aim other than the explicitly social one of bringing about a particular relationship between its agents.

For this reason, a structural model of condescension would have much in common with the model of gift exchange proposed by Mauss, and we might even posit that the social force of condescension derives from the way in which it evokes the inalienability of the gift within a modern economy of alienable commodities. Mauss values archaic gift exchange over modern economic exchange, in that economics attempts to isolate itself from the moral aspects of social life, while gift exchange is centrally concerned with these moral aspects.[41] Jacques Godbout, a disciple and critic of Mauss, radicalizes Mauss's distinction between the gift and economic exchange: "The gift is the embodiment of that system of relationships that is strictly social, in that these relations cannot be reduced to factors of power or economic interest."[42] For Mauss, the relational aspect of gift exchange derives from the idea that gifts (unlike economic commodities) are inalienable: they retain the identity of their original owners. Mauss expresses it thus: "It follows clearly from what we have seen that in this system of ideas one gives away what is in reality a part of one's nature and substance, while to receive something is to receive a part of someone's spiritual essence."[43] Mauss structuralizes this personal quality by claiming that every gift bears with it a *hau*, or spirit of origins, that marks the presence of the giver. The gift has no intrinsic or generic value but derives its value entirely from the *hau*. Mauss's investment in the *hau* can be read as a disinvestment from the given object, and Mauss correspondingly takes great pains to show that reciprocal exchange (gift giving) never produces a material gain or loss.

Like gift exchange, condescension is performed solely for the purpose of refining a social relationship. Claude Lévi-Strauss demonstrates the relational essence of gift exchange in a passage that could well be applied to the condescension act, as he analyzes the exchange of wine between two strangers seated together at a restaurant table. Here gift exchange serves the purpose of establishing one's relationship to a stranger. If one stranger accepts the wine offering of the other, the relationship has become cordial; if he instead refuses the wine offering, the relationship has become hostile. In either case, the offering has ended the "relationship of indifference."[44] Likewise, the condescension act, whether it engenders reconciliation or conflict, is a strategy for bringing to light relationships of social authority that have not been fully explored or articulated, validating or challenging these relationships where they are already visible, and creating these relationships (whether hostile or friendly) where they do not exist.

Because condescension is a relation, it must be studied in two perspectives, that of the one who condescends and that of the one condescended to.[45] Peter Mandler, in his introduction to *The Uses of Charity*, complains that studies of Victorian philanthropy have routinely adopted the middle-class perspective, and he describes the need for a study of charity from below.[46] We might adapt Mauss's terms to this task by proposing that if the gift-given is inalienable from the giver, so is the gift-received inalienable from the receiver. The project of a social analysis of condescension is therefore to understand both how the condescension-subject (the "superior") gives of herself, and how the condescension-object (the "subordinate") receives of (or as) herself.[47] Neither subordinate nor superior has an advantage with respect to this process of identity formation. As in Hegel's master-slave dialectic, each agent depends on the recognition of the other.[48] In the condescension act, then, identity is formed on the crucible of relation. As an agent in such an interaction, my whole purpose is to create and control my relational identity, to produce a particular who-I-am-to-you. This act of creation is the entire content of condescension.

How is the transaction of identity accomplished, and how can it be said to fail? We can answer this question by further specifying the kind of exchange that condescension involves. Consider this passage from Maria Edgeworth's *Patronage:* "[W]ith his whole heart and soul he thanked his majesty for this gracious condescension—this testimony of approbation—these proofs of sensibility to his attachment, which paid—overpaid him, in a moment, for the labours of a life."[49] Here condescension is presented as the supreme reward, ample compensation for a lifetime of labor. And yet the monarch's condescension is not mere payment but overpayment; it is not just a reward but a gift besides. As we know from Mauss and Malinowski, gifts confer a debt, demanding the receiver's further participation in a cycle of obligation.[50] When Edgeworth's Lord Oldborough corrects himself—he is not paid but overpaid—he acknowledges that his past duties to the crown have not been enough and that the king's condescension is sufficient to purchase the labors of the future along with the ones of the past. To be overpaid is in this case rather less than to be paid. Edgeworth's phrase "paid—overpaid" reveals a rift within the condescension act, which unites a sense of excessive generosity with an uneasy confusion as to what kind of payment is being offered anyway, and what is being purchased with it.

As we have seen, for Mauss the value of a gift resides in the *hau,* the spirit of origins that designates the giver. When an inalienable gift is accepted, when it is even apprehended to be a gift, it thereby purchases the recipient's recognition. In other words, whenever I receive a gift of any kind, the immediate return I make is to recognize the giver. Ralph Waldo Emerson (in an essay that puzzled but intrigued Mauss) understands recognition to be the essence of gift-receiving:

> Rings and other jewels are not gifts, but apologies for gifts. The only gift is a portion of thyself. Thou must bleed for me. Therefore the poet brings his poem; the shepherd, his lamb; the farmer, corn; the miner, a gem; the sailor, coral and shells; the painter, his picture; the girl, a handkerchief of her own sewing. This is right and pleasing, for it restores society in so far to its primary basis, when a man's biography is conveyed in his gift, and every man's wealth is an index of his merit. But it is a cold, lifeless business when you go to the shops to buy me something . . . as a kind of symbolical sin-offering, or payment of black-mail.[51]

Despite his dire statement of the case—"Thou must bleed for me"—Emerson's list of acceptable gifts includes items that are not necessarily sacrifices but are simply characteristic of the person offering. This confusion over what counts as a portion of oneself suggests that there is room for variation in the carrier of the *hau;* it seems sufficient that the given object should bear the mark of the giver. Such marks, signs of the giver's identity, secure and acknowledge the fact that every gift makes a purchase of recognition.

In the case of condescension, recognition is not only the thing purchased but also the thing given. Of course, I may give something else at the same time that I condescend: a salutation, a donation of money, or even a plea for help. But what marks my act out as condescension is that it involves my recognizing someone who is normally beneath my notice. Consider the following passage from *Martin Chuzzlewit,* in which Mark Tapley denounces the newly unmasked hypocrite Pecksniff. "Pecksniff! Why, I wouldn't see the man myself; I wouldn't hear him; I wouldn't choose to know he was in company. I'd scrape my shoes on the scraper of the door, and call that Pecksniff, if you liked; but I wouldn't condescend no further" (663). Tapley's refusal to "condescend," as he describes it, amounts to a refusal to see, hear, and know—in fact a refusal to recognize.

We see, then, that condescension involves an exchange of recognition in both directions. To be sure, the whole transaction is set in motion by the superior, but it is ratified by the subordinate, and we can try to understand the phenomenon from both perspectives. When I condescend, I temporarily abdicate my privilege of self-definition. I grant recognition to another and make a plea for recognition in return. Condescension is a momentary rechanneling of recognition outward, an expansion of the circuit of recognition, but always with the presumption that it will lead back to the one who condescends. For the subordinate, condescension is a momentary emergence into the realm of visibility but also an emergence into a particular role constituted by the recognition of the superior. In other words, condescension is a kind of mirror, an encounter through which both subordinate and superior see themselves as constituted by the recognition of the other.[52]

Of course such recognition is subject to distortion, and this distortion is precisely what produces the failure of condescension. This failure most commonly takes place when one party uses condescension to claim a superiority that the other party may not acknowledge. In such cases, the one who condescends cannot be sure that he or she will be properly recognized as superior and must therefore link the appeal for recognition with an attack against the other person as someone who is indeed subordinate. Thus, my recognition of you as my subordinate is in fact a tactic for subordinating you, a projection disguised as recognition. This is the condescension we know and hate, an act that appeals to the other for approval even while subjecting the other to disdain. Of the Victorian novelists, Dickens was the most keenly sensitive to the psychology of a condescension designed to subordinate. For instance, in *Martin Chuzzlewit,* Pecksniff pawns off his condescension on Tom Pinch as a gift, but we understand it to be a characteristic power play: "He made the promise with so much condescension and patronage, that Tom felt he had asked a great deal (this had not occurred to his mind before), and thanked him earnestly" (90). Along the same lines, Miggs the maid (in *Barnaby Rudge*) describes the demonically manipulative Mr. Chester as "[s]o upright and noble, that he seems to despise the very ground he walks on! and yet so mild and condescending, that he seems to say 'but I will take notice on it too'" (211). The ironic resources of an exploitative condescension were certainly a comic gold mine for Dickens, but the irony had its tragic uses too, as in this passage from *David Copperfield:* "We were all extremely glad to see Traddles so put down, and exalted Steerforth to the skies: especially when he told us, as he condescended to do, that what he had done had been done expressly for us, and for our cause, and that he had conferred a great boon upon us by unselfishly doing it" (101). Here there is no insult but something more threatening still; Steerforth's recognition of the younger students is a simultaneous allocation of privilege and guilt, a tactic of charismatic exposure that brands David even into his adulthood.

Our discussion of recognition (and its distortions) has enabled us to see the mechanism whereby condescension succeeds or fails. But we have yet to consider the qualitative experience of condescension, the motives out of which the act arises and which it fosters in turn. This phenomenological qualification of the condescension structure follows a course proposed by Marshall Sahlins, in his influential revision of Mauss's work. After discussing the possibility of a "purely formal typology of reciprocities," Sahlins explains that such a typology would be incomplete: "It ought to be recognized from the beginning that the distinction of one type of reciprocity from another is more than formal. A feature such as the expectation of returns says something about the spirit of exchange, about its disinterestedness or its interestedness, the impersonality, the compassion. Any seeming formal classification conveys these meanings: it is as much a moral as a mechanical scheme."[53] Sahlins goes on to describe various types of reciprocity that share the same formal structure (donation → receipt → return) but are marked by a different set of attitudes and consequently seem, from the performer's perspective, entirely distinct. For instance, donation might be understood as "sharing" or "payment" or "losing," depending on the context of the transaction.

One might mistakenly yoke condescension to a particular social attitude—deference, for instance. By this account, condescension is a tool with which authority figures produce deference among their subordinates, a mechanism of social control. Yet we cannot claim that this is always, or even typically, the case. For one thing, condescension is by no means acknowledged to be the best method for generating deference: sometimes the schoolmaster must be strict rather than generous to ensure the pupil's obedience; the employer must be unyielding to ensure the worker's respect or docility. What appears to be calculated condescension may instead be an unintended compromise on the part of the authority figure, a genuine capitulation of power rather than a power play. Conversely, what appears a deferent response on the part of a subordinate might mask resentment—or indeed it might indicate gratitude and an affirmation of authority. In this way, condescension comprises such diverse practices as sacrifice and degradation, deference and blackmail. In itself, condescension is not necessarily conciliatory, nor is it necessarily antagonistic. Yet these two qualities do represent the moral spectrum of condescension, and we will consider them in turn.

Traditional condescension is based on the premise that a ritualized recognition of existing authority relationships can work toward their moral justification. In some ways this is hard to grasp; we tend to think that power, when it is working, hides itself from view. But traditional condescension requires a situation where there is no confusion about the facts of authority. It is only possible between subjects whose authority relationships are clearly established—servant and mistress, son and father, tenant and landlord, hopeful lover and unrequiting beloved. In such situations, the authority figure has every reason to expect the obedience of the subordinate. Condescension therefore lays no new obligation on the subordinate; instead, it makes comprehensible, and even desirable, an obligation that is already felt. One such instance takes place at an earlier moment in *Patronage*, in which the young barrister Alfred Percy praises the chief justice under whom he serves: "Before the chief justice was so high as he is now, without a rival in his profession, he was ever the most generous man to his competitors. I am sure he is now the most kind and condescending to his inferiors. In company he is never intent upon himself, seems never anxious about his own dignity or his own fame. He is sufficiently sure of both to be quite at ease.—He excites my ambition, and exalts its nature and value" (271). Because the chief justice is not anxious—because his dignity and fame are secure—his condescension is compatible with real generosity, genuine humility. In condescending, he refuses to take his inferiors for granted but suggests instead that their labor is something to be earned. In this case, condescension to inferiors is given as the moral equivalent of generosity to rivals; it is a way to recognize the worth of the other in the face of a structural antagonism.

Even later in the century, condescension is sometimes able to retain its traditional, conciliatory quality. This is possible, for instance, when one party wants to be under obligation to the other. In Kingsley's *Yeast*, Lancelot Smith is glad to have been graced with the "sunshine" of Argemone's condescension, because he wants to serve her.[54] Lancelot's devotional use of the word carries a religious intonation, captured directly by Kingsley in the same novel, with a reference to God as "the Spirit of order, obedience, loyalty, brotherhood, mercy, condescension" (261). In *Romola*, Nello is accused of playing the sycophant to Lorenzo, in order "that he may be affable and condescending to you."[55] And in *Far from the Madding Crowd*, Boldwood appeals to Bathsheba Everdene's "kindness and condescension" partly to convince her (and himself) that if they marry, he will be able to subordinate his desires to her will.[56] In cases such as these, the problematic opposition between giver and receiver is nullified by the petitioner's willingness to put himself under an obligation.

Victorian condescension more commonly displays an adversarial quality, where the interests of superior and subordinate are felt to be opposed and the condescension act becomes a contest of wills. Emerson explains how easily gift giving can provoke an adversarial response: "For, the expectation of gratitude is mean, and is continually punished by the total insensibility of the obliged person. . . . It is a very onerous business, this of being served, and the debtor naturally wishes to give you a slap" ("Gifts," 537). Mauss too is fully cognizant of this condition of gift exchange; his theory, in fact, is meant to account for all societies of total prestation (in which all wealth is shared in the form of gifts), even where prestation takes a particularly agonistic form. In such cases, the exchange is called "potlatch," a straightforward competition—still in the form of gift exchange—for the benefit of one's own clan.[57] Condescension is often just this sort of competitive exchange, with both the one who condescends and the one condescended to seeking to turn the encounter to advantage.

We have already looked at a number of these adversarial cases, cases in which the superior condescends to control and manipulate the subordinate. In such cases, the acceptance of the condescending gesture is felt to be a capitulation to authority, and the subordinate may thus reject the gesture out of hand, or indeed demand more, as in the following exchange from *Lady Audley's Secret:* "'Tell my lady how thankful you are, Luke,' she said. 'But I'm not so over and above thankful,' answered her lover savagely. 'Fifty pound ain't much to start a public. You'll make it a hundred, my lady.'"[58] Here Luke Marks lays bare the adversarial nature of Lady Audley's proposal, denying her the appearance of generosity and characterizing her offer as a capitulation to blackmail. Henry Jekyll is similarly compromised when he remarks, "There comes an end to all things; the most capacious measure is filled at last; and this brief condescension to my evil finally destroyed the balance of my soul."[59] His condescension betokens his own defeat and his enemy's ascendancy. In the battle for authority, it is occasionally the subordinate who condescends, as at the moment in *Frankenstein* when the creature returns to punish his creator: "Slave, I before reasoned with you, but you have proved yourself unworthy of my condescension. Remember that I have power; you believe yourself miserable, but I can make you so wretched that the light of day will be hateful to you. You are my creator, but I am your master;—obey!"[60] Condescension is here at its adversarial peak. It is the vehicle whereby the creature reveals his dominance, and the word itself fires a semantic revolution after which the father and creator is no longer to be supplicated but simply tolerated.

Issues of concord and discord are perhaps the most obtrusive aspects of the phenomenology of condescension, but they are not the only ones. Also central is the traversal of space. Whereas gift exchange involves, at least superficially, the transfer of an object, condescension is entirely concerned with attitudes and relations; consequently, the spatial relation between the agents is foregrounded. Several spatial factors should be considered: Is the condescension-subject (literally and metaphorically) descending to the level of the object or raising the object to a higher level? Does condescension bridge a gap between subject and object, or does it in fact hold the gap open and even make it useful? Does condescension occur at the place of the subject or the place of the object? Here we can observe a key difference between invitation and invasion. When Mauss discusses the tribal potlatch, for instance, he argues that the chief invites others into his tent to save them from the ignorance of his own name or importance. In other words, the gift he gives them is the recognition of himself. Charitable visits, by contrast, take place in the homes of the needy. Does this fact constitute a recognition of the subordinate that invitation does not, or at least a more complete kind of recognition? In the case of Eliot's Janet Dempster ("Janet's Repentance"), it is Janet's homelessness—her eviction—that makes her a proper (or approachable) object; neither invitation nor visiting is a viable avenue of interaction. And what about condescension that involves no space at all, such as that which takes place in a written correspondence? Do begging-letters, for instance, attempt to evade a physical approach that would somehow preclude or preempt condescension?

Equally important is the element of time, which is frequently discussed both pragmatically and abstractly in relation to the gift. As is discussed in later chapters, the spontaneity of the gift was an active idea in the public discourse of Victorian charity; it has also been central to theory. Godbout refers to spontaneity as "that element . . . that is found in all varieties of gift."[61] The gift transaction (and condescension as well) must be over in an instant; any residue becomes debt and turns the gift into an economic exchange. Paradoxically, in classical theories of the gift, there is always a return, and a long delay between the original and the return donation is what, in fact, makes it a gift exchange instead of an economic one. Jacques Derrida develops this idea: the gift is only a gift until it is returned, at which point it becomes an economic transaction. The progress of time, says Derrida, makes the gift impossible, bringing a return and causing it to cycle back into economics. The gift thus freezes time, momentarily breaking out of the economic cycle. Thus, the important fact about the thing given—its very structure—is the delay it causes.[62] Yet because the gift always meets with a return in less than an instant (it is returned even as it is recognized or thought), the delay allowed by the gift takes no time at all, and it is really only the sense of a delay, the already-forfeited possibility of an escape from the economic, that is given. This abstract approach is directly relevant to the analysis of condescension acts, partly because they are threatened by their extension or even their remembrance in time (which creates the suspicion that the act is calculating, looking for a return), but additionally because they also, as they approximate instantaneity, can seem like they have transacted nothing of substance, if anything at all.

The Argument

In recent years, philanthropy has become a vibrant sector of Victorian studies. Organized charity is applauded by those who see it as having contributed to cross-class sympathy, a redistribution of wealth, public vocations for women, and the foundations of modern social work. Conversely, charity is deplored by those who see it as a tool for middle-class hegemony, political complacency, and social stratification. Critics have used these various ideological paradigms as a way of contextualizing and complicating the seemingly simple, manifest aims of Victorian philanthropists: to spread the gospel, feed the hungry, teach thrift and economy, and prevent the deserving poor from slipping into pauperism. What is not always recognized are the deep divisions within the philanthropic imagination itself, and the ways in which the texture of charity changed from one generation to the next. Condescension is a case in point: when critics discuss the tendency of volunteer workers to condescend, they present condescension as if it were an obvious and perennial impediment to philanthropy, whereas in fact the very condescension that alienated the Victorian poor had been seen, just decades earlier, as the best sign of charity's success. *Charity and Condescension,* then, attempts to expand our perception of charity's ideological purposes by examining the deep structural tensions within philanthropy's image of itself.

This book is inspired by the work of other literary critics who have explored the cultural and ideological resonance of Victorian philanthropy. Many scholars have used charity as a lens through which to gain insight into the desires and achievements of middle-class women and to investigate the complex negotiations of gender and sexuality that permeated the Victorian public sphere, once thought to be exclusively masculine. Judith Walkowitz's *City of Dreadful Delight* set all of these issues in motion, revealing the powerful late-century emergence of a discourse of urban spectatorship and showing how W. T. Stead's 1885 exposé of child prostitution drew mainstream readers into a charged dialogue about women, sex, and urban life. Deborah Epstein Nord's

Walking the Victorian Streets brings many of Walkowitz's themes to bear specifically on philanthropy, as she considers the transgressive aspects of slum visiting, in which the middle-class woman was transformed from spectacle to spectator. Dorice Elliott's *The Angel Out of the House* sees philanthropy as both sanctioning and trying to circumscribe women's "ambitious desires," desires centered on fulfillment through vocation. In *Giving Women*, Jill Rappoport considers the social networks that Victorian women created through alternative economies of gift exchange. And Seth Koven's *Slumming* considers the ways in which the social experimentation involved in slumming tracks with the emergence of modern sexual identities. *Charity and Condescension* draws on these studies, revisiting some of the philanthropic scenes that feminist and gender critics have brought into focus and considering how charity's "gender trouble" relates to the structures of authority and deference endemic to condescension.[63]

Other cultural studies work has looked at charity in relation to the state, citizenship, and nation building; especially notable is Lauren Goodlad's 2003 *Victorian Literature and the Victorian State*. Goodlad focuses on the tensions inherent within liberal ideology, arguing that the perpetual struggle between the bureaucratic poor laws and the self-organizing initiatives of philanthropy was an effect of the liberal state's determination to govern indirectly.[64] I believe that the failure of condescension and, more broadly, the instability of the charity narrative very much reflect the tensions Goodlad discusses, in that they register the attempts of the philanthropic establishment to maintain its traditional conciliatory influence while denying any claim of authority. *Charity and Condescension* also engages with critical work on the politics of sympathy and sentimentality, literary tropes that were essential to the traditional condescension scene. In "Dismal Pleasure," Miriam Bailin offers a profound analysis of sentimental pathos, asserting that the conventions of sentimentality are a response to the anxieties surrounding social mobility and stratification. Audrey Jaffe's *Scenes of Sympathy* subtly examines the complex symbolic negotiations by which the sympathetic spectacle allows identification (positive and negative) across class lines and activates fantasies of social climbing and fears of falling. Mary Lenard, Ellen Argyros, and Daniel Bivona and Roger Henkle all consider the ways in which sympathy relates to narrative authority. Amit Rai locates sympathy in the service of colonialism, while Brigid Lowe sees it as an engine of political subversion. What unites these studies is that they explore the particular mechanisms through which relations of power are constructed; they forgo aerial views and attempt to capture the workings of authority at the ground level. Such a perspective is only possible when we bracket the structural equations that would reveal all acting subjects to be the interpellated agents of a class ideology, and reconstruct the ways in which particular social exchanges ask their subjects to manipulate an array of familiar roles, conventional gestures, and legible attitudes.[65]

My argument diverges from the existing work on charity and Victorian literature in two ways. The first has to do with the relationship of charity to broader ideological structures such as class and gender: it is my hypothesis that the charity narrative, while very much entangled with other cultural narratives, has its own set of trajectories and conventions—its own horizon of meaning—and that these structures (condescension, conscription, settlement, restitution, and so forth) can be recognized and described separately from the social purposes that they serve. Such descriptions ultimately benefit even the most sociologically inflected literary criticism, in that the semantic contours of a text condition the ways in which it becomes available to ideology. My argument also differs from some others in its emphasis of narrative over discourse. While I often look to discursive structures (the connotations of the word *condescension*, arguments about the timing of charity, the Salvationist concern over backsliding, and so forth) as a way of providing context for my literary readings, I see both the problem of condescension and the imagined resolutions to that problem as fundamentally narrative transactions. This is equally true of all the narratives I examine, from the tightly structured novels of Dickens and Eliot, to Tennyson's evolutionary narrative of King Arthur's conquest of Britain, to Octavia Hill's episodic record of her own conquest of the slums. In positing that writers look to narrative as a solution to the deep strains within ideology, I aspire to the method of studies such as Fredric Jameson's *Political Unconscious*, Nancy Armstrong's *Desire and Domestic Fiction*, Rosemarie Bodenheimer's *The Politics of Story in Victorian Fiction*, and Audrey Jaffe's *Scenes of Sympathy*. At the same time, although I make frequent reference to philanthropic discourse, my work stops well short of the detailed discursive analysis that is the emphasis of some of the best literary studies of Victorian charity, including Mary Poovey's *Making a Social Body*, Dorice Elliott's *The Angel Out of the House*, and Lauren Goodlad's *Victorian Literature and the Victorian State*.[66]

Charity and Condescension draws on the work of social historians, who have, over the past two decades, created increasingly complex accounts of the role played by institutional charity in the functioning of the state and in the lives of the poor. The traditional Marxist analysis of charity is best exemplified by Gareth Stedman Jones, who argued in 1971 that Victorian philanthropy existed to increase the status and authority of liberal middle-class professionals and to create a deference community among the urban poor, reproducing the hierarchies of subordination that are characteristic of traditional English society. Many social historians have worked to revise this view, both by taking seriously the explicit motives of philanthropists and by showing the complexity of the relationship between philanthropic agencies and the liberal state.[67] Others have attempted to see charity from a working-class perspective, on the premise that just as charity served complex social and economic purposes for the rich, so too did it serve complex purposes for the poor, purposes that were not necessarily condoned or understood by middle-class philanthropists.[68] Among these historical perspectives, literary critics have generally found the social control thesis most congenial, often taking charity's disciplinary functions as a backdrop against which one can spot more destabilizing or subversive phenomena.[69] My own argument accepts, and even relies on, the idea that charity contained multitudes: it was an attempt at social control but also a sign of commitment to the physical and spiritual health of the poor, a site of working-class deference but also of working-class resistance. This dialectic did not merely surround philanthropy; it also animated it, creating much of the narrative instability that I locate in the condescension scene. In addition to the more polemical studies, *Charity and Condescension* draws substantially from the monumental work of social historians to recover the people and institutions of Victorian charity: Octavia Hill and the housing debates, the vast enterprise of home visiting and missions to the slums, and the Salvation Army.[70]

This book is not a history of charity. It is a study of the way in which a certain kind of scene, fundamental to the traditional plots of British literature, shed its conciliatory meanings and took up disruptive ones. But the transformation of the literary condescension scene only makes sense in light of related transformations in the social world; indeed, these were so marked as to make the failure of condescension in literature seem natural. The movement against condescension took place in many regions, not only in the realm of charity. We might as easily trace the failure of condescension in the discourse of marriage, with the emergence of a doctrine of separate spheres, questions of coverture and property, and debates over the meaning of Christian subordination. Or we could look at attempts to remove condescension from education, with, for instance, the community schools at New Lanark, the Working Men's Institutes, the pupil teacher system, and the educational systems of reformers such as Johann Pestalozzi and Maria Montessori. Condescension came under fire in the struggles of women and working men to get the vote; conversely, it maintained its force and even gained traction in the missionary and racial discourses of empire. But while charity is only one of many arenas in which condescension comes into the spotlight, it seems to me the most crucial. In charity, condescension was most likely to be embraced or rejected for its own sake—considered not just for what it did but for what it *was*. In other words, the issue is not simply that condescension was seen to endanger the relationships engendered by charity; rather, it had itself provided the content of those relationships, and the failure of condescension created not merely a logistical challenge for philanthropists but a need to reexamine the purpose and meaning of charity. For this reason, throughout the book, I use charity as a touchstone for the fortunes of condescension in nineteenth-century literature. One chapter is specifically devoted to philanthropic experiments that would rewrite the visiting scene; other chapters invoke other developments in Victorian charity, insofar as they shed light on the literary uses of the condescension scene.

Condescension, and in particular the condescension of the powerful to the helpless, is only one of several philanthropic "scripts." Charity took many different shapes in Victorian England, and by emphasizing this one, I run the risk of implying that Victorian philanthropy was entirely, or even mainly, a matter of the prosperous classes offering their social inferiors aid or advice that could never be reciprocated. Scholars have repeatedly debunked this description as a myth, and one that occludes much real philanthropic work. Frank Prochaska has been foremost in insisting on the enormous role played by working-class philanthropy, "the charity of the poor to the poor," both spontaneous and organized.[71] And as Colin Jones observes, "The time-honoured assumption that donors are from within the elite and their recipients situated at the base of the social pyramid consigns the middling sort, who could be at once recipients and donors, to a charitable limbo."[72] I readily acknowledge that the idea of a philanthropy that flows exclusively from rich to poor is a myth, one of many competing myths—many narrative paradigms—that Victorians summoned when they thought about charity.[73] It is, though, the myth that most often undergirds the condescension scene. As a consequence, when I look at the dilemma that condescension presented for Victorian philanthropy, I refer to a specific sort of charity narrative, one in which a person with some tangible social advantage helps a person with some tangible social disadvantage.

Just as the discourse of charity provides a rich context for the changes I trace in Victorian narrative fiction, so too does fiction offer a useful template for thinking about the phenomenology of charity. The Victorian philanthropy debates were largely procedural: a good deal of the disagreement among philanthropists dealt with practical matters such as how one might properly "time" the charitable visit, how a middle-class visitor should comport herself in the homes of the poor, what other kinds of places were most conducive to charitable interactions, and what sorts of people would make the best agents of charity. The procedural thrust of these questions can send them shuttling beneath our radar, but they touch on larger questions about the nature and purpose of charity. And significantly, matters of procedure tie in very directly to matters of narration, such that the way the literary work deals with questions of setting and pace reflects the ways the charity writer discusses procedure. The protocols of charity have much to do with the protocols of fiction.

In the pages that follow, I attempt to show how some of the most nuanced Victorian treatments of charity were predicated on the unraveling of the condescension scene. In place of condescension, writers looked to alternative forms of association—all the while exploring the costs of these more modern protocols and registering a sense of loss at the failure of a social script that had been so deeply entrenched in traditional English life.

The loss is most bitterly evident in the works of Dickens, who began as a champion of "personal charity" but, I argue, eventually came to see all acts of patronage as abusive. Critics have traditionally read Dickens as a general advocate of the philanthropic spirit, of the spontaneous outpourings of benevolence that preserve the bonds of humanity against the heartless machinery of the state. And indeed, in his early novels, Dickens ardently subscribes to the notion of personal charity, a Victorian embodiment of the traditional condescension act that centered on personal relationships between the powerful and the powerless. Yet at the height of his career, Dickens lost considerable faith in the aspects of charity he advocated throughout his early works. The ideal of personal charity is extremely complicated in the novels of his middle period, in which personal encounters between rich and poor remain essential but their character changes: instead of manifesting a kind of mutual goodwill across the social spectrum, these encounters expose prior histories of abuse and neglect and, through such exposures, provide an avenue for restitution and recovery. In Dickens's later novels—particularly *Little Dorrit*—personal charity is seen no longer as a vehicle to restitution but as a kind of mystification that forestalls restitution by obscuring any proper recognition of social justice. A charity based on personal relation utterly loses its power to reconcile; intimacy itself is unmasked as a tool whereby the poor can be manipulated. Like Beatrice Webb and other late-century critics of philanthropy,

Dickens ultimately saw condescension as bereft of any productive possibilities, contending that even the exertions of the most earnest benefactors were finally performed in the interest of their own security.

The works of George Eliot exhibit a more divided view, as I explore in the second chapter. Her first novel, *Adam Bede,* represents the dangers of a desultory, disorganized charity built on spontaneous acts of condescension. George Eliot's uneasiness with scenes of condescension echoes a pragmatic contemporary concern: that the moment of charity, as a disruption of the ordinary social and economic relationships between rich and poor, would necessarily be ephemeral and ineffectual. Yet in *Adam Bede,* even as Eliot endorses a systematic approach, she reinscribes the extraordinary potential of the interruptive moment. She thus engages with distinctly modern questions about forms and procedures, specifically, with the relationship between charity and proper timing. The problem of timing haunts *Adam Bede* at every level—from the straightforward matter of making and keeping appointments, to the strategic management of arrivals and departures, to the career-making moments of inheritance and marriage. Characters must decide when to grasp fulfillment and when to recede into expectation, and miscalculations in these matters can steer a benevolent impulse into destructive channels—a fear that would soon be recapitulated by the Charity Organisation Society in its campaign against indiscriminate charity. And yet, while Eliot agrees that the success of charity is a matter of timing, she continues to value the interruptive power of condescension, the sense in which the exceptionality of the condescension scene creates an arena of freedom within the mechanical clockwork of official welfare. For Eliot, charity thus becomes a negotiation between transience (its necessary condition) and fixity (its only guarantee), a negotiation that sheds light on the struggle, throughout Eliot's work, between modern idiosyncrasy and the fixed forms of convention.

Such questions are foundational to the intriguing philanthropic experiments of Octavia Hill and Samuel Barnett, whose different methods of slum settlement attempted to undo the condescension that they felt plagued other sorts of charity work. The third chapter considers Hill's and Barnett's initiatives as correctives to home visiting, whose necessary superficiality, in the view of Kingsley and others, had become a way of concealing rather than revealing the personality of the visitor. Whereas the aim of home visiting was to tear down the barriers between rich and poor, many writers argued that it produced an opposite result, encouraging the visitor to insulate herself with protocol or to immerse herself within her administrative role, and prompting the poor to perform a ritual of docility and gratitude. One alternative to visiting was settlement, a practice in which middle- and upper-class volunteers took on a permanent presence in the poorest neighborhoods. Periodic visits would be replaced by a perpetual intimacy, and in the shared spaces of residence halls and tenements, the identities of rich and poor would be forced out into the open. Paradoxically, and against the logic of the condescension scene, the social worker would become more approachable, more available to others, precisely by asserting his or her own opinions, tastes, and desires. For Barnett, this amounted to creating a simulacrum of Oxford in the streets of Whitechapel; for Hill, it amounted to entangling herself in the daily provocations of building management. Hill and Barnett ultimately imagined ways of life in which the relations between rich and poor would flourish by ceasing to be special; the only conspicuous element of their operations would be how utterly routine they were.

The final chapter looks at what was perhaps the most ambitious Victorian treatment of volunteer work and community, Alfred Lord Tennyson's *Idylls of the King*. Tennyson attempts to replace condescension with conscription, a process in which the disaffected and disenfranchised are themselves enlisted as agents in the struggle for the social welfare. Most notable in this regard was the Salvation Army, which recruited its soldiers in the working-class streets and neighborhoods. These workers would trade in the currency of the slums, serving as a link between the philanthropic establishment and the unwelcoming poor. To be effective, many Salvationists planted themselves on the thin line between rescue and perdition; unlike the pious working-class visitor, they were rowdy, uncouth, and convincingly capable of falling back into sin at any time. Tennyson's *Idylls* reflects this fraught notion of conscription, the idea that the commissioned agent himself is necessarily caught between public duty and independent impulse. As King Arthur's civil and military corps, the knights are public men, men whose interior lives must be wholly synchronized with their public commission. When these two things come into conflict, the knight must bury his errant self if he is to remain a knight. But conscription cuts both ways: while it holds out the promise that any renegade subject might in an instant grab hold of a kind of public intimacy that includes both the king's knights and the sovereign himself, it also presents the constant possibility that even the king's most loyal agents will lapse into rebellion. For this reason, much of the *Idylls* concerns Arthur's efforts not to win control of the kingdom but to win back the hearts of his own knights. By depicting a political culture in which even the best knights resist or revise the work that they are called upon to do, Tennyson illustrates the degree to which new modes of governance that attempt to forgo condescension thrust the public servant into a particularly ill-defined and embattled position. In the voluntaristic milieu of the liberal Arthurian state, condescension is divested of its power both to sting and to secure.

CHAPTER ONE

Help Wanting

The Exhaustion of a Dickensian Ideal

"When you have sat at your needle in my room, you have been in fear of me, but you have supposed me to have been doing you a kindness; you are better informed now, and know me to have done you an injury."

—Dickens, *Little Dorrit*

In July 1860, Dickens published a piece in *All the Year Round* containing a devastating scene of philanthropy gone wrong. The article relates Dickens's own experiences as, during a night of insomnia, he rambles "houseless" through central London and Southwark. A bell tolling three o'clock finds him on the steps of St. Martin's:[1]

> Suddenly, a thing that in a moment more I should have trodden upon without seeing, rose up at my feet with a cry of loneliness and houselessness, struck out of it by the bell, the like of which I never heard. We then stood face to face looking at one another, frightened by one another. The creature was like a

> beetle-browed hair-lipped youth of twenty, and it had a loose bundle of rags on, which it held together with one of its hands. It shivered from head to foot, and its teeth chattered, and as it stared at me—persecutor, devil, ghost, whatever it thought me—it made with its whining mouth as if it were snapping at me, like a worried dog. Intending to give this ugly object money, I put out my hand to stay it—for it recoiled as it whined and snapped—and laid my hand upon its shoulder. Instantly, it twisted out of its garment, like the young man in the New Testament, and left me standing alone with its rags in my hands.[2]

What is gained, what even is learned, in this encounter? Imagine the cold March night in Trafalgar Square, a young man in rags, harried by the elements and by his imagination, faced suddenly by—not a Brownlow or a Cheeryble but the father of all the Brownlows and Cheerybles, the very conscience of philanthropy. For decades Dickens had urged readers to reach out to lost souls like this beetle-browed youth. Yet now his own helping gesture comes to nothing. It does not matter that Charles Dickens passed by; an alderman or policeman, or an actual devil or ghost, would have done just as well. The futility of the scene seems to forfeit the social mission of the earlier Dickens, for there can be little hope for charity when the poor recoil from help as they would from harm. The benefactor too is called into question as a possible "persecutor," his companionship becoming theft as he inadvertently seizes the youth's only garment.[3] Philanthropy is no longer a solution to the failures of society; it has proven itself a failure as well. And yet, while this scene is a testament to that failure, it contains traces of the hope that has been abandoned: the ideal of personal charity.

I use the phrase "personal charity" to denote a particular strain in Victorian discussions of philanthropy. Borrowing the logic of condescension, proponents of personal charity held that the primary (or exclusive) function of philanthropy should be to multiply the points of contact between rich and poor, a contact that had been increasingly attenuated by the stratifications of modern urban life. Rather than contribute to the economic relief that was the sole province of the state, philanthropists should personally visit hospitals, prisons, schools, workhouses, and, of course, the homes of the poor. Through individual scenes of personal contact, each class would exert a salutary influence on the other. The rich would advise the poor on matters spiritual (scripture, doctrine, prayer) and temporal (economic and domestic management, health, hygiene), while the poor would remind the rich of the necessity of

Christian charity and would often provide examples of fortitude, dignity, and (paradoxically) independence.

Dickens embraced the personal approach to philanthropy, particularly in what I call his middle period, from *Dombey and Son* (1846–48) to *Bleak House* (1852–53).[4] During these years, Dickens moved away from the vision of general benevolence he had supported in his earlier novels and looked for solutions that would draw rich and poor into a much tighter scheme of relation. Yet Dickens's brand of personal charity reached beyond the regular philanthropic ideas of familiarity and influence to incorporate the idea of restitution—action that proceeds from a recognition of another's claims. In Dickens's middle novels, charity leads directly to restitution through the exposure of shared personal histories between rich and poor, histories that hinge on a primal moment of injury or failed paternity. Far from merely activating the powers of influence, charity effects an actual or symbolic resumption of paternity or reversal of some prior wrong.

Dickens's narratives of restitution temporarily find their expression in the operations of personal charity, but in the later novels, restitution presents a serious challenge to the entire philanthropic enterprise. This new attitude reflects the incipient socialism that, in the decades after Dickens's death, would convince the nation at large that philanthropy was an insufficient means of maintaining the social welfare. The proponents of state regulation (in matters such as housing and wages) argued that relief to the poor must be seen not as a philanthropic measure at all but as an assertion of economic justice. Charity was a palliative for the consciences of the rich, who could thereby demonstrate their solicitude for the poor without compromising the foundations of their own economic dominance. As an example of the new socialist thinking, I cite Arnold Toynbee's famous 1883 confession (excerpted from Beatrice Webb's autobiography):

> We—the middle classes, I mean, not merely the very rich—we have neglected you; instead of justice we have offered you charity, and instead of sympathy we have offered you hard and unreal advice; but I think we are changing. If you would only believe it and trust us, I think that many of us would spend our lives in your service. You have—I say it clearly and advisedly—you have to forgive us, for we have wronged you; we have sinned against you grievously—not knowingly always, but still we have sinned, and let us confess it; but if you will forgive us—nay, whether you will forgive us or not—we will serve you, we will devote our lives to your service, and we cannot do more.[5]

Toynbee's account names charity the enemy of restitution, a designation that was forecast by Dickens's own late-career change of heart. In *Little Dorrit* (1855–57) and afterwards, Dickens attacked the very form of personal charity that had previously proven so vital, showing it to perpetuate precisely the kinds of failures that it had earlier served to expose and expiate. The following pages consider the uses to which Dickens put the idea of personal charity during his middle period, and the reasons he later abandoned it.

Haunted Philanthropy

When *Dombey*'s Alice Marwood, a fallen woman, angrily rejects the alms offered her by Harriet Carker, she performs an act that will be frequently rehearsed throughout Dickens's later novels. Jack Maldon, Jo, Richard Carstone, Amy Dorrit, Miss Wade, Lizzie Hexam, Betty Higden, and even Silas Wegg find occasion to refuse or resist offers of charity. Yet Alice's refusal of help, conventional as it would later become, is far from automatic; it takes her several hours to return the money, hours that carry her into and back out of London and involve her in emotions ranging from intense gratitude to agonized rage. The whole transaction can be charted as follows:

1. Alice is "contemptuous and incredulous" toward Harriet's kindness;
2. Alice relents, becomes grateful;
3. Harriet gives Alice money, which Alice accepts as a token of her benefactor;
4. Alice delivers the money over to her mother;
5. Alice learns that Harriet is the sister of her enemy;
6. Alice seizes the money from her mother;
7. Alice returns to Harriet and replaces her gratitude with a curse;
8. Alice throws the money to the ground.

By opening a significant gap between Harriet's offer and Alice's refusal, Dickens suggests that the rejection of charity is not the spontaneous expression of a particular attitude but the culmination of multiple motives, attitudes, and effects. Even a first reading of the list above prompts various speculations about the psychological process of such a rejection: that the recipient's anger is predicated on an initial relenting; that the recipient must accept the money before she can reject it (cast it back); that it is not *general* suspiciousness but a *particular* suspicion (or allegation) against the donor that causes the recipient to turn on her; and that in the encounter between a donor and a recipient, other voices and interests (represented here by the mother) may be brought to bear. All of these issues complicate our picture of charity and its failures.

One conspicuous aspect of the transaction is that, whether Alice accepts or returns the alms, the money cannot stay in her hands. At the instant Alice arrives in the city, her mother asks her for money: "The covetous, sharp, eager face with which she asked the question and looked on, as her daughter took out of her bosom the little gift she had so lately received, told almost as much of the history of this parent and child as the child herself had told in words" (491). The demands of an avaricious mother are surely meant to signify the inescapable cycle of criminal poverty—the idea that when one is forced continually to revisit her degraded origins, she has little chance to reform. But the profits of charity are ephemeral in a more mundane sense as well, as they are quickly lost to the hard contingencies of urban survival.[6] A little money can do nothing to improve Alice's connections, erase her crime, find regular work for her. Rejecting the donation therefore becomes a way for her to repossess it. As she seizes the money from her mother, Alice ensures that it will nourish a private and sacred cause—the cause of her anger and vengefulness—instead of feeding the parasitic demands of her ordinary life.

It is not just the money that Alice repossesses at that moment; she instantly returns in her mind to the very moment of the donation, so that she can construct a new image of what actually happened:

> "Stop!" and the daughter flung herself upon her, with her former passion raging like a fire. "The sister is a fair-faced Devil, with brown hair?"
>
> The old woman, amazed and terrified, nodded her head.
>
> "I see the shadow of him in her face! It's a red house standing by itself. Before the door there is a small green porch." (493)

The scene unfolds anew before Alice's eyes, but differently; Harriet is now a "fair-faced Devil." Such an epithet may well have suggested itself to Alice in her initial "contemptuous and incredulous" apprehension of Harriet. If so, it has remained with her, ready to resurface if her interpretation of the scene should require it. The rejection of charity, then, involves not only a repossession of the alms but also a reconstruction of the past. Once arrived at Harriet's house, Alice further exercises the drive to reconstruct: "If I dropped a tear upon your hand, may it wither it up! If I spoke a gentle word in your hearing, may it deafen you! If I touched you with my lips, may the touch be poison to you! A curse upon this roof that gave me shelter!" (495). The battle for the present—who will have the money?—is revealed to be a battle over the past. To refuse charity, Alice must look backward.

For Dickens, acts of charity are fundamentally concerned with this backward-looking reconstruction of the past. Harriet cannot look at Alice's "reckless and regardless beauty" without imagining the state she has fallen from, and Alice, in describing her own abjection to her mother, links together scenes of her past history as a child, then a girl, then a criminal, now a woman. In the same novel, Polly Toodles fears that Biler's tenure at a charity school will sever him from his family, and she wants to reach him before he loses hold of his past: "She spoke, too, in the nursery, of his 'blessed legs,' and was again troubled by his spectre in uniform. 'I don't know what I wouldn't give,' said Polly, 'to see the poor little dear before he gets used to 'em'" (60). Both the desire to help out and the willingness to be helped are connected with memories of the past. Thus, John Carker takes an interest in Walter, who reminds him of the hopeful days of his own youth; Edith Dombey looks after Florence, a daughter who may still, unlike herself, be rescued from parental neglect; the prostitute Martha (*David Copperfield*) helps rescue Emily after she too falls; and Redlaw (*The Haunted Man*) finds, through Edmund Longford, a way to forgive the injuries of his own past. A study that wishes to integrate Dickens's scenes of charity with the most profound aspects of his narrative and social imagination must begin by asking what charity has to do, specifically, with reconstruction and revision.

Critics have noted that Dickens's class aspirations, and the hopes and fears generally held by a precariously mobile lower middle class, make the question of origins a vexed one.[7] For those struggling upward, the past supplies alternating images of shame and security, images available to be sorted, selected, forgotten, and recovered. Complementing these impulses is the novelist's conventional turn to the personal past as a setting for the most outrageous fantasies of suppressed identity and improbable affiliation—not merely in the sensation novels that surrounded Dickens in his final decade but in the great novels of his youth, in Jane Fairfax's secret love affair and Roland Graeme's hidden ancestry. But it is Dickens's brazen innovation to use such a past—the personal as opposed to the cultural past—as a framework for the utopian reconstruction of social relations in the present. Dickens removes the act of charity from the utilitarian realm of policy and measured outcomes and reveals it to be the reenactment of some primal and specific scene of alienation. The benefactor and the needy are invariably linked by a set of concrete circumstances that take three characteristic forms: (1) the object of solicitude sparks a remembrance in the benefactor of his or her own early life, as with Martha and Emily; (2) the benefactor turns out to share a suppressed kinship with the needy, as with Alice's eventual intercession on behalf of Edith Dombey; and (3) the benefactor has had some actual role in causing the suffering of one she intercedes for, as with Mrs. Clennam and Amy Dorrit. Personal charity in Dickens advances far beyond the standard philanthropic program of forging a better acquaintance between rich and poor. It thrusts both classes upon an imaginary landscape in which they are always already related, whether through identification, kinship, or criminal culpability.

The Haunted Man (1848) bears out Dickens's conviction that the success of charity depends on the reconstruction or recovery of a shared past. At the story's opening, Redlaw (a chemist) is a haunted man, suffering from the memory of a past injury. Redlaw is granted his wish to forget the sorrow of his past life and remember only the good, but he gradually finds that in the process of forgetting injury, he has lost his ability to feel compassionate toward others' sorrows.[8] Meanwhile, the chemist passes on his forgetfulness to all who come near him, always with the same effect: as soon as the sorrows of the past vanish, so does the compassion of the moment. This reprieve from sorrow proves fatal to the capacities both to help and to be helped. A mother loses interest in her infant children; a father has no pity for his dying son; a patient cannot tolerate his nurse; a prostitute slips beyond the pale of recovery. The hauntedness (shame, guilt, indignation, regret, loss) that had seemed a problem turns out to be a desirable condition, the only possible means to a constructive benevolence. While trying to escape his sorrowful past, Redlaw comes to realize that he has endangered his moral integrity—"integrity" in a chemist's sense of the word—and has cut himself loose from the community of suffering humanity. The story thus vindicates hauntedness and denounces any cure that would sever the ethics of the present from the trauma of the personal past.

The practical consequences of such a break are serious indeed, and the story traces these consequences, in allegorical fashion, across the diverse landscape of human life. For instance, Redlaw meets a fallen woman who is haunted by sorrowful memories of better days but loses all of her qualms of conscience once she begins to forget her past. "'Sorrow, wrong, and trouble!' he muttered, turning his fearful gaze away.'All that connects her with the state from which she has fallen, has those roots!'" (367). The chemist is "afraid to think of having sundered the last thread by which she held upon the mercy of Heaven" (367). Similarly, when Redlaw encounters a criminal who, softened by the pleadings of his father, is at the point of renouncing his career, Redlaw's presence restores to the man the boldness to eschew repentance and salvation. In another scene that is less sensational but even more pointed than these, Mrs. Tetterby, a mother of eight, ceases to care for her children and grows contemptuous of her husband. As she is later to describe it, "I couldn't call up anything that seemed to bind us to each other, or to reconcile me to my fortune. All the pleasures and enjoyments we had ever had—*they* seemed so poor and insignificant, I hated them" (349). Mrs. Tetterby's indifference to her family is wrenchingly portrayed in Tenniel's illustration, which shows her surrounded by her clinging children, who try to get her attention as she sits motionless and stares vacantly out of the frame.

FIGURE 1. Mrs. Tetterby, from John Tenniel's "Illustrated Double-page to Chap. II," in *The Haunted Man and the Ghost's Bargain.* Charles Dickens, Christmas Books (London: Chapman and Hall, 1913). Mervyn H. Sterne Library, University of Alabama at Birmingham.

The mother has drifted away from her family and can only recognize afterwards that it was her sorrow, sweetened by memory, that had anchored her to her home. Severing the link to sorrow, then, does not simply impair a person's benevolence; it reconfigures her whole ontology, such that she becomes a creature of the moment. As in Dickens's other Christmas narratives (such as the earlier *A Christmas Carol* and the later "What Christmas Is as We Grow Older"), the authentic life is shown to be the one that holds past, present, and future together at every moment and along with these includes failed hopes, lost ambitions, pasts that might have been but weren't.

"'The past is past,' said the Chemist. 'It dies like the brutes. Who talks to me of its traces in my life? He raves or lies! What have I to do with your distempered dreams? If you want money, here it is. I came to offer it; and that is all I came for. There can be nothing else that brings me here'" (356). With these words Redlaw reprimands Edmund Longford, the sick student to whom the chemist has paid a visit. Longford has just revealed his own hidden association with Redlaw's sorrowful past—a past that Redlaw can no longer remember—and welcomes the chemist's visit as a fulfillment of his long-nurtured hopes and expectations. But Redlaw rejects this account. He wishes to give a gift but refuses to enter into (or to be implicated within) a cycle of reciprocity, a process that has prepared for his participation before Redlaw ever thought of offering it. This cycle would be most famously described a half-century later by Marcel Mauss, who saw the process of gift exchange as constantly rehearsing the three phases of giving, receiving, and reciprocating. In Mauss's analysis, every aspect of the gift cycle is performed in response to an obligation. Correspondingly, in *The Haunted Man*, the escape from the past serves to liberate one from the burdens of the reciprocity cycle, making it possible to give without feeling obliged to do so and to receive without feeling compelled to repay the gift.[9] Once Longford is infected by Redlaw's forgetfulness, he too resists the gift cycle (described below by Milly Swidger) that would extend the act of charity beyond its immediate circumstances:

> "When I have seen you so touched by the kindness and attention of the poor people down-stairs, I have felt that you thought even that experience some repayment for the loss of health, and I have read in your face, as plain as if it was a book, that but for some trouble and sorrow we should never know half the good there is about us. . . ."
>
> "We needn't magnify the merit, Mrs. William," he rejoined slightingly. "The people down-stairs will be paid in good time, I dare say, for any little

extra service they may have rendered me; and perhaps they anticipate no less." (359)

The student objects to the drag of a charity that, even as it heals him, demands that he always remember his illness—a charity that far exceeds the moment of necessity and wishes to take back as much as it gives.

The hauntedness of Dickens's story is therefore the hauntedness of Mauss's gift, a sense in which every new encounter somehow recapitulates a moral drama that has come before. Redlaw's mistake is to think that he can become part of the solution without ever having been part of the problem. He enters Longford's sick chamber intending to relieve a stranger's distress, only to discover that he was present at the primal scene of catastrophe and that he has suffered by it for years alongside the student. Indeed, it is Redlaw's desire to help that sets the story in motion; as he contemplates Milly Swidger's seemingly untroubled benevolence, he becomes fixated on his own troubles, which seem to remove him from the community of others. If he could forget his sorrows, he could train his efforts outward, providing for others' peace and comfort as Milly does so easily. But the story's final revelation is that Milly is not untroubled—that she is in fact haunted by the greatest of sorrows, the loss of a child. Milly is the paradigmatic benefactor of Dickens's middle period, an avatar of personal charity whose itinerant social activism never ceases to look backward, attempting to recover an earlier scene of interrupted maternity. Figures such as Milly and the reconstructed Redlaw are absent from Dickens's earlier novels, in which natural benevolence—of the kind demonstrated by John Browdie (who defends Smike), Mr. Garland (who employs Kit Nubbles), and the schoolmaster who takes care of Nell—does not have its sources in trauma. Yet the perfect solution represented by Milly and Redlaw would be short-lived; with later figures such as Arthur Clennam, Miss Wade, and, most important, Miss Havisham, Dickens loses all confidence in the effects of a haunted solicitude that proceeds from suffering.

The beginnings of this shift can be traced to the philanthropic discourse of *Bleak House*. Like the other books of the middle period, *Bleak House* rigorously examines the motives and strategies that constitute personal charity, suggesting at every point that rather than pursuing the "telescopic" course of philanthropy, benefactors should place their own intentions and interests under the microscope. As in *Dombey* and *The Haunted Man*, the sufferers of *Bleak House* harbor secret histories of criminal neglect or failed paternity. Consider the case of Gridley, who, as the Man from Shropshire, has witnessed the dissolution of his property by the Court of Chancery; or the case of the Neckett children, whose father's untimely death casts them upon the mercy of their neighbors; or the case of Jo, who doubles as a figure for the wandering orphan (his parentage comes under investigation) and a figure for the semicriminal class of vagrant poor (the police call him "Toughey"). Acts of help uncover prior moments of abandonment, and casual interference reveals the inexorable pattern of identification that binds rich to poor, an identification crystallized by Lady Dedlock's impersonation of Jenny. But while the logic of personal charity continues to cast those who would help back upon their consciences, *Bleak House* ultimately doubts whether refinements of conscience can produce a constructive charity.

Personal charity is primarily endorsed within the context of the novel's multiple attacks against the impersonality of institutional philanthropy. Dickens's treatment of the shortcomings of his London philanthropists can easily be read as a general complaint against the narcissism of charity at large, but in fact his complaint is much more specific than that. The real problem is that because of the flamboyance (and simply the scope) of the philanthropic enterprise, philanthropists are inevitably caught up in the commotion produced by their colleagues, in much the same way that the American social elite in *Martin Chuzzlewit* are caught up in the enthusiasm of their mutual idealism. Certain of *Bleak House*'s philanthropists hold their colleagues' missions in contempt (423), while others do not: "[N]othing respecting them was half so clear to us, as that it was Mr. Quale's mission to be in ecstasies with everybody else's mission, and that it was the most popular mission of all" (203). But whether contemptuous or ecstatic, the philanthropists are too concerned with one another. John Jarndyce finds the "noise" of the whole enterprise intolerable:

> Mr. Jarndyce had fallen into this company, in the tenderness of his heart and his earnest desire to do all the good in his power; but, that he felt it to be too often an unsatisfactory company, where benevolence took spasmodic forms; where charity was assumed, as a regular uniform, by loud professors and speculators in cheap notoriety, vehement in profession, restless and vain in action, servile in the last degree of meanness to the great, adulatory of one another, and intolerable to those who were anxious quietly to help the weak from falling, rather than with a great deal of bluster and self-laudation to raise them up a little way when they were down; he plainly told us. (204)

Against a philanthropy spasmodic and loud, Jarndyce makes it his mission to keep quiet—and here already we can see the double bind. If personal charity is to be explicitly constructed as an alternative to other forms of philanthropy, it must become concerned with itself—with its own justification—in a way that duplicates the self-centeredness of every other philanthropic agenda. In its passage from feeling to form, from the pre-articulate to the deliberately silent, Jarndyce's tenderness becomes merely another philanthropic style.

Throughout the novel, Jarndyce awkwardly navigates between participation and self-effacement: he works to put the family legacy to rights, but he will not attend the Court of Chancery; he throws in with a fleet of philanthropists but keeps his contributions secret; he looks after the welfare of Esther, Ada, and Richard from their early childhood but only gradually (and sometimes reluctantly) reveals his own role in their lives and his intentions for their future. His generosity forces him into contortions:

> The notes revived, in Richard and Ada, a general impression that they both had, without quite knowing how they came by it, that their cousin Jarndyce could never bear acknowledgments for any kindness he performed, and that, sooner than receive any, he would resort to the most singular expedients and evasions, or would even run away. Ada dimly remembered to have heard her mother tell, when she was a very little child, that he had once done her an act of uncommon generosity, and that on her going to his house to thank him, he happened to see her through a window coming to the door, and immediately escaped by the back gate, and was not heard of for three months. (61)

It is not only the united chorus of the philanthropic mob that Jarndyce cannot tolerate; he cannot, in fact, "bear acknowledgments for any kindness" at all. Jarndyce pursues the absolute purification of the philanthropic act, an act that cannot be acknowledged without being compromised.[10] But his qualms cause problems greater than an occasional disappearance. For instance, Richard finds it easy to resent Jarndyce's concealment and effacement of his own interests, interests that Richard's imagination can readily supply. Jarndyce's unwillingness to ingratiate others—to place them under an obligation—thus becomes a convenient avenue for Richard's defection. Somewhat more unsettling is the phenomenon of Harold Skimpole, a kind of emanation of Jarndyce's obscure benevolence. A Derridean impossibility, Skimpole accepts gifts *as* gifts yet makes no return at all—of gratitude, recognition, or substance—to the giver. Skimpole short-circuits the gift cycle, deciding that every offer of charity is, at its source, a boon to the giver, and thus depriving the gift of its compulsion to be repaid. As he explains, "I almost feel as if *you* ought to be grateful to *me*, for giving you the opportunity of enjoying the luxury of generosity. I know you like it. For anything I can tell . . . I may have been born to be a benefactor to you, by sometimes giving you an opportunity of assisting me in my little perplexities" (71). The "luxury of generosity" without recognition or thanks is indeed a rare and welcome gift to John Jarndyce, but it is a luxury that can accomplish nothing, a pure but stillborn philanthropy.[11]

All of Jarndyce's work to manage the "noise" of philanthropy compensates for, and sometimes competes with, the more difficult problem of constructive social action. The novel thus fears that the personal charity that Dickens has so ardently defended might be no more than a science of attitudes. Rescue operations may be able to keep their integrity, but what if that is all they can do? As Esther and Ada realize in the brickmaker's cottage, "between us and these people there was an iron barrier, which could not be removed by our new friend. By whom, or how, it could be removed, we did not know; but we knew that" (108). Here Esther's social astuteness attunes her to a broader narrative phenomenon, whereby the restitution plot has separated itself from the drama of benefaction. No longer is society restored through the relenting of a Scrooge or Dombey or through the intervention of a Harriet or Martha. The fall of the Dedlock dynasty and the dissolution of the Jarndyce estate are inevitable. In the midst of this, charity struggles to keep its conscience clear. Like the walker in "Night Walks," the helpers of *Bleak House* come under the hard scrutiny of those they would reach. Increasingly, the complaints of people like Jo, Gridley, Miss Flite, and the brickmaker cannot be satisfactorily met. To recognize the claims of the distraught—to be haunted—is unproductive concern, unredeemed guilt. It remains for *Little Dorrit* to transform that guilt to resentment; to reveal a philanthropy in which benefactors are at war with their dependents; to propose that charity is (as Toynbee would have it) not a recognition, but a denial, of the claims of the poor.

Little Dorrit and the Dangerous Patron

The third number of *Little Dorrit* concludes at sunrise outside the Break of Day inn, where we spot "John Baptist Cavalletto running away from his patron" (134). The chapter is called "Let Loose," and the new morning—inaugurated by John Baptist's flight "among the flaming pools of rain-water" (134)—is an unmistakable image of transformative liberation. In this context, the choice of words is conspicuous; why "his patron" rather than "his tormentor"? Dickens's irony requires us momentarily to suppose that patrons wish to hurt and exploit their dependents, rather than help them. Echoing Cavalletto's Italianized English, Dickens invokes the most sinister connotations of the Italian *padrone*, connotations of covert negotiation and cruel mastery. Cavalletto himself certainly considers Rigaud a threat, frequently addressing him with the "conciliatory" expression, "my master" (7–8). Patron and master are interchangeable.

The novel abounds with such mobile authority figures—patrons, patriarchs, benefactors, masters, and proprietors, whose "helping" gestures betray their intentions to command. Authority is universally mistrusted in the novel, in a way that causes charity, even when it is not intentionally exploitative, to forfeit all of its effectiveness. Attempts at social reconciliation actually work to sustain authority conflicts. This reconstitution of the problem is most explicitly realized in Miss Wade, as David Suchoff explains:

> False sympathy and cheer, and the will to spurious social reconciliation, thus become Miss Wade's avowed enemies. . . . Given the primacy of goodwill and benevolence in the appeal of Dickens' fiction, this set toward exploding the fictions of middle-class amity explains Dickens' assertion of her importance to the novel, since she constitutes a strong part of its challenging voice. . . . Ascetic discipline in Miss Wade's character is, as for Kafka, less pathology than a commitment to live without any social illusions; and a social skepticism that renders her unable to cherish the myths of middle-class home that Dickens himself produced.[12]

The "will to spurious social reconciliation"—a reconciliation that inhabits "the myths of middle-class home"—is everywhere present among Miss Wade's social betters. Yet gestures of reconciliation only frustrate Miss Wade; they have become indistinguishable from the root causes of her degradation. This continues throughout the novel: when authority relents in any way, it is instantly suspected of doing so to maintain its own dominance. Failed acts of help make the very project of reconciling authority conflicts seem self-defeating and even perverse.

The British novel is deeply rooted in the tradition of misguided authority, a tradition that is manifest but perverted in *Little Dorrit*. Many of the great novels deal with the problems that arise when authority figures (such as fathers, landlords, and aristocrats) neglect or underestimate those situated below them. Henry Fielding's *Tom Jones* is the paradigm case; Squire Allworthy banishes his adopted child out of a mistaken idea about Tom's character. In *Guy Mannering*, the laird of Ellangowan evicts the gypsies from his estate, but when his son is kidnapped, he is forced to seek help from an old gypsy woman. In Edgeworth's *The Absentee*, Lady Clonbrony removes her family to London, disregarding the fact that her social position depends on her family's income from their tenants back in Ireland. While the authority figures of *Little Dorrit* abuse their dependents, they do not forget or underestimate them. In *Little Dorrit*, authority is fascinated with the poor and the needy, and authority figures programmatically cultivate their relationship with those below them. Unlike those of Ellangowan, *Little Dorrit*'s well-established householders and men of business are intensely aware of the disaffected multitudes on the streets and under their own roofs and devote considerable attention to the proper management of these disaffected. Yet with this new awareness on the part of the authority figure, the novel propounds a dismal antithesis to those earlier books: careful attention to the poor and disaffected has become a mercenary activity of political prudence; charity is the most effective means of exploitation and self-exaltation.

The novel's great virtuoso of self-exaltation is William Dorrit, who receives charity as if it were homage and treats others as beggars to exalt himself. Dorrit is at his characteristic best in his conversation with his "pensioner," Old Nandy. Clennam notices

> the relishing manner in which [Dorrit] remarked on the pensioner's infirmities and failings. As if he were a gracious Keeper making a running commentary on the decline of the harmless animal he exhibited.
>
> "Not ready for more ham yet, Nandy? Why, how slow you are! (His last teeth," he explained to the company, "are going, poor old boy.")
>
> At another time, he said, "No shrimps, Nandy?" and on his not instantly replying, observed, ("His hearing is becoming very defective. He'll be deaf directly.")
>
> At another time he asked him, "Do you walk much, Nandy, about the yard within the walls of that place of yours?"
>
> "No, sir; no. I haven't any great liking for that."
>
> "No, to be sure," he assented. "Very natural." Then he privately informed the circle ("Legs going.") (373–74)

Besides the intangible benefit that Dorrit derives from the homage of such as Old Nandy and Henry Gowan are the important financial "contributions" he collects from Arthur Clennam and others. Dorrit, like Harold Skimpole, makes his very begging appear to be a form of patronage, and any exposure of the illusion becomes a concrete threat to his livelihood. Thus, when Tip plans to attack Clennam for refusing him money, Dorrit lashes out in protest, on the logic that the Dorrit family must demonstrate a nobility of Spirit by "forgiving" Arthur's temporary indisposition, and hitting him up once again. In constantly reducing the claims of the people around him, William Dorrit echoes Henry Gowan, who sees bankruptcy everywhere. "The worst class of sum worked in the every-day world," says the narrator, "is cyphered by the diseased arithmeticians who are always in the rule of Subtraction as to the merits and successes of others, and never in Addition as to their own" (488). Gowan, reasoning thus, makes a companion of Blandois, whom he thoroughly detests. Like Dorrit, Gowan perceives himself to be elevated by the degradation of the people around him.

In the world of *Little Dorrit,* it is difficult to distinguish between false perception and false representation; where they diverge, they are respectively labeled "diseased arithmetic" and "mystification."[13] Diseased arithmetic, as we have seen, is a strategy in which a person comes to believe in his own authority by treating others as beggars and debtors. Mystification is another strategic deception, aimed outward rather than inward. As Henry Gowan is Dickens's diseased arithmetician, Henry's mother is the great mystifier, maintaining that her son's marriage is a descent and a disappointment when in fact it works much to her advantage:

> "And how do you both do, Papa and Mama Meagles?" said she, encouraging her humble connexions. "And when did you last hear from or about my poor fellow?"
>
> My poor fellow was her son; and this mode of speaking of him politely kept alive, without any offence in the world, the pretence that he had fallen a victim to the Meagles' wiles.
>
> "And the dear pretty one?" said Mrs. Gowan. "Have you later news of her than I have?"
>
> Which also delicately implied that her son had been captured by mere beauty, and under its fascination had forgone all sorts of worldly advantages. (519–20)

Mr. Meagles, like the narrator, finds Mrs. Gowan's scheme transparent and asks "to have no such mystifications played off upon me" (522). The narrator's cynical gloss on Mrs. Gowan's "concern" for Pet is later duplicated by Miss Wade, who, in her History, claims that her own supposed benefactors are actually working to demean her. Wade's claim cannot be dismissed as willful perversity; it accords perfectly with the novel's analysis and critique of mystification.

Often enough, mystification enables the appearance of gentility or, in Mrs. General's terms, the formation of a surface. Rigaud's "swagger," Dorrit's "genteel fiction," the Chief Butler's "supercilious eye," the "red-brick dungeon at Hampton Court"—all of these assume a gentility that does not disguise its material reality but actually reveals it, almost mesmerically demanding the complicity of observers: "Callers looking steadily into the eyes of their receivers, pretended not to smell cooking three feet off; people, confronting closets accidentally left open, pretended not to see bottles; visitors with their heads against a partition of thin canvas, and a page and a young female at high words on the other side, made believe to be sitting in a primeval silence" (311). Many times, the uses of mystification extend beyond gentility to a more tangible gain. Patriarchal Casby projects benevolence; he meanwhile lends money at 20 percent interest (411–12). And Dorrit drops his genteel fiction as soon as he discovers his fortune, inadvertently revealing his full awareness of his children's vocational activities outside the prison (420). In this case, Dorrit's presumed ignorance turns out to have been not the self-deception of the diseased arithmetician but a conscious mystification, a deliberate lie for profit.

Much criticism of *Little Dorrit* has discussed the novel's gallery of mystifications; "their purpose," explains George Holoch, "is to conceal the sources of wealth and the past histories of the characters."[14] Yet the connection between mystification and philanthropy has not been drawn as tightly as it might be. Holoch notes that "benevolence itself, in the person of Mr. Casby, is nothing but a fraudulent disguise for exploitation" (336), and others agree that generosity, when it appears, is often simply a mask for self-interest.[15] But we must recognize also the degree to which the prosperous *need* to exercise benevolence to maintain their authority. In other words, while it is true that philanthropy is grounded in self-interest, it is also true that self-interest cannot survive without the philanthropic gesture.

Consequently, philanthropy even pervades the mind of the solipsist, in the form of self-torment. The impulse to self-torment is infectious and ubiquitous in this novel. Tattycoram, tearing at her own face, reflects the "self-tormentor" Miss Wade, even as Arthur reflects Mrs. Clennam's relentless self-torment when he refuses to leave the Marshalsea for a better prison. Yet self-torment is at best a degenerate form of philanthropy, in that it amplifies the value of renunciation to such an extent that it loses sight of an object of charity. The authority figure no longer even pretends to be a benefactor but simply makes sacrifices as if her own spirit required it. For instance, Mrs. Clennam understands "reparation" only as it afflicts herself; she has no thought for those who might benefit from her reparation. Self-torment, like mystification and diseased arithmetic, is finally performed for the sake of the self-tormentor; it is another means by which a fragile authority empowers itself. The self-tormentors of *Little Dorrit* use their own suffering as a vehicle for legitimation (or, in religious terms, justification).

The advantages of suffering are elaborated in Mrs. Clennam's Calvinism, which threatens all worldly authority as a usurpation of Heaven and holds out affliction as man's best security. For Mrs. Clennam, to have power is to owe a debt, and to suffer is to be redeemed. Mrs. Clennam keeps a balance sheet, where those on top are always bound to fall and those below are always ascendant. She deplores any philanthropy that leaves the benefactor unimpaired, that emphasizes the raising up of the weak at no cost to the strong. This explains her mysterious hatred for Frederick Dorrit, who, she claims, "was the beginning of it all" (779). Mrs. Clennam elaborates:

> "If [Frederick Dorrit] had not been a player of music, and had not kept, in those days of his youth and prosperity, an idle house where singers, and players, and such-like children of Evil, turned their backs on the Light and their faces to the Darkness, [Arthur's mother] might have remained in her lowly station, and might not have been raised out of it to be cast down. But, no. Satan entered into that Frederick Dorrit, and counselled him that he was a man of innocent and laudable tastes who did kind actions, and that here was a poor girl with a voice for singing music with."

In the transaction described, the real criminal is the girl's patron; along these lines, when Gilbert Clennam wishes to take pity on the girl, he does so by rewarding her patron. It is as though, for Mrs. Clennam and her father-in-law, patronage itself is on trial, and it cannot coexist with the balance sheet.

For all of his family resentment, Arthur is too much his stepmother's son, accepting wholeheartedly the balance-sheet ideology.[16] Arthur imagines every part of his life to be integrated with every other in his great scheme of restitution. Thus, on his first approach to Twickenham, his thoughts fly from his occupation, to his inheritance, to his concerns about a family debt, to his relations with Mrs. Clennam, to Little Dorrit, to Pet (187–88). For Arthur, all thoughts of charity and social service are subsumed by thoughts of debt and reparation. We learn more of his state of mind in the eighth number:

> The shadow of a supposed act of injustice, which had hung over him since his father's death, was so vague and formless that it might be the result of a reality widely remote from his idea of it. But, if his apprehensions should prove to be well founded, he was ready at any moment to lay down all he had, and begin the world anew. As the fierce dark teaching of his childhood had never sunk into his heart, so that first article in his code of morals was, that he must begin, in practical humility, with looking well to his feet on Earth, and that he could never mount on wings of words to Heaven. Duty on earth, restitution on earth, action on earth; these first, as the first steep steps upward. (319)

Although the text contrasts Arthur's worldview with his childhood lessons, we must remark how closely the two are aligned. Like Mrs. Clennam, Arthur sees the whole world around him for the claims it makes upon himself, just as he sees self-inflicted restitution as a ladder to absolution. It must be a relief to Arthur when his amorphous sense of obligation is replaced by the tangible debt that sinks him in the Marshalsea.

Despite their impulses to self-punishment, Arthur and Mrs. Clennam both pursue courses of self-acquittal that compete with the novel's restitution plot. Having suppressed Amy's claims to inherit, Mrs. Clennam assuages her guilt by taking the girl on as a servant. Meanwhile Arthur—whose suspicions of wrongdoing at first caused him to abandon the family business—eventually becomes the chief defender of the House of Clennam, working to silence the claims of Rigaud. And yet it is finally Rigaud's extortion, not Arthur's reparation, that restores Amy to her fortune. From a narrative point of view, Arthur and Mrs. Clennam are allies in one struggle, and Amy and Rigaud are allies in another. While one of the novel's trajectories centers on the enlightenment, repentance, and reparation of the Clennams, another trajectory—which supersedes the first—involves the destruction (by Rigaud) and forgiveness (by Amy) of the House of Clennam from the *outside*. The guilt-ridden self-torment of the Clennams is finally at odds with the restitution plot, which is accomplished instead by Rigaud, who has no guilt, and by Amy, who bears no blame.

Thus, in *Little Dorrit* the refinement of the philanthropic conscience proves unconstructive, fulfilling a pattern that had begun in *Bleak House*. The "haunted philanthropy" of the middle period, through its revelations of shared histories and suppressed crimes, enabled authority figures to transcend interests narrowly personal or particular to their own class. But in *Little Dorrit* Dickens recognizes that hauntedness (or, in one manifestation, liberal guilt)[17] does not necessitate an emergence into the social—that it harbors its own private life. Authority may be self-serving (Casby, Gowan) or self-punishing (the Clennams), but in neither case does it pursue a social aim. Real restitution must indeed come at the expense of the authority figure, but it is not within the hands of authority to achieve, whether by help or by sacrifice. The novel's central question becomes whether it is possible to perform an act of charity for the sake of the object, an act that is neither a vehicle for personal gain nor an exaction of penance. And while *Little Dorrit*'s indictment of the hollow show of benevolence is clear and bracing, its attempts to preserve the ideal of philanthropy are profoundly complex.

In the Best of Families

So far we have examined *Little Dorrit*'s deep skepticism toward the idea that poverty and social alienation can be constructively addressed by the exertions of a benefactor. We might notice at this point that the failure of philanthropy takes much the same form in family life as it does in public life. William Dorrit's delusional patronage is extended to the Marshalsea prisoners and to his children alike; Casby's patriarchal mystification is equally active in Bleeding Heart Yard and under his own roof. Likewise, Mrs. Clennam runs her domestic affairs with the same balance sheet she uses for her business associates. On Arthur's homecoming, the narrator muses, "Woe to the suppliant, if such a one there were or ever had been, who had any concession to look for in the inexorable face at the cabinet" (47). Just as Dickens uses family life to add poignancy to his depictions of subjection and sham philanthropy, he also looks to the family for a possible justification of the philanthropic ideal. The whole philosophy of paternalism is, of course, built on the model of a parent's solicitude for a child, so the parent-child relationship is the ultimate testing ground for an attack against charity. If the parent has the power to ameliorate the child's distress, then charity cannot be altogether dismissed as a principle of social action. If, however, parental care is subject to the same failings as public philanthropy, then the whole principle of personal charity loses its grounding. In the character of Mr. Meagles, who is both an itinerant philanthropist and the head of a household, Dickens analyzes the capacities and the costs of an earnest, active charity.

By confronting the parent with the same set of issues that face the philanthropist, Dickens departs from the strategy, common to his late novels, of constructing domestic life as an alternative to the marketplace. This is not to say that the homes of these novels are impervious to outside forces. In *A Tale of Two Cities,* Lucie Darnay hears her conjugal peace disrupted by the footsteps of the Revolutionary Army; in *Great Expectations,* Pip's home with Herbert is invaded by Provis; and in *Our Mutual Friend,* Lizzie Hexam's cottage is papered with the unwholesome documents of her father's trade. Yet in each case there is a tension between the domestic and the economic, a struggle that finds temporary relief in such abodes as Wemmick's castle, Boffin's Bower, and John and Bella's Greenwich house. In *Little Dorrit,* by contrast, domestic life does not exist in tension with economic life.[18] Essentially, *Little Dorrit* uses the family not as a sanctuary from social abuse but as a laboratory for social experimentation. In the process, parental care becomes subject to the same dangers that beset philanthropic interest.

The most important participant in this experiment is Mr. Meagles, not because he abuses his authority but because, even with the best intentions, he finds it impossible to exercise his authority in a way that elicits the "right" response from the people closest to him. "I am like a sane man shut up in a madhouse," he complains (15). Meagles's authority fails most visibly in his unsuccessful attempts to integrate Tattycoram into his household, attempts directly tied to the economics of philanthropy. In Tattycoram, Meagles is able to perceive most starkly the greatest danger that besets his household: the defection of the child. Meagles tries to manage Tattycoram through the exercise of parental condescension, a practice that is premised, as we shall see, in the belief that the parent can intervene usefully to solve problems that are not of his own creation. But Tatty, in the course of her rebellion against the Meagleses, challenges this idea of intervention, suggesting that the parent is much more responsible for the suffering of the child than the logic of condescension will allow. While it is perhaps impossible to determine the justice of Tatty's challenge, it is most significant that Mr. Meagles cannot actually recognize her claims for what they are; his generosity requires him to imagine Tattycoram as a suffering girl who does not know her own mind. This particular blindness becomes even more marked as Meagles tries to understand the defection of his own daughter. Rather than view Pet as a danger to his household, Meagles submerges her in a series of displacements and projections, all in the attempt to imagine a daughter who could be a proper object of charity.

Meagles is a philanthropist in the literal, public sense of the word; it is, in large degree, what he means by describing himself and his wife as "practical people." Of course, his (and Mrs. Meagles's) adoption of Tattycoram stands out as his great act of philanthropy. But Meagles's charity ranges beyond this act. He is the novel's primary meddler, intervening on behalf of Daniel Doyce, Miss Wade, and the incarcerated Arthur Clennam.[19] Meagles also falls prey to the busy gluttony of schemers who lay traps for philanthropists: when he advertises for Tattycoram, Meagles is flooded by responses from eligible young people, and he is solicited by a "swarm of begging-letter writers" for enterprises completely irrelevant to his search.[20] Beyond his deeds, Meagles has what we might call a philanthropic temperament. When he faces dissent or insurgency, he does not circumvent it in the manner of the Circumlocution Office, nor does he ignore it in the manner of William Dorrit, nor is he destroyed by it in the manner of Mr. Merdle. Meagles disarms such conflicts simply by being magnanimous. He is constantly pardoning the affronts of those around him; his signature is the munificent handshake, which he deploys on every possible occasion.[21] Meagles instinctively forgives Tattycoram for running away, altogether disregarding the injury to himself:

> "Yes, assuredly; I want to give her another chance; Mother and Pet want to give her another chance; come! You yourself," said Mr. Meagles, persuasively, as if the provocation to be angry were not his own at all, "want to give the poor passionate girl another chance, I know, Clennam."
>
> "It would be strange and hard indeed if I did not," said Clennam, "when you are all so forgiving." (323)

Meagles expects his forgiveness to be met with contrition and gratitude. The process of condescension is able to set his home to rights because his own spirit of generosity is met (among his subordinates) with a spirit of patience and a conciliatory hope. "Patience" and "duty" are Meagles's lessons to Tattycoram; with these, conflicts can be managed without any final cost. "'Here we are, you see,' said Mr. Meagles, 'boxed up, Mr. Clennam, within our own home-limits, as if we were never going to expand—that is, travel—again. Not like Marseilles, eh? No allonging and marshonging here!'" (192)

Like Toynbee's philanthropists, Meagles intercedes so readily and good-naturedly as to put his own authority and intentions beyond doubt. While he does not pretend to have a share in—or even to understand—the suffering around him, he will happily forgive it and provide what relief he can. Here we see the limits of personal charity, a paternalist practice that makes no actual claims of paternity. Whereas Dickens had once used charity as a means of revealing the actual claims of the poor upon the rich (or the child upon the parent), in *Little Dorrit* he describes a charity that denies or defers those claims.

The philanthropist is a not a father but a paternalist, intervening in a situation that is in fact the province of someone else. Mr. Meagles is by nature such a caretaker, ready to intervene in troubles that are not his own.

Miss Wade attacks Meagles for just this philosophy of intervention, which is used, in her view, as a way for culpable authority to exonerate itself. "You can be," she tells Tattycoram, "a toy in the house showing the goodness of the family. . . . You can recover all these advantages . . . by telling these gentlemen how humbled and penitent you are, and by going back to them to be forgiven" (328). Every act of forgiveness is also an attribution of blame; the weakness of the child is invoked to obscure the fault—or even the cruelty—of the parent. Wade articulates this strong charge in her "History of a Self-Tormentor," which explicitly references Mr. Meagles's constant concern for Tattycoram's bad temper: "Did [Charlotte] say, 'It is I who am wearing [Miss Wade] to death, I who am keeping her on a rack and am the executioner, yet she tells me every night that she loves me devotedly, though she knows what I make her undergo?' No . . . She began sobbing and weeping (to secure the aunt's sympathy to herself), and said 'Dear aunt, she has an unhappy temper; other girls at school, besides I, try hard to make it better; we all try hard'" (664). According to this account, Charlotte is blind to her own instrumentality in Miss Wade's dejection; Charlotte's sympathy is predicated on (or productive of) this blindness. Likewise, throughout the "History," the philanthropist—in the aspect of friend, foster parent, or employer—sees herself as taking measures to mollify Miss Wade's intractable temper. Miss Wade asserts that this language of intervention disguises the power that the benefactor has over the afflicted. In her formulation, the one who intervenes becomes responsible for the welfare of the other. There is no portable paternalism: helping gestures lead to a full emotional custody, a principle that Miss Wade adheres to in her own "adoption" of Tattycoram.

Meagles's sympathetic recognition of Tatty's difficult origins allows him to assign the sources of her present discontent securely to her tattered past, a past that has nothing to do with him. When things go wrong with Tattycoram, according to Meagles, it is due to a defect in the girl's temper. He explains: "We are practical people. So if we should find her temper a little defective, or any of her ways a little wide of ours, we shall know what we have to take into account. We shall know what an immense deduction must be made from all the influences and experiences that have formed us—no parents, no child-brother or sister, no individuality of home, no Glass Slipper, or Fairy Godmother" (18). While in Meagles's account Tattycoram's bad temper has social causes, it is a thing already established by the time he adopts the girl; that its causes may originate or persist under his own roof does not occur to him. "Temper" is not a quarrel; it is simply a condition. From the beginning, Tattycoram's unfortunate temperament is presented as an affliction—more specifically, as a disease. For her to make her first appearance in quarantine is fitting. When Miss Wade finds her by herself, Tatty is "freshly disfigured with great scarlet blots," having torn at her skin in an outbreak of ingratitude (26). If Tattycoram is ill, then her complaints are significant not for what they say about the Meagles family but what they say about herself. They are the symptoms of her disease, the empty inarticulate signs of suffering: "The girl raged and battled with all the force of her youth and fulness of life, until little by little her passionate exclamations trailed off into broken murmurs as if she were in pain" (27).

Yet even while burying itself in the private experience of suffering, Tattycoram's passion carries a social threat very different from self-torment. At present Marseilles is a prison hospital of quarantine, but in the very recent past, as Meagles well recalls, it was a cradle of insurrection. "The bolts and bars of the old Bastille couldn't keep her": Tattycoram's "illness" invokes images of class conflict and resistance, and her blots are the color of the Revolution (320). Tattycoram's abandonment of the Meagles house is deeply resonant, seeming to set off a string of insurrections over the course of the next two monthly numbers. Pet sees betrayal in her own intention to marry: "[I]t is strange, even to me, that loving [home] so much and being so much beloved in it, I can bear to cast it away. It seems so neglectful of it, so unthankful" (335). Blandois, having entered the Clennam household as a distinguished guest, begins to show the features of a blackmailer. Tip is rebuked for pursuing a "parricidal" course of begging, which humiliates the Father of the Marshalsea ("Are you—ha—an Atheist?" asks Dorrit) (376–77). And Dorrit himself, through the agency of Pancks, achieves emancipation from his prison, only to begin (like Tattycoram) his long journey back.

Thus, despite its impulsive manifestations, Tattycoram's bad temper can be seen as a displacement of her social discontent. The submergence of the social within the impulsive is sensationally represented in Pancks, Casby's agent. Pancks, the man who eventually does take action to reform Bleeding Heart Yard, has no ideals, no programs, no words. He serves his proprietor and prepares his proprietor's overthrow at the same time yet does both as speechlessly and inexorably as a force of nature: "Perspiring and puffing and darting about in eccentric directions, and becoming hotter and dingier every moment, he lashed the tide of the yard into a most agitated and turbid state" (279). When he meditates an action against Casby, Pancks draws a parallel between himself and the "angry, passionate, reckless, and revengeful" Miss Wade:

> "The wonder is to me . . . that [Miss Wade] has never done for my proprietor, as the only person connected with her story she can lay hold of. Mentioning that, I may tell you, between ourselves, that I am sometimes tempted to do for him myself."
>
> Arthur started and said, "Dear me, Pancks, don't say that!"
>
> "Understand me," said Pancks, extending five cropped coaly finger-nails on Arthur's arm. "I don't mean, cut his throat. But by all that's precious, if he goes too far, I'll cut his hair!" (541)

It is significant that Pancks sees Miss Wade as the epitome of passionate violence; his portrait of her as Casby's cutthroat evokes the image of Gaspard exacting brutal revenge against the Marquis d'Evrémonde. And truly, Miss Wade (perhaps along with Rigaud) represents the novel's most primal impulse toward insurrection. But while Tatty's insurrectionary strain is reflected in the violent passion of Miss Wade, it is also reflected in the devastating action of Pet, the good daughter.

Although Tattycoram questions what the Meagles family feels for her, she is convinced that they are happy among themselves. Her own exclusion only further convinces her of the contentment that the Meagleses find in each other. The family does, indeed, come onto the novel's stage as a harmonious group. For instance, when Pet privately offers Miss Wade her father's assistance, Meagles steps in to sanction the offer, having overheard the conversation (24). The whole interaction plays out as a choreographed scene, in which Pet acts as her father's operative. Pet, in her maid's eyes, is the idol of her parents' affection: "I am younger than she is by two or three years, and yet it's me that looks after her, as if I was old, and it's she that's always petted and called Baby!" (26). Tatty leaves the household just after Mr. and Mrs. Meagles have "said Good Night to Pet in her presence (very affectionately, I must allow)" (322). By Meagles's account, the burden of Tattycoram's complaint is her jealousy of Pet: "She was younger than her young mistress, and would she remain to see *her* always held up as the only creature who was young and interesting, and to be cherished and loved? No. She wouldn't, she wouldn't, she wouldn't! What did we think she, Tattycoram, might have been if she had been caressed and cared for in her childhood, like her young mistress?" (322–23). Miss Wade supports Tattycoram in the view that the Meagles family is content without her. In fact, Miss Wade goes a bit further and claims that the Meagleses have purchased a sort of complacency and family unity at Tatty's expense: "You can be, again, a foil to his pretty daughter, a slave to her pleasant wilfulness, and a toy in the house showing the goodness of the family. . . . You can again be shown to this gentleman's daughter, Harriet, and kept before her, as a living reminder of her own superiority and her gracious condescension" (328). Miss Wade sees the girl not just as neglected but as exploited to showcase the family's "goodness" and to give them an object upon which to practice their condescension.

But Tattycoram and Miss Wade are both wrong to think that the only negotiations taking place in the Meagles house are between the family and the maid. Despite appearances, all is not well between Pet and her parents. Ever since the infant death of Pet's twin sister, Mr. and Mrs. Meagles have struggled to manage Pet properly. The family habit of international travel was originated for Pet's health and amusement, and the decision to adopt Tattycoram was similarly motivated. Much as she pleases her parents, Pet sharply opposes their wishes by committing herself to Henry Gowan. When Gowan visits Twickenham, Meagles is stricken to the heart. Despite Pet's attempts at conciliation (to be repeated three numbers later), Meagles cannot come to terms with her decision, and he and his wife are torn over the issue of managing Pet: "Mother and I have tried all we could to get the better of it, Clennam. We have tried tender advice, we have tried time, we have tried absence. As yet, of no use" (321). In fact, Tattycoram disappears on a night when the Meagles household is particularly fraught, Meagles having upset Pet by stating his desperate intention to take her abroad once more. We must assume from Meagles's account that the several nights preceding Tatty's disappearance have been especially uncomfortable. This challenges Tattycoram's account of the Meagleses' tender devotion to Pet; it is significant that Tattycoram runs away when Meagles's tenderness has given way to helpless frustration and his devotion seems most fragile.

Pet's discomfort with her parents' orchestrations causes a particular problem for the magnanimous Meagles. In general, when Meagles's amnesty is not met with gratitude—when his authority is rejected—he is completely disarmed. He is removed from a position to forgive others' resentment and is forced to cope with the resentment within himself. "To suspect me of the plague is to give me the plague," Meagles says (15). He grows agitated as he recounts Tattycoram's rebellion, becoming "almost as flushed and hot by this time as he described her to have been" (323). As much as Meagles wants to help Doyce, in doing so he must maintain his own superiority—in this quality,

Arthur famously detects the "mustard-seed that had sprung up into the great tree of the Circumlocution Office" (194).[22] As soon as Mrs. Gowan affects superiority over the Meagleses, all of Mr. Meagles's schemes of magnanimous reconciliation are thwarted, leaving him paralyzed with resentment at having been suspected of strategy.

We can now understand why Meagles is at once so sensitive and so incapacitated with respect to his daughter. Meagles is very ready to acknowledge Pet's unhappiness and to give her his sympathy. But Meagles will not acknowledge his strong sense that Pet is a threat to his home and his authority. Pet is his image of calm obedience; her touch immediately curbs his temper (29). Meagles is outraged by the suggestion that Pet could be considered dangerous: "DID you ever hear of such damned nonsense as putting Pet in quarantine?" (16). Yet even while raising this objection, Meagles himself quarantines Pet in the image of her dead twin sister. Since this twin died, Meagles has nourished her image alongside Pet's. She is like Pet in every way, only she, unlike Pet, is safe. The twin has matured in her parents' imagination, but she has also remained the same, a daughter "who died when we could just see her eyes—exactly like Pet's—above the table, as she stood on tiptoe holding by it" (19). Her infant image is a perfect object for Meagles's parental condescension. She is well below him, very much needing his support, but at the same time standing on tiptoe and looking up, acknowledging the favor that is to be conferred and the authority of the one who confers it. This twin is Meagles's elect child, standing tiptoe as his inheritor but still holding by the table as a pet would.

Growing up in the Meagles home, Tattycoram has long been aware of the spectral presence of the dead twin. Insofar as Tatty sees herself as Pet's counterpart, the twin is a counterpart to both girls. Tatty's involvement with the twin is evident when Arthur first visits Twickenham, as he looks at a double portrait of the two sisters: "The picture happened to be near a looking-glass. As Arthur looked at it again, he saw, by the reflection of the mirror, Tattycoram stop in passing outside the door, listen to what was going on, and pass away with an angry and contemptuous frown upon her face that changed its beauty into ugliness" (194). Tatty does not, as one might suppose, simply envy the twin for being Pet's equal in her father's eyes. For although Tattycoram so often complains that Meagles favors Pet over herself, Tatty actually identifies closely with Pet. On the night Tattycoram runs away, she objects that the Meagleses do not "have a right to name her like a dog or a cat" (323); here she could just as well be speaking of Pet's own name. Tatty does not run away during an episode when Pet is being "spoiled"; she leaves exactly when Pet is most in conflict with her parents. "I hate you all three," Tatty says. "I am bursting with hate of the whole house" (322). It is the revolution in the Meagles house that frightens Tattycoram. Without understanding the particulars of Meagles's struggle with Pet, Tattycoram feels it all intensely. She is frightened by the fierce insistence of Meagles's solicitousness and by her own sense that this generosity, particularly as it is extended to Pet, conceals the father's profound doubts about the security of his household.

With his invocation of the dead twin, Meagles illustrates a tendency inherent to philanthropy: the imaginative projection of a certain kind of dependent. As we have seen, the sham philanthropists of *Little Dorrit* are masters of mystification, advertising their exploitative schemes as helpful measures. But with Meagles, Dickens suggests that projection is not merely a strategy of deception, but that it is in fact a necessary prelude to any condescension act at all. By this logic, constructive intervention is not possible unless both benefactor and dependent play their roles appropriately.[23] The question of the benefactor's fault must never come up; the needy must never make demands. The benefactor cannot understand the plight of the needy from their perspective, since to do so would be to abandon the superior perspective of the outsider, to cede the mastery over the situation that the philanthropist requires.[24] Mr. Meagles actually alerts Clennam to the difficulty of understanding Tattycoram on her own terms: "As to how it happened, it's not so easy to relate: because you must have the unfortunate temperament of the poor impetuous girl herself, before you can fully understand it" (320). To help Tattycoram, Meagles must project a particular image of her, that of the mistempered child. Likewise, to benefit from Meagles's kindness, Tatty must capitulate to that projection, must acknowledge it to be true—as indeed the novel itself must do if it is to cede a victory to Meagles's benevolence. In order, too, to help Pet, Meagles must project onto her the image of the grateful supplicant, an image that Pet, for better or for worse, will not inhabit.

The gap between Meagles's projection and the actual, dangerous Pet is inhabited for a time by the fantasy of the dead twin, but by the end of the novel it comes to be inhabited by Amy Dorrit, Meagles's ideal of the obedient child. This displacement, which is prepared over the whole course of the novel, is actualized in the last number. Tattycoram has just absconded from Miss Wade and returned to the Meagleses,[25] at which point Meagles refers her to the passing figure of Little Dorrit and urges Tatty to make a model of her behavior. Moments later, Meagles offers Amy his continued intervention; she leans forward and kisses his cheek, just as Pet had always done. Meagles's associations instantly fly to Pet: "'You remind me of the days,' said Mr. Meagles, suddenly drooping . . ." (814). Meagles believes that Amy exemplifies the perfect object of condescension—which, in fact, she does not. The rest of this chapter will look at the ways in which Amy undoes Meagles's narrative of philanthropy.

Restitution

Reeling from his failures with Tattycoram and Pet, Mr. Meagles sees Amy Dorrit's behavior as an alternative to that of his own daughters. Meagles does not meet Amy until the end of the novel, when he and she work together to recover Mrs. Clennam's stolen box. At this point, Meagles immediately notices Amy's exceptionality. He uses her as an object lesson for Tattycoram, drawing special attention to the effects of her image on those who see her:

> "You see that young lady who was here just now—that little, quiet, fragile figure passing along there, Tatty? Look. The people stand out of the way to let her go by. The men—see the poor, shabby fellows—pull off their hats to her quite politely, and now she glides in at that doorway. See her, Tattycoram?"
>
> "Yes, sir."
>
> "I have heard tell, Tatty, that she was once regularly called the child of this place. She was born here, and lived here many years. I can't breathe here. A doleful place to be born and bred in, Tattycoram?"
>
> "Yes indeed, sir!"
>
> "If she had constantly thought of herself, and settled with herself that everybody visited this place upon her, turned it against her, and cast it at her, she would have led an irritable and probably an useless existence. Yet I have heard tell, Tattycoram, that her young life has been one of active resignation, goodness, and noble service. Shall I tell you what I consider those eyes of hers, that were here just now, to have always looked at, to get that expression?"
>
> "Yes, if you please, sir."
>
> "Duty, Tattycoram. Begin it early, and do it well; and there is no antecedent to it, in any origin or station, that will tell against us with the Almighty, or with ourselves." (812–13)

Meagles's description implies several comparisons between Amy and Tattycoram, all with the idea of correcting Tatty's behavior. He refers to Amy's "origin," comparing her Marshalsea childhood with Tatty's life in the foster home, or possibly with Tatty's life as an adoptee in the Meagles house. He draws attention to Amy's silent consequence as she glides past—in contrast to Tatty, who broods in isolation. He claims that Amy's eyes are fixed on duty, a discipline reminiscent of the one he urges on Tatty: to count five-and-twenty. And in characterizing Amy's life as one of active resignation, Meagles tacitly approves the latest chapter in Tatty's progress, her decision to steal the box back from Miss Wade and resign it to him.

By making the comparison, Meagles conflates Amy's "duty" with the gratitude that he has tried to purchase from Tattycoram and Pet. But resignation is not gratitude, and Amy's Marshalsea childhood is a far cry from the charitable jurisdiction Meagles attempts to maintain. In an economy of charity—the economy of Mr. Meagles—the gratitude of the subordinate is purchased by the generosity of the superior. Amy's history, by contrast, is a story of survival under the despotic demands of her relatives. In fact, Amy has been manipulated and exploited in much the same way that Miss Wade claims to have been. It is *because* Tattycoram sees her own story in this light—because she fears that the kindness of Mr. Meagles masks something more threatening—that she leaves the Meagles home. Resignation, then, is exactly what Meagles must convince Tatty no one is asking of her. With his appeal to Amy, Meagles unwittingly chooses for Tatty a role model whose story, if it were known, would confirm the child's worst fears about the attentions of her foster family.

Meagles's error raises a broader question: to what degree does Amy Dorrit support a philanthropic ideal? The moment that best seems to capture the character of Amy's charity is in her last encounter with Mrs. Clennam, in the novel's last number. Mrs. Clennam describes herself as "hard" and calls Amy "merciful" (twice), "gentle," and "kind" (790). These attributes cast Amy in the image of Christ, an association that she makes explicit in her plea to Mrs. Clennam: "Angry feelings and unforgiving deeds are no comfort and no guide to you and me. . . . Let me implore you to remember later and better days. Be guided, only by the healer of the sick, the raiser of the dead, the friend of all who were afflicted and forlorn, the patient Master who shed tears of compassion for our infirmities" (792). Amy's plea supports the practice of compassion, intervention, care; but it is a care that bears an uncertain relationship to philanthropy. The progress of the passage—showing Christ as healer, then as friend, and ultimately as compassionate Master—moves away from help and toward sorrowful identification, with the suggestion that the highest capacity of the master is to take the sorrows of the servant upon himself. This is a far cry from the sponsorship of the Cheeryble brothers; it is, too, rather different from the ministry of Mr. Meagles. Amy's benevolence exists apart from charity in a conventional sense; she has been neither the object nor the agent of philanthropy. When Mrs. Clennam kneels to Amy in supplication, the younger woman becomes uncomfortable: "'Not in that posture,' said Little Dorrit. 'It is unnatural to see your grey hair lower than mine. Pray rise; let me help you'" (790). Rather than grant forgiveness in a way that would secure her own authority, Amy wishes altogether to disregard (or erase) Mrs. Clennam's crime, lowering herself to the level of her supplicant. Here—and afterwards, with the burning of the codicil—Amy removes herself from the negotiations of a philanthropy in which both parties ultimately pursue their own interests, yielding as much as they can afford to purchase their own security. As we have seen, *Little Dorrit* establishes such negotiations as charity's inevitable course, even a charity as well-meaning as that of the solicitous father. But Amy, first as a prison-child and later as an heiress, resists the relations of charity—a resistance that is formulated most explicitly in her story of the Princess and the cottager.

If Arthur Clennam is usually placed at the center of *Little Dorrit*—resembling the novel's author and readers, with respect to both his own social agency and his normalizing comprehension of the world around him—Amy Dorrit has always been placed at the novel's limits. For some critics, Amy introduces the possibility of responsible social action into the novel; for others, she occupies an exclusive perspective (marked by her gender, class, size, and family history) that uniquely enables the novel to transcend the usual limits of popular social analysis. Traditionally, Amy has been seen to provide an escape clause in the rigid logic of abuse that governs most of the novel's social relationships. J. Hillis Miller sees her as a figure for a preserved childhood, "the one stage of life which escapes the shadow of the prison."[26] Amy has been called the perfect servant.[27] She has been shown to be immune to the taint of acquisition that marks the novel's property seekers.[28] She has been seen as embodying the ideal of the domestic woman, an alternative to the male authority figures of the liberal, paternalistic order.[29] In fact, critics have traditionally answered Clennam's desperate injunction that Amy not call the prison "home" (258) with a sense that such an identification with the lower world of the novel is not, after all, a danger to which Amy is susceptible. More recently, the critical focus has shifted away from claims that Amy is a moral resource for untainted action within the novel, toward claims that she is a touchstone by which the world of *Little Dorrit* is made to reveal itself for what it is.[30] In this formulation, Amy makes visible (by virtue of her compulsive submission and conspicuous silences) the violence common to the conditions of working-class life and to the repression of women in an economy of liberal, middle-class paternalism.[31] The difference between these two critical positions depends largely on opposing characterizations of the novel itself as a fantasy of reform or as an analysis of an existing situation; both positions, though, make strong arguments for Amy Dorrit's marginal status.

In all of these arguments, Amy is treated as a static image. However inscrutable her motives, however inexplicable her peculiar sensibility, and however ambiguous the effects of her actions, Amy's identification as an "image" is never questioned. The novel itself fosters this approach to Amy, drawing and redrawing her portrait within the Marshalsea walls, in Arthur's quarters, in the streets, and on the Iron Bridge. Various characters question the effect of Amy's very presence: Fanny says that Amy carries with her the prison's "tone and character" (262); Arthur says that Amy has brought the spirit and influence of the outside world into the prison (260); William Dorrit feels Amy's presence to be a reproach.[32] The nature of this reproach is theorized by Suchoff, who claims that the novel's descriptions of Amy "serve the function that Benjamin found in the dialectical image: fetishized visions identify their own escape from the culture of the marketplace, and point out the very urban history they evade."[33] For Suchoff, the popular novel's attempts to describe and account for a pauper's daughter expose middle-class blindness both within the novel and within its readership.[34] This characterization of Amy as a "dialectical image" accords well with other critical assessments of Amy as an image, a figure, a model, or an ideal. Yet to treat her exclusively as such is to assume that Amy's marginal relationship to the common humanity of the novel—that her subordination within the abusive authority structures that dominate the novel—is consistent throughout the narrative.

Is this assumption justified? Amy's experiences within the space of the narrative proper are more completely heterogenous and transformative than those of any other character in the novel. She graduates from extreme poverty to extreme wealth, from emotional isolation to friendship, love, and marriage, from a life of ritual repetition inside a prison to a whirlwind excursion through France, Switzerland, and Italy. Her night (in the fourth number) outside the prison walls is said to be literally epochal to her. She loses a father, wins a husband, and gains control of a fortune that derives from neither. The Amy of the final number is not the Amy of the early numbers, and her new scope of action has significant consequences for any attempt to understand the social principle behind her behavior. Amy's transformations enable Dickens to dismantle the ideal of charity from the perspective of rich *and* poor, presenting her at first as a sacrificial victim who reveals the poverty of her benefactors, and later as an authority figure who resists the temptations of philanthropy.

Amy fills the role of a kind of household sacrifice for the first third of the novel, and she continues in this capacity up through the conference on the Iron Bridge (no. 6). She is called the Child of the Marshalsea, a badge of abjection that causes even the prisoners to pity her. Her domestic operations are figured as a kind of extremism, rather than a common filial attitude: "It is enough that she was inspired to be something which was not what the rest were, and to be that something, different and laborious, for the sake of the rest. Inspired? Yes. Shall we speak of the inspiration of a poet or a priest, and not of the heart impelled by love and self-devotion to the lowliest works in the lowliest way of life!" (71). Amy's family affections are thus distinguished from the usual set pieces of the Victorian hearth. She is inspired, otherworldly—like the poet or priest, perhaps, except that Dickens never drew an inspired poet or priest.[35] As the Child of the Marshalsea, Amy is "born and bred, in a social condition, false even with a reference to the falsest condition outside the walls" (71). She lives below the threshold of gain, with no real prospect of domestic or social tranquility. The extremism of her psychic life corresponds to the extremity of her situation.[36] Her "self-devotion to the lowliest works" is possible because she has nothing to hope for. Amy's sacrifice—that is, the sacrifice *of* Amy—purchases her no security, no reward.

In this phase of the novel, several attempts are made to help Amy, but those who try to help are exposed as lacking either the ability or the intention of doing her any good. As early as the second number (where Amy is first introduced), the turnkey struggles to find a way to leave some money to the girl such that the father cannot get at it. It is an unsolvable riddle, and the man dies intestate. Other attempts to help fare no better. Arthur cannot intervene without encouraging William Dorrit's rapacity. Flora gives Amy work but torments her with a fabricated account of Arthur's renewed devotions. Meanwhile, Mrs. Clennam's attentions to Amy constitute an elaborate subterfuge, as indicated in the epigraph to this chapter.

Most interesting of all are the efforts of Pancks, whose inquiry uncovers the vast wealth of the Dorrit family. Even as the agent's charitable efforts begin to bear fruit, Amy expresses her skepticism toward his investigations: "'I have heard him called a fortune-teller,' said Little Dorrit. 'But I doubt if he could tell many people, even their past or present fortunes'" (295). This verdict aptly follows Amy's own fortune-telling episode, a story she invents for

Maggy—and one, I argue, that implicitly challenges Pancks's philanthropic enterprise. The story concerns a "poor tiny little woman" who lives by herself in a cottage, spinning at her wheel and guarding a secret "shadow of Some one"—a man—"who had gone long before." She is confronted by a Princess who "had the power of knowing secrets." The Princess continues to visit the cottager until her death, and the cottager's secret is interred in her grave.

The fable is most remarkable for what it does not include, for the narrative possibilities that are introduced but never realized. In particular, the "Some one" who is the primary object of memory and desire never returns to the cottage, and the story comes to focus much more on the interaction between the cottager and the Princess than on the absence of "Some one." Even more mysteriously, the Princess, in her repeated visits, never helps the little woman; she simply looks in to "see what came of it." Essentially, Amy has rewritten the Cinderella story, an important action because Cinderella has been invoked several times in the novel already in reference to the daughter's fortune. Tattycoram, according to Meagles, has had "no Glass Slipper, or Fairy Godmother" (18). Three numbers later, in a chapter entitled "Little Dorrit's Party," one of the running titles of the 1868 edition reads "Cinderella's Shoes," referring ironically to Amy's "thin, worn shoe" (167). Amy has told her father she is out at a party—a reversal of Cinderella's ball, which Cinderella attends under the pretence of having stayed home. Like Tattycoram in her early childhood, Amy is without Glass Slipper or Fairy Godmother, and the novel suggests that these things are the sign of rescue. In this light, it is significant that Amy's fable features no Fairy Godmother and no change of fortune. The story is offered up in explicit contrast to the lucrative godmothering of Pancks. In effect, Amy offers her fable as a truer vision than Pancks's; the attentive Princess and the settled cottager replace the bountiful Godmother and Cinderella ascendant.

If Amy's fable is not the Cinderella story, it is in fact not a story about charity at all. What the Princess discovers, when she looks in at the door, is not a scene of need but a scene of contentment. The cottager's shadow "was bright to look at; and when the tiny woman showed it to the Princess, she was proud of it with all her heart, as a great, great, treasure" (294). The strange fact is that the cottager already has a treasure, and so the Princess has nothing more to offer, no crisis to rectify. While Dianne Sadoff has argued that the shadow signifies a secret shame associated with incest and molestation,[37] Amy describes it as an object of pride, explaining that the reason the cottager keeps it hidden is that she is afraid someone will take it away (a condition that recalls the turnkey's conundrum). The revelation is that condescension is unnecessary—that, when the Princess looks into the cottage, the cottager can look back at the Princess not with vacant submission but with a secret treasure of her own.

In fact, the primary activity of the fable is this back-and-forth looking, which is so insisted on that Maggy decides that the two women are "trying to stare one another out" (293). The Princess and the cottager are thus linked by identification, not charity. Amy reiterates this: on the cottager's death, the Princess muses that "there was nobody to look at her now, and nobody for her to look at . . ." (294). The fable's trajectory of fulfillment is not inheritance or fortune but the development of a fuller identification between rich and poor. Amy emphasizes the power of identification in the first encounter between cottager and Princess:

> "The Princess was such a wonderful Princess that she had the power of knowing secrets, and she said to the tiny woman, Why do you keep it there? This showed her directly that the Princess knew why she lived all alone by herself spinning at her wheel, and she kneeled down at the Princess's feet, and asked her never to betray her. So, the Princess said, I never will betray you. Let me see it. So, the tiny woman closed the shutter of the cottage window and fastened the door, and, trembling from head to foot for fear that any one should suspect her, opened a very secret place, and showed the Princess a shadow." (293)

The nature of the communication between the two women is cryptic and extraordinary. The Princess mysteriously demonstrates her knowledge by asking a question and goes on to duplicate the cottager's speech ("she asked her never to betray her"; "I will never betray you"). Basic communication acts are transformed into an erotically charged secret sharing that obliterates the limits of identity. Of course this passage maintains the language of subjection, but it is an image of subjection without power and exposure without threat, a fantasy in which the stares of the Princess can be fully returned by the cottager. Amy's suggestion is that when the rich look at the poor, they are looking into a mirror, and that once identification takes place, the purpose of charity falls away. For Little Dorrit, the pretences, projections, and mystifications of charity are themselves the crisis; in response, she creates a narrative of intervention without help.

The story of the Princess serves as a narrative hinge, linking the trials of poverty to the trials of wealth. The story can be read, and usually is, as Amy's synthesis of her own prior experience, a narrative both describing and enacting her feelings of guilt and desire. In this reading, Amy *is* the tiny woman, and the story is about her "state of mind" (to borrow the novel's terms). Of course, it is natural to imagine that Amy is the cottager, and Phiz's illustration endorses this assumption, presenting Amy (as she tells the story) in the attitude of the little woman, peering out the window of her shabby room. But by telling this story rather than making a confession, Amy simultaneously invokes a powerful image of the sacrificial victim and casts some doubt as to her own immersion *within* this image.

FIGURE 2. Amy and Maggy, from Hablot Browne's [Phiz's] "The Story of the Princess," in *Little Dorrit*. Charles Dickens, *Little Dorrit* (London: Chapman and Hall, 1914). Mervyn H. Sterne Library, University of Alabama at Birmingham.

With this in mind, it is surprising that so many readers see, in the Amy that emerges in the second book of the novel, the tiny woman of the cottage. Although throughout her continental travels she remains more concerned for others (such as Fanny, her father, and Pet) than for herself, her concern is no longer offered on the altar of her self-sacrifice. Her authority is predicated entirely on her personal qualities—particularly her keen observation—in the manner of an Anne Elliot or a Daniel Deronda. Amy becomes newly important as a vehicle for articulating the truth;[38] her carefully stated "advice" (so referred to in the chapter title) that Fanny not marry sharply contrasts her short, qualified statements to Fanny after the first meeting with Mrs. Merdle. I would suggest that, especially in relation to Pet, Amy's "dream-life" should be taken as an exact complement to her fable to Maggy. Now in the role of the Princess, Amy, the powerful knower of secrets, dips in and out of Pet's life as both comforter and observer. In a letter to Arthur, Amy keenly describes the Gowans' uncomfortable lodgings in Rome and proceeds to analyze the deep sources of Pet's unhappiness: "She is so true and so devoted, and knows so completely that all her love and duty are his for ever, that you may be certain she will love him, admire him, and conceal all his faults, until she dies. I believe she conceals them, and always will conceal them, even from herself" (552). The reversal is remarkable: Pet has become the ill-fated harborer of secrets, while Amy has assumed the role of the Princess—with reference not only to her external social situation but also to her entire presentation as a knower of secrets and a conveyor of articulated wisdom. Like the Princess, Amy carries out a program of observation and identification, never entering into the negotiations of power that inhere within the economy of the gift.

Accordingly, when Amy burns the Clennam codicil, she reiterates the futility of charity. Amy is poised between poor and rich—she has inheritance within her grasp but has not yet inherited—and this position allows her to correct what Dickens sees as the necessary failures of both parties to the philanthropic exchange. She chooses destruction over donation: she will neither receive nor give a legacy. Also, by choosing not to inherit the money that should have been hers from childhood, Amy is effectively choosing never to have had—a choice unavailable to the wealthy. Most important is that Amy counteracts the mutability of philanthropy: the philanthropist always leaves the homes of the poor, but Amy will stay. If, as Suchoff claims, "the tiny woman's isolated 'cottage' evokes the Marshalsea prison" (*Critical Theory*, 62), then Arthur Clennam finally plays the role of the cottager, imploring Amy to leave him: "You belong to much better and brighter scenes. You are not to look back here, my Little Dorrit; you are to look away to very different and much happier paths" (761). Arthur's torment exposes the yearnings of the philanthropic imagination at its most tragic, most sublime. To the mind of philanthropy, the intimacy between poor and rich is fleeting; the gift is a reminder of difference, and the visit must give way to the real state of things. Arthur's fate (like Dickens's) is to believe in but despair of the gift. Of course, this is why Amy cannot tell him about the codicil, cannot offer the inheritance to him, cannot even let him see her renounce. Amy must not help her husband—not because the *property* is corrupt but because her act of charity would live on as a conquest ever afterwards.[39]

To destroy a codicil, erase an inheritance—what sort of agency do such acts indicate? What is left after charity fails? With Charles Darnay and Lucie Manette (*A Tale of Two Cities*), Dickens will revive the predicament of *Little Dorrit*. Like Arthur, Charles is burdened with a superfluous reformism; his efforts to repair his family crimes are rejected, and he (like Arthur) can do nothing more useful than place himself in custody. Lucie, like Amy, waits, watches, and hopes; she is a reader of portents, a domestic savant. Restitution will come of its own accord. It has ceased to be the province of the charitable conscience. Debts can no longer be paid; they will be collected, and with interest. The trajectory of Dickens's career thus anticipates the trajectory of late-Victorian poor relief, which determined that the claims of the poorer classes could be met neither by the workhouse nor by the generosity of philanthropists and volunteer workers. To say that charity disappears from Dickens's later novels would be to overstate the case. But where acts of charity *do* succeed—of the sort performed by Biddy in *Great Expectations* and by Riah and Jenny Wren in *Our Mutual Friend*, for instance—they are removed from the realm of authority. Dickens continues to marvel at "what the poor are to the poor" (*Bleak House*, 109), but at the same time he decries the effects of social paternalism. So, too, is there a place left below the radar for Amy and Arthur, who "went down into a modest life of usefulness and happiness . . . went quietly down into the roaring streets, inseparable and blessed" (826). Beyond the far fringe of Dickens's narrative, Amy and Arthur resuscitate simple helpfulness; they pick up the pieces of paternity, raising "Fanny's neglected children" along with their own and watching over Tip. In a home without foundlings or "parricides," without pensioners or runaways—without authority—help works. It is hard to imagine, though, that Mr. and Mrs. Clennam will attempt to be helpful in the roaring streets, if they have learned the lesson of *Little Dorrit*. The thing for the streets is to go quietly.

Preacher's Vigil, Landlord's Watch

Charity by the Clock in Adam Bede

> All honour and reverence to the divine beauty of form! Let us cultivate it to the utmost in men, women, and children—in our gardens and in our houses. But let us love that other beauty too, which lies in no secret of proportion, but in the secret of deep human sympathy.
>
> —George Eliot, *Adam Bede*

CHAPTER TWO

If condescension, as Dickens contends, concealed histories of neglect and mystified social relations, it drew its power to do so from the discourse of spontaneity. As I discuss in the introduction, the condescension scene unfolds as a spontaneous, interruptive moment, relying for its force on the sense that something out of the ordinary is taking place. The gesture of condescension is affecting precisely because it is surprising: it could not have been foreseen, and it is sadly but beautifully ephemeral. The wonder of the moment will subside and both rich and poor will reenter the routines of their ordinary life. Condescension marks the moment of charity as a moment apart. And by standing apart, Dickens suggests, charity essentially deflects responsibility and disowns the social causes of poverty and distress.

This sort of spontaneity came under considerable fire in the mid-Victorian decades from the practitioners of scientific charity, a movement to base particular acts of charity on a systematic social analysis. While these reformers occasionally commented on the motives of spontaneous or impulsive charity, they were more concerned for its results and insisted that anyone who would intervene in a situation of poverty or distress must take a full measure of the consequences of intervention, both immediate and over the long term. The situation at hand can never be divorced from the whole network of conditions in which it is imbedded. This way of thinking runs counter to the logic of condescension, which embraces the exceptional moment. Such exceptions, according to Victorian social analysts, were likely to cause more harm than good. A particular act of charity serves its purpose only if it is integrated within the broader enterprises of organized poor relief, social uplift, and civic development.

As we consider particular acts of charity in the context of complex and evolving social systems, it is inevitable that we think of George Eliot, who, like the proponents of scientific charity, labored to trace the abiding consequences of unconsidered, impulsive actions. And nowhere is Eliot's analysis more acute than in her ubiquitous discussions of sympathy. While sympathy and charity are not identical, Eliot often uses the words interchangeably, as at the moment in *Adam Bede* when she asks her readers to be in "perfect charity" with Mr. Irwine.[1] Indeed, an act of charity can be seen as an instantiation of sympathy, the shape sympathy takes when it enters into practice. Although throughout her works Eliot discusses sympathy as a structure of feeling, she is equally concerned with the mechanics of sympathetic action, the conditions and protocols under which fellow-feeling can be turned to account—and in this way, she shared much with the charity reformers of her day. Her narrators wield their sympathy reflectively, chastising readers and characters who base their judgment on uninterrogated emotion. In addition, Eliot believed that true sympathy could not be achieved through the inherited conventions of literature but must arise out of an accurate and diverse picture of the human condition. Sympathy required the subject to rise above a provincial point of view and to comprehend her neighbors' virtues and failings within a larger web of historical and social patterns.[2] In its call for an ever-widening perspective, Eliot's sympathy was to an earlier Victorian sentimentality what the new charity was to the old.

But alongside her commitment to a sympathy well-informed, analytically ambitious, and subtle—essentially, a realist sympathy—Eliot provides a counterdiscourse, which is visible in the epigraph to this chapter. Contrasting sympathy with proportion, Eliot suggests that the wider perspective can create ethical distortions of its own.[3] This claim accords with certain emerging concerns about the methods of the new social work: as public policy was increasingly predicated on a growing body of sociological research, many feared that social relations were at risk of becoming too programmatic, too impersonal, even too efficient. With this in mind, I would like to present a counternarrative to our usual understanding of Eliotic sympathy. Even as it expands the individual's perspective, sympathy stops well short of an integrated social vision; it creates an escape clause from the normative patterns of historical process. In this way, Eliot preserves the particular instance of charity as a realm of narrative freedom, working against the determinist thrust of analytical realism. By loosening the scene of sympathy from the historical chain of causes and effects, Eliot addresses a commonly felt need to protect charity from the worst consequences of its systematic administration. Although Eliot's realism resonates with the methods of the social scientists, her moments of sympathy maintain the exceptionalism of the condescension scene.

When we assume that Eliot presents morality as a corollary to social integration, we tend to associate her theory of personal moral development with her theory of social progress. Moral growth—signified by the transcendence of the self, the awareness of an external world, the shift from egoism to altruism—is seen as both analogous to and continuous with a broader social movement away from atomistic individualism and toward community consciousness.[4] Accordingly, the climactic moment of personal conversion—the moment when the accumulated weight of suffering brings about a spontaneous and powerful extension of sympathy—heralds the individual's accession to a higher life of reciprocal relations and social forms. Barbara Hardy sees this process epitomized in the growth of Adam Bede's sensibility, an organic development that culminates in Adam's forgiveness of Hetty Sorrel and then progresses further: "Adam's pity and awe moves even beyond Hetty towards the true tragic generalization which embraces all poor wretches."[5] Thus, Adam's highly particular act of charity is a sign of his new capacity for generalization. Bernard Paris describes the same moral/social process as having three stages: an egoistical stage, where "the distinction between the inward and the outward is obscured"; a stage of disillusionment and alienation, where the individual is "overwhelmed . . . by the hard reality of the world"; and an integrated stage, where the subject "may relate to the world at once meaningfully and objectively, seeing the world as an autonomous existence of which it is a part."[6] Many more-recent critics have seen sympathy as enabling a modern, liberal model of affiliation in which the individual voluntarily demarcates his or her involvement within a broader social network.[7] Indeed, the socializing power of the sympathetic moment is implied in Eliot's "Natural History of German Life," where the *Philister*'s egoism is pitted against an ideal of social participation. In all of these accounts, self-transcendence may be galvanized in a particular encounter, but it ultimately becomes a permanent principle of communal living; sympathy is both a revelatory visitation and the standard stuff of social cohesion.

And yet we can hardly view sympathy as fundamentally integrative when, throughout Eliot's works, acts of charity are inhibited not just by egoism but by social form and community consciousness. In a study that focuses on Eliot's attraction to *Gemeinschaft* (integrated, premodern) notions of community, Suzanne Graver aptly concedes that even in the "pastoral" novels, Eliot "does . . . explore how the fixity of ways in Gemeinschaft can deny individuality."[8] "Custom," Graver explains, "encourages one kind of solidarity, but it discourages the fellowship that has its origins not in the group response but in 'individual feeling.'"[9] The workings of custom, while congenial to the "group response," preclude the very particular relations formed through sympathy. In fact, the shock of Eliotic sympathy typically takes place not merely when the egoist faces a psychological crisis but when available social forms prove unable to accommodate some intensely felt interpersonal need (for example, Lydgate's need to prove himself innocent before his wife in *Middlemarch*, or Hetty's need to confess in *Adam Bede*). Sympathy thus releases the subject both from egoism and from community in the broadest sense; it creates momentary possibilities of association outside of society. Furthermore, it is often inaccurate to see Eliot's moments of sympathy as setting in motion any enduring trajectory of new, broader, and better social affinities. The more usual pattern (typified in the Lydgate household) is that the charitable breakthrough is strikingly ephemeral, a taste of some new mode of relation that has no place in ordinary life.[10]

Eliot's refusal to depict a self-sustaining and integrated sympathy gains significance within the context of nineteenth-century attempts to regiment the operations of charity. Throughout the century, charity workers and organizers struggled to develop a philanthropy that was neither impulsive nor desultory but a routine function of a well-regulated society. Such a philanthropy (the argument went) would offer members of all classes the political stability and moral satisfactions of social cohesion. An anonymous pamphlet of 1836 promises that rich and poor "only require to know each other more, that they may love each other more"; the author argues that besides learning about the poor, the charity worker will learn about himself and his species.[11] Another guide to home visiting, written two decades later, touts the author's ability to enter into perfect sympathy with poor mothers.[12] This desire for identification and integration marks even the early career of Beatrice Webb, who embraced her job as rent collector because poor tenants regarded her and her colleagues "not as visitors of superior social status, still less as investigators, but as part of the normal machinery of their lives."[13] Of course, the great drive to regiment charity came from the Charity Organisation Society (COS), whose members believed that only a philanthropy that was judiciously planned and professionally administered could make independent citizens of the respectable poor.[14] Helen Bosanquet, the society's most eloquent spokesperson and historian, argued that under the reign of disorganized attempts at philanthropy, the East End had become "the field for many strange adventures, and much noble though too often misguided chivalry."[15] In truly Eliotic terms, Bosanquet urged charity workers to understand "the local institutions and customs which do so much to make the people what they are, and to which it is due that a district can be worked, not as a chaotic agglomeration of atoms, but as an organic whole" (6). For the COS, sympathy became productive precisely when it fused the separate worlds of rich and poor, allowing the social worker to enter the organic life of the people she wished to help.

But even as the COS tried to regulate the practice of charity with strict timetables, careful geographical boundaries, and procedural guidelines, they and other philanthropists remained wedded to the idea of charity as an exceptional moment. In fact, it is one of the unremarked paradoxes of COS doctrine that while the caseworker had to be completely systematic, the poor aid recipient had to be economically mobile, poised to regain independence quickly. In other words, a primary condition of charitable donation was that it was not to become ordinary or expected. Charity had to be carefully planned by the donor, but it would have to be nowhere in the plans of the recipient. This insistence on the mobility (or "helpability") of the poor was largely a response to the concern that poor families were "working" the various charitable agencies with no intention of ever going off the dole, a concern epitomized by the figure of the professional vagrant who had made an industry of collecting handouts.[16] Thus, the terminally dependent poor—the *permanent* poor—were to be left to the Poor Law, while the charities made it their exclusive function to help the deserving (that is, *mobile*) poor weather the crisis of the moment (typically, illness or loss of employment).[17] The need of the deserving poor was "temporary,""exceptional,""causeless."[18] As C. S. Loch (a long-time COS secretary) remarked,"[H]ow needless and inadvisable is relief provided to meet the ordinary contingencies of life."[19] In the complicated rhetoric of the COS, the lives of the poor were organic, but their troubles were causeless; the visits of the social worker were routine, but each visit was extraordinary.

Under the leadership of the COS, the charity industry struggled to ensure that the newly regimented casework would maintain an aura of exceptionalism. Loch, for instance, argued for the necessity of surprise visits (70–71). In response to applications for relief, Loch asserted, "[T]he question asked should be 'Ought I not to refuse?' rather than, 'Ought I not to give?'"[20] When the caseworker takes this approach, the administration of charity necessarily becomes the exception, a departure from the ordinary—and a departure that is perceived as such. Thus, Bosanquet explained that the right kind of charitable encounter often required two visits in sequence: the first one to demonstrate to the poor woman that she could not expect help of the type and amount she wished, and the second to establish a relationship that the poor woman could never have wanted under her initial, "ordinary" attitudes toward the charity worker. And it was not just the visited, but also the visitor, for whom charity would be an exceptional encounter. Bosanquet saw value in the initial surprise of the social worker entering the London slums, and she wished she could conduct an experiment in which West End inhabitants were moved to East End homes and vice versa: "One hardly knows which would be most at a loss; the rich woman brought suddenly face to face with the necessity of lighting the fire and preparing the breakfast, or the poor one confronted with the task of directing a West End establishment."[21] Many critics (including Martha Vicinus, Brian Harrison, Debra Nord, and Dorice Elliott) have discussed the rare opportunity that philanthropic visiting gave middle-class women to engage in a professional and social sphere outside of the home; in many women's narratives (such as *Aurora Leigh* and *North and South*), visiting among the poor becomes an occasion for a broad social awakening. An early episode in her autobiography shows Beatrice Webb having found "a certain charm and restfulness in [a poor family's] simple piety and absolute ignorance of the world" (154). In the dawning days of a career battling against provincialism, Webb's endorsement of absolute ignorance is telling; she saw her extended visit among the mill hands and miners as time out, a temporary escape from her normal modes of social engagement.

Eliot employs exactly this sense of surprise and anomaly in her own scenes of charity. Whereas much of the tragedy in Eliot's fiction unfolds in a naturalistic mode—the painfully inevitable outcome of irrevocable actions—her charitable encounters belong to a totally separate economy. They have no narrative inevitability, and can even therefore be seen as dramatically excessive (as attested to by the number of critics who have wished to separate the "plots" of *Daniel Deronda*). The moment of sympathy is not part of an organic history—rather, it is the convergence of independent trajectories, separate stories, foreign sensibilities. Eliot's agents of sympathy are rarely involved in one another's lives before the moment of connection, and their meeting invariably seems less a plot event than a resolution of vectors, a strange interlude between people on different schedules. In fact, their very contingency in an otherwise naturalistic world is what gives them their poignancy. In *Middlemarch*, Dorothea and Rosamond have no shared sense of purpose either before or after their meeting, no tangible or emotional object that brings them together; and yet their meeting signifies a great deal to each. Often the benefactor seems strange and unfamiliar to the character in distress, not at all the type of person expected. In "Janet's Repentance," Tryan is a far cry from the canting hypocrite Janet has ardently imagined. In *Romola*, Romola is surprised to see Savonarola's calm glance, and the "impression from it was so new to her, that her anger sank ashamed as something irrelevant."[22] And in *Adam Bede*, Hetty Sorrel, despite her many months living with her aunt's niece, is surprised by the sudden thought of Dinah as someone who might help her: "Dinah did not seem to belong to that world of Hetty's, whose glance she dreaded like scorching fire."[23] In other words, when Hetty cannot bear to see any of the people she knows and fears, she is for the first time capable of opening a door for her vaguely understood cousin to enter.

In almost all of Eliot's works, sympathy follows this exceptionalist paradigm. But this was not initially the case. Her earliest work of fiction, "The Sad Fortunes of the Reverend Amos Barton," charts a different course for charity, a road Eliot rarely takes in the later books. In this novella (the first of Eliot's *Scenes of Clerical Life*), charity is both a product of and an aid to the broadest kind of social identification. The critical episode of the narrative is Milly's death, an event that draws the sympathy even of Amos's detractors: "There were men and women standing in that churchyard who had bandied vulgar jests about their pastor, and who had lightly charged him with sin; but now, when they saw him following the coffin, pale and haggard, he was consecrated anew by his great sorrow, and they looked at him with respectful pity."[24] With Milly's death, the novella's series of piercing conversational vignettes gives way to an integrated picture of a community restored to fellow-feeling. The inhabitants of Shepperton are no longer distinguished from one another by act or temperament; they have become a single social body, ethically and affectively unified. Sympathy is anything but an exceptional moment; it is the very bridge between two epochs in Sheppertonian evolution.

But the following novella, "Mr. Gilfil's Love Story," dispenses with the idea of a historically significant charity and instead propounds a vision of sympathy as personal, fragile, and mainly unnoticed. Whereas Shepperton's sympathy with Barton is presented as a permanent transformation of public opinion, the sympathetic eruptions in "Mr. Gilfil" are fleeting and take place behind closed doors: in a *poveraccio*'s garret, a coachman's farmhouse, a parsonage drawing room. The difference between the sketches is perhaps most pronounced in the first pages of "Mr. Gilfil," which effectively picks up where "Amos Barton" left off: once again (though at an earlier historical moment) the people of Shepperton are gathered at the cemetery to pay tribute to their vicar. This time it is the clergyman himself who has died, an event of broad significance because of Mr. Gilfil's universal popularity. But while the loss is felt individually throughout the community, it has no power to bind the mourners together; Gilfil's funeral is a site for precisely the kind of petty bickering that Milly's funeral undermines. Whatever unhistoric acts of charity consecrated the vicar's life have begun to dwindle with his death. The fading of Gilfil's small charities parallels the disappearance of his earlier "drama of hope and love," which, in the vicar's later decades, "long ago reached its catastrophe, and left the poor soul, like a dim and dusty stage, with all its sweet garden-scenes and fair perspectives overturned and thrust out of sight" (87).

"Janet's Repentance" (the third of the *Scenes*) revives the pure pathos of "Amos Barton," but its picture of sympathy takes up the exceptionalism of "Mr. Gilfil." True sympathetic feeling cannot be guaranteed by any proper ordering of society; it is instead the product of extreme circumstances. This idea is articulated in a dialogue between Janet and her mother. Praising the broad-minded attitudes of the local curate (Mr. Crewe), Janet suggests that "[t]hat is the best Gospel that makes everybody happy and comfortable, isn't it, mother?" to which her mother responds, "Ah, child, I'm afraid there's no Gospel will do that here below" (236). And of course Janet is quickly to learn that Mr. Crewe's gospel—and its supporters, the broad-church community of Milby—cannot keep her happy or even safe. There are places in the world where such good-natured clergymen as Parson Irwine, Mr. Farebrother, and the Reverend Lyon can have no effect. Mr. Tryan is a different matter, qualified to enter into Janet's troubles by his own extraordinarily troubled past. Yet Tryan's public ministry hinders, rather than enables, his contact with Mrs. Dempster. Tryan's followers, who knew Janet before she was married, pity her for her catastrophic marriage, but this publicly circulated pity has no power to create the sympathetic association that Tryan seeks. Only when Janet is cast out of her home—when she becomes mobile, in the terms of our discussion of institutional philanthropy—does she become alive to Tryan's charity. Janet's utter lack of affiliation with Tryan is turned to the greatest account: "The impulse to confession almost always requires the presence of a fresh ear and a fresh heart; and in our moments of spiritual need, the man to whom we have no tie but our common nature, seems nearer to us than mother, brother, or friend" (293). The fact that Janet had earlier ridiculed Tryan in Orchard Street makes the young curate a most fitting object for a sympathy that escapes from the public.

The romance of sympathy rescues Janet from domestic violence, and it also, strangely, removes Tryan from the role of charismatic lieutenant of the new dispensation in Milby. In a larger sense, their shared revelations lift both of them above any integrated Comtean species history.[25] "Our subtlest analysis of schools and sects," explains the narrator, "must miss the essential truth, unless it be lit up by the love that sees in all forms of human thought and work, the life and death struggles of separate human beings" (267). This separation of beings—this dissolution of the social body—is a central project of the sympathetic imagination, just as historical rupture is a project of the act of charity. In this, charity is of a piece with other exceptional moments of crisis (such as Janet's eviction), "when we are cut off abruptly from the life we have known, when we can no longer expect tomorrow to resemble yesterday" (286). Thus, while for Janet Dempster the moment of charity is caught between an earlier moment of alienation and a later one of social integration, it would be wrong to see charity—or sympathy—as a transitional act that confirms the wayward individual's domestication within the social. If, for Eliot, charity is incompatible with narcissism, it is equally incompatible with an integrated social consciousness. Throughout Eliot's works, the moment of sympathy remains just that, a moment, emerging gloriously out of the swamp of psychic isolation and disappearing under a tide of new affiliations and social forms. Romola's encounter with Savonarola, Dorothea's conferences with Rosamond and Lydgate, Daniel's last meeting with Gwendolyn: these crucial sympathetic episodes bear as little relation to the affairs that follow as they do to the circumstances that came before. Charity cannot be sustained.

While "Janet's Repentance" establishes an exceptionalist paradigm of sympathy, *Adam Bede* attempts to understand the exceptional moment alongside the evolutionary history of a community. In turn-of-the-century Hayslope, Eliot imagines a set of social conditions that make unexpected associations possible and a community calendar that makes unconscripted time all too available. Hayslope is a village that, to its own mind, exists between epochs, and the community's fixation on a future age of paternalistic reform fosters a general spirit of laxity about the social forms of the present day. The casualties of Hayslope's experiments in negligence are well documented: a murdered infant, a young woman transported, a broken estate. Yet it is precisely in this environment, at a moment when social protocols are brittle, that charity can take shape. The following discussion argues that against Eliot's evolutionary sociology runs a competing discourse of the charitable moment, a moment that can coalesce only within a social rift—not so much the gap between classes as the gap between fact and formula, social models and daily practice. In this sense, Hayslope's incessant plans and predictions are as necessary (from a narrative point of view) as they are shortsighted. For even if sympathy never takes the form expected, it always arises out of a culture of expectation; it is the apotheosis of a social desire that has overrun the ordinary channels of association. Like the pioneers of Victorian social work, then, Eliot believed that the sublimest effects of charity were predicated on the practical business of making and keeping philanthropic appointments—except that for Eliot, the appointment kept is never the appointment made.

Hayslope, Progress, and Postponement

The village of Hayslope, along with its satellites Donnithorne Chase and the Hall Farm, has benefited from a wealth of critical attention, much of which was written in response to Ian Gregor's still-influential discussion of the "two worlds of *Adam Bede*." According to Gregor, the novel's moral study is irreconcilable with its idealized, pastoral image of Hayslope, which cannot be touched by tragedy or historical realism. "We don't," explains Gregor, "think of Arthur as being rich or of the Bedes as being poor."[26] A subsequent generation of critics, concurring with some of Gregor's claims, attempted to see an idealized Hayslope as part of a unified analytical enterprise: thus, John Goode argues that Eliot's "dehistoricization" of Hayslope is a conservative historian's effort to reify a set of particular social conventions as natural law, while Ian Adam shows that the "pictorial realism" of the pastoral is complemented (rather than corroded) by the "analytic realism" of the sociologist. Eve Sedgwick inaugurated the latest phase in Hayslope studies, describing Gregor's "two worlds" as overlapping moments that signify England's historical transition to an industrialized society, a transition in which "apparently timeless gender roles" gave way to "extinction" and "reorganization."[27] Critics since Sedgwick have continued to focus on Hayslope as a society in transition, which both expresses and challenges the assumptions of an emergent middle-class hegemonic culture.[28]

I would like to complicate these studies by considering the ways in which Hayslope imagines *itself* as existing within a transitional moment, as it looks ahead to the restoration of a paternalistic order that has fallen into disrepair. More complicated still is the phenomenon whereby the community's glee over the fantasy of the new squire is both tapped into and challenged by the unsettling claims (spiritual and temporal) of the newly emergent Methodist ministry. Hayslope's millennial hopes destabilize the social forms of the present, nourishing a culture of idiosyncrasy and social improvisation. In this way, the community's fascination with its own destiny breaks the rhythms of historical inevitability and opens the narrative to possibilities of the exceptional moment.

Eliot's world of supposed pastoral stability and cyclicity is actually a world of broken rhythms and bad timing. The novel's first chapter famously shows Adam's indignation at the readiness with which the other carpenters throw down their tools at the stroke of six. Adam's tirade impugns the clock as an agent of alienation, distracting the workmen from any satisfaction they might find in their labor. The calendar itself is an uncertain signifier, as evidenced in chapter 18's various deliberations on churchgoing. Alick, the Poysers' shepherd, feels that the responsibilities of management prohibit him from going to church of a Sunday: "[H]e had a general impression that public worship and religious ceremonies, like other non-productive employments, were intended for people who had leisure" (187). One such person is Mr. Poyser himself, who, like Alick, would prefer to stay home and keep working but knows by experience and hearsay "that work on sacred days was a wicked thing" and that "money got by such means would never prosper" (193). It might therefore seem that work on the Sabbath is justified only when it is necessary—yet Old Martin stays home to look on after the milking, precisely because he is *un*necessary; the rest of the family's churchgoing allows him to recapture the importance of his earlier days. Thus, calendars and clocks ring out a number of discrepant protocols. More tangibly, the discrepancies among particular clocks play an important role in the circumstances of Hetty's tragedy. Hetty's lateness returning from the Hermitage is due mainly to her encounter with Arthur in the Chase, yet it also owes to the fact that the clock at the Hermitage is considerably slower than that of Mr. Poyser (which, we are reminded later, takes time "by the forelock"

[194]). Arthur's watch reminds the two lovers that it is growing later, but the caution does little good, because he knows the watch to be fast. And while Hetty's return home at half past nine—as the rest of the household anxiously await her—might well have flustered her into revealing her dalliance with Arthur, the speed of Mr. Poyser's clock (as compared to the one at the Hermitage) gives Hetty an excuse for having lost track of time.

Hayslope's uneven timing is matched by its uncertain choreography, as farmers, tradesmen, and their wives struggle to assemble themselves on various occasions. Here Eliot's depictions of rural protocol are reminiscent of Scott's, but whereas Scott's characters treat local custom as a second nature, Eliot's villagers are uneasy in these matters. At the young squire's birthday feast, for instance, the men at the upper table debate who is to sit at the head and who at the foot. Mr. Casson argues matter-of-factly that such an arrangement is always determined by age, but old Martin is unsatisfied with this proposal; Luke Britton suggests that the man with the most land should have precedence, and no one backs his suggestion. The men happily settle on giving the coveted space to the "broadest" man, a practical solution that skirts the edgy question of authority. The whole problem of orderly association has been raised in the novel twice before, once at Dinah's meeting on the green and again at Thias Bede's funeral. In both cases, observers refuse to cluster together and instead deport themselves over a range of places and attitudes that both announce and disguise their relationship to the scene. Regarding Dinah's preaching, the narrator explains, "The men were chiefly gathered in the neighborhood of the blacksmith's shop. But do not imagine them gathered in a knot. Villagers never swarm: a whisper is unknown among them, and they seem almost as incapable of an undertone as a cow or a stag. Your true rustic turns his back on his interlocutor, throwing a question over his shoulder as if he meant to run away from the answer, and walking a step or two farther off when the interest of the dialogue culminates" (21). Eliot's ethnographic portrayal draws attention to the men's unwillingness to form an aggregate, a behavior that will persist, and gain in importance, throughout the novel. The villagers' reluctance to swarm amounts to an evasion of both intimacy and confrontation. The "true rustic" retreats even as he engages; he courts conversation by resisting it, and, always on the move, he postpones the moment of crisis.

Thus, the ostensible nearness of God—and the intimacy of the preacher—are what give Dinah's sermon its discomfiting effectiveness within her circle of listeners. Dinah believes in visible manifestations of Jesus (31) and argues that the poor in particular need to cultivate their awareness of God's grace, to work against their reasonable fears that their condition is a divine judgment against them.[29] Jesus shows the poor the hidden part of God: "[W]hat God's heart is, what are his feelings toward us" (28). The second, severer stage of Dinah's sermon—her exhortation against sin—does not at all retreat from her rhetoric of God's nearness but emphasizes it all the more.[30] As Dinah rants, Chad's Bess "began to feel very much as if the constable had come to take her up. . . . She had a terrified sense that God, whom she had always thought of as very far off, was very near to her, and that Jesus was close by looking at her, though she could not see him" (31). The terrifying allure of God's almost-tangible presence attaches to his messenger as well, who both frightens and attracts her hearers: "Wiry Ben was feeling very uncomfortable, and almost wishing he had not come to hear Dinah; he thought what she said would haunt him somehow. Yet he couldn't help liking to look at her, though he dreaded every moment that she would fix her eyes on him, and address him in particular" (30). A perfect example of Eliot's true rustic, Ben patrols the outskirts of intimacy, swayed by Dinah's words but dreading her approach.

In this way the preacher recapitulates the role of the landlord, another public figure in Hayslope whose approach fascinates but is rarely desired. Although people complain of the squire's neglect, they have had little reason to be glad for his interference. Whenever the squire does come around, his tenants regret it; several of the men, for instance, complain that old Donnithorne "had the meanness to collect his own rents" (195), and his rare visit in chapter 32 to the Hall Farm is to serve a kind of eviction notice. The community prefers to deal with the squire in the speculative realm of rumor, complaint, and prediction. It is in this realm that Mrs. Poyser most frequently confronts him: "The old Squire's visits to his tenantry were rare; and though Mrs. Poyser had during the last twelvemonth recited many imaginary speeches, meaning even more than met the ear, which she was quite determined to make to him the next time he appeared within the gates of the Hall Farm, the speeches had always remained imaginary" (342). Paternalism thus takes a strange shape in Hayslope, as something to be wished for but not really to be trusted. The reverence for rank is revealed most often in connection with Adam and Mrs. Poyser, yet Adam's reverence is strongly accompanied by fantasies of personal upward mobility, while Mrs. Poyser's "awe of the gentry" (83) has no power to check her conversation with either the young squire or the old. While the people of Hayslope are certainly prepared to collect the ransom—at least in moral, conversational terms—for paternalism's failure, they are in no hurry to bring it back.[31]

What, then, are we to make of the community's (and particularly of the tenant farmers') constant invocations of the day when Arthur Donnithorne will gain control of his grandfather's estate? "Every tenant was quite sure things would be different when the reins got into his hands—there was to be a millennial abundance of new gates, allowances of lime, and returns of ten per cent" (87). When Mr. Poyser proposes Arthur's health at the birthday feast, the aggregate of tenants who could not even agree where to sit join together to savor the expectation of Arthur's eventual governance.[32] But just as the tenants are content to complain about the old squire in his absence, they are also content to relegate Arthur (and "improvement") to the millennial future. An exchange occurs to this effect when Arthur, in his visit to the Hall Farm, refers to the coming days when he would be "a bald old fellow"—to which Mrs. Poyser emotionally returns, "O dear sir, that 'ull be a long time first" (86). By using the language of millennialism, Eliot connects Hayslope's views of reform with the social attitudes associated with evangelical theology. Such an equation is difficult to interpret, particularly because postmillennialist thought at the turn of the century (when the novel is set) tended to be aligned with social activism, whereas the premillennialism of the nineteenth century took on connotations of political quietism.[33] Notwithstanding this ambiguity, Hayslope's millennialist adoration of the young squire clearly enables the community to put off the urgency of any present reform. While the moment of reform is assiduously held in view, it is held there at arm's length.

The Exceptional Moment

Dinah Morris and Arthur Donnithorne, Hayslope's millennial messengers, are the two figures who are not thrown into difficulties by this gap between promise and fulfillment. In fact, both characters rely on this gap to shape their extraordinary careers. Each is the bearer of a new dispensation, a promise of epochal change; as such, they are the "visible manifestations"[34] of Hayslope's fantasies of reform. They enter and depart from the community at strategic moments, manipulating presence and absence in the service of their particular vocations. Thus, Arthur and Dinah are masters of the exceptional moment, and it is in the medium of unforeseen intervention that the two "benefactors" disseminate their charity and sympathy with such overpowering force. But while Dinah understands the power of such moments, Arthur misjudges their significance completely until it is too late.

Despite their parallel functions in the social and narrative web of *Adam Bede,* Arthur and Dinah have very rarely been the subject of critical comparison. To the contrary: in discussions of the tragic quartet comprising Hetty, Adam, Dinah, and Arthur, the latter characters are the only ones to have been denied concourse. Hetty and Dinah are discussed (most extensively by Dorothea Barrett in *Vocation and Desire*) as representing the fate of women's sexual and vocational desires within the patriarchal order; Adam and Arthur are seen to demonstrate the historical transmission of patriarchal authority from the aristocracy to the middle class; Arthur and Hetty perform the novel's too-conventional tragic seduction, while Dinah and Adam enact its too-conventional comic union; and finally, Hetty and Adam (according to Barbara Hardy) strike the characteristic Eliotic chord of disillusionment and reconciliation.[35] Focusing on these combinations makes perfect sense; they are the pairings around which Eliot constructs her dramatic scenes, in the bedchambers, on the hill, in the wood, in the cottage, and of course in the prison cell. Arthur and Dinah, by marked contrast, have little to do with one another. In his visit to the Hall Farm in chapter 6, the captain does not so much as glance at Dinah; by the end of the novel, the two still have not exchanged words and probably have not met. They have, of course, communicated through Adam, and Arthur has passed on to Dinah his watch—a point to be discussed shortly.

For the moment, though, we should note that although they never interact—and in some sense *because* they never interact—Dinah and Arthur are the subjects of an important metonymic displacement. On several occasions, Dinah serves Hetty as a substitute for the absent Arthur—once in the "Return Home" of chapter 14, again in the fevered hopes of Hetty's diasporic wanderings of book 5, and finally in the Stoniton jail. In all of these cases, Dinah's presence explicitly addresses the condition of Arthur's absence. And Dinah's and Arthur's alternating passages into and out of Hetty's life mirror their relationship to the community at large. Their movements to and from Hayslope make their very absence and presence into matters of general interest. At the beginning of the novel, Arthur is both the prodigal son and the wandering king; like Prince Hal or Michael Corleone, his temporary dissociation from the community serves to prepare his eventual and permanent advent. Dinah begins the novel much in the opposite position; she is both a visiting niece and an itinerant preacher, prepared at any moment to return to her native Snowfield. These temporary conditions will be jarringly solidified at the novel's end, as Arthur's wanderings and Dinah's residence are made perpetual. But for most of the novel, their comings and goings create wrinkles in Hayslope's business-as-usual.[36]

Arthur's consistent ethical practice is to dissociate the present from the future, deferring the time of consequences and capitalizing on the license his "prematurity" affords him. Thus, his every interaction is consecrated by an aura of exceptionalism, as if he were good-naturedly condescending to the probational circumstances which happen to be the only circumstances he has ever known.[37] Under the promise of his inheritance, Arthur is not bound by immediate concerns; in fact, to be too preoccupied with the present would be meanness, an unmindfulness of his millennial importance. As for the latter, he plans diligently for the day when he will inherit, pledging to be a model landlord (124), reading treatises on manure (168), and at every opportunity reiterating his plan to make Adam his grand vizier (63–64, 102–3). Of course, initiating such improvements in the present is largely beyond Arthur's control, and his efforts to do so are repeatedly rebuffed by the old squire. But Arthur's postponements are not just imposed piecemeal from without; they have become his standard operating procedure. He cannot square his actions with his intentions, as depicted in chapter 12, when Arthur lunches in Norburne to miss Hetty, then races back to the Chase to defy his own arrangements and meet her after all. Goode makes a strong case that Arthur's public liberality toward the Poysers (among others) is undermined by his private liberality toward Hetty,[38] but it may be even more accurate to see Arthur's relations with both Hetty and the Poysers as self-indulgences borrowed against the dutiful prospects of the future. This construction is implied in Goode's elaboration of the problem: "The old Squire's threat to turn out the Poysers is, it is true, never realized, but this is precisely because structurally it is highly ironic. It is the new Squire, with his millennial promise, who is destroying the basis of the Poysers' world" (Goode, "*Adam Bede,*" 25). Parson Irwine, who perceives the conflict between what Arthur wants now and what he intends later, believes that the captain's wish to be well regarded in the community will protect him against indiscretions with Hetty (Eliot, *Adam Bede,* 172). But what Irwine fails to perceive is that Arthur's projections of consequence actually underwrite, rather than excluding, his ethical lapses—and that the community sees a confirmation of these projections in the fact that Arthur currently lives as if on borrowed time.

Arthur's failed confession to Irwine is the first of a series of events that uncover the hidden collusion between the proprieties of the young squire's future and the indiscretions of his present. The narrator attributes this failure to the casual nature of modern protocols. "The progress of civilisation," we find out, is such that one might now make a confession over eggs and coffee:

> Still, there was this advantage in the old rigid forms, that they committed you to the fulfilment of a resolution by some outward deed: when you have put your mouth to one end of a hole in a stone wall, and are aware that there is an expectant ear at the other end, you are more likely to say what you came out with the intention of saying, than if you were seated with your legs in an easy attitude under the mahogany, with a companion who will have no reason to be surprised if you have nothing particular to say. (161)

The problem with the confession, then, is that it is formless, a telling deficiency considering Arthur's constant tendency to form plans. For Arthur, the future is anything but formless; his wish to be a "model landlord"—a resonant term in the 1850s, when model housing associations matched architectural specifications with instructions as to how tenants and landlords should behave—is accompanied by a profusion of concrete intentions concerning the improvement of the estate. Thus, Arthur's postponement of responsibility is also a postponement of *form*. In thinking this way, Arthur subscribes to the trajectory discussed earlier in this chapter, in which the individual's life progresses from a chaotic self-centeredness to an integrative social affiliation. He does not understand that in his exceptional relationship with Hetty, he is manufacturing situations that are no less consequential for their irregularity. Even after the relationship has transgressed all bounds of intimacy, Arthur objects to Adam that the affair is protected from consequence by its exceptionality: "The wider the distance between [the man and the girl] the less harm there is, for then she's not likely to deceive herself" (300). Arthur's ethical lapse actually grows out of his sense of perspective and his awareness of his place within the community; these things, he thinks, create a kind of destiny for him that will be a safeguard against any mistakes he might make in this probationary period.

If Arthur's exceptionalism carelessly diminishes the significance of the present moment, Dinah's does the opposite. Like Arthur, Dinah lives for the moment, yet in her theology the moment is not a postponement but a time of heightened importance. The millennium is now rather than later; plans and expectations fall away before the insistent force of the divine leading. "We mustn't," she explains, "be in a hurry to fix and choose our own lot; we must wait to be guided" (38). The effect of Dinah's total mobility is to make every instant an intermediate one, but not in a way that strips it of its consequence: in fact, its intermediacy gives it urgency and distinction. Dinah's exceptionalism therefore gains its power not by intimating better days to come but by conspicuously emerging from and merging back into the very ordinary. In some ways, her pattern speaks to a duality inherent in early-century Methodism: the balance between social disruption and political conciliation.[39] From the beginning, the movement swung between radicalism and conservatism, schism and integration. Such a dialectic clearly characterizes Dinah's modes of interaction; she is at once calming and terrifying, a disturber and a reconciler.[40] Critics have responded to Dinah's intractable intermediacy in a variety of ways: Gregor, for instance, believes that Dinah cannot (at first) perceive that she "must submit herself to the claims of the healthy as well as the needy," while Barrett claims that Dinah starves her own needs for the needs of others.[41] Most analyses boil down to the idea that Dinah must learn to take the long view, planning her interventions more carefully, weighing their cost against their benefit, and recognizing that the needs of the moment should always be considered in view of times to come. Indeed, the novel seems to endorse this lesson as it engineers her ultimate decision to marry. But Dinah's later policy of integration serves to vindicate, rather than discredit, her earlier exceptionalism.

In fact, Dinah's sympathetic intervention in Hetty's life owes its effectiveness to the preacher's overseriousness in the fifteenth chapter and to her misapprehension of Hetty's state of mind. Late in the evening, hearing stirrings in Hetty's bedchamber, Dinah begins to let her mind wander over her cousin's future, and, opening her Bible to Paul's dramatic parting at Ephesus, decides to supply Hetty's dwindling minutes of consciousness with an emotional exhortation. With her unexpected gravity, Dinah upsets and frightens Hetty, who begins to sob—a reaction that Dinah misinterprets as "the stirring of a divine impulse": "It is our habit to say that while the lower nature can never understand the higher, the higher nature commands a complete view of the lower. But I think the higher nature has to learn this comprehension, as we learn the art of vision, by a good deal of hard experience, often with bruises and gashes incurred in taking things up by the wrong end, and fancying our space wider than it is" (159). Here Dinah's relative blindness is important; her misunderstanding allows for the exceptional encounter—the distressing confrontation—that never takes place in Arthur's "confession" to Irwine. Whereas Arthur undervalues the importance of the present moment, for Dinah the moment is overcharged with consequence. Her misreadings of Hetty lead her to sound notes that Hetty cannot interpret. "You may some day be in trouble" (158): Dinah plants the seeds of sorrow in Hetty's mind, and her consolations serve only to heighten Hetty's panic at the ominous picture. Dinah's ministrations finally provoke an impatient response from her cousin: "Don't talk to me so, Dinah. Why do you come to frighten me? I've never done anything to you. Why can't you let me be?" (160). But out of this failure, out of Dinah's extraordinary inability to understand Hetty, are set the conditions for a later moment of rescue. The kind of sympathy Hetty will require is incompatible with neighborly familiarity; it requires blindness, lack of perspective—what Barrett would call Dinah's egoism.[42]

In the shadow of the gallows, Hetty has no use for perspective. While Hetty's repentance in the Stoniton jail is certainly a kind of self-transcendence, it is not an induction into the social realm. Instead, that moment—a culmination of the process begun in Hetty's bedchamber—is protected from the punishing claims of society and held completely apart from the progressive narrative of community. To suppose that social awareness would be a fitting remedy for Hetty's all-consuming egoism, however, is inaccurate; her strongest desires are for social recognition and admiration, just as her strongest fears and regrets have to do with the ways in which she will be judged by the community.[43] Hetty's main concern is that she will be abandoned by the people who have nurtured her; she is absorbed in exactly the drive toward social "adaptation" that, for Goode, is the great motive of *Adam Bede* and the great signifier of Hetty's moral failure. The confession to Dinah, however, breaks out of the integration narrative and suggests that there is a release from community, from her assimilationist hopes—a release from plans and prospects. We might even see Dinah's repeated appeal to the Divine Presence (449–50) as a gesture meant to liberate Hetty from both the drive toward integration and the anticipation of her sentence. The intervention of the Divine separates Hetty from these things and consecrates the moment of repentance.

Thus Dinah is able to offer Hetty solace and refuge in the face of a social network and narrative system that are totally unable to assimilate her; this fact alone raises serious doubts about critical claims that Dinah's ministry is "ineffectual" (Barrett) or "aberrant" (Herbert). In Herbert's view, Dinah's religion represents a Calvinism that, by trying to separate man from a corrupt nature (in both senses of the word), disables a more humanistic sympathy. The Wordsworthian metaphysics of Parson Irwine, Herbert argues, best represent Eliot's own values of love and harmony.[44] James Eli Adams makes a related argument, claiming that as long as Dinah is steeped in doctrinal language her sympathy is limited: "The faltering of Dinah's eloquence thus comes to mark a resistance to the specific character of Dinah's vocation."[45] But this doctrinal language, this aberrant theology of separation, is what enables Dinah to be charitable to Hetty even after the young mother's "unnatural act" has disqualified her from any prospect of Wordsworthian harmony—has placed her in an exceptional circumstance that recalls Mrs. Dempster's lament for a gospel of happiness and comfort, "[T]here's no Gospel will do that here below" (236). In the same way, the transience of Dinah's career as a Methodist preacher should not be read as a judgment against either women's preaching or evangelical religion, much as our acquaintance with the author urges us toward the latter opinion. Dinah's ending—her reentry into the ordinary life of middle-class marriage—is the means by which Eliot foregrounds and secures the exceptionalism of the character's earlier career. Of course, Dinah could very plausibly have joined a breakaway sect (as did Eliot's Aunt Samuel), and it would be strange indeed to argue that Dinah's continued affiliation with the Wesleyan Conference signifies a greater sympathy on Eliot's part with the social reactionism of Bunting than with the apostolic liberalism of the Primitives. But by making Dinah a reformer whose career punctuates the illiberal trajectory of turn-of-the-century Methodism, Eliot is able to create exceptional moments of sympathetic association that can interpenetrate the most uncompromising narrative of social evolution.[46] Dinah's radicalism, in other words, is especially profound because it is not perpetual, not part of a revolutionary movement. The greatest effects of her sympathy, likewise, are never allowed to become a simple matter of character; instead, they owe everything to the strangeness of her ministry in Hayslope and the uncertainty of her tenure in her aunt's home.

When Arthur rushes home after hearing of his grandfather's death, he realizes the time for waiting is over: "[N]ow he would have room and opportunity for action, and he would use them" (439). He will be "the severe upbraider of negligent landowners" (439), as if all along the landowners were the ones who had the power to help and harm, while incumbents such as himself looked on helplessly. Yet Arthur has already had his room for action; he has spent his life trading on the future. The bargain Arthur finally makes with Adam and the Poysers is a remarkable one, particularly from a generic standpoint: after years of complaining about their landlord's negligence, the tenants will be satisfied only by his removal altogether. That the landlord's disappearance should be the best atonement for his crimes goes against a long tradition of fiction, epitomized in the novels of Maria Edgeworth, in which the landlord's only possible restitution is a return to the estate, an assumption of custodianship. But Arthur's crime has never been absence or indifference: he has all along indulged himself under the sign of the social. His accession to sympathy comes finally when he realizes that it is in his social role that he has done so much harm and that his only recourse lies in dissolving every social bond, evacuating his future, and giving himself over to the power of the moment, the force of contingency.

In this respect, the most important symbolic transmission of the novel is not Arthur's delegation of Adam to work out the affairs of his estate with the Poysers[47] but Arthur's resignation of his watch to Dinah. At the point in the narrative when Eliot is ready to put Dinah on the clock—the point after the preacher's exceptional charity has both interrupted and subsided back into the organic history of the community—Arthur must learn, for the first time, to stop looking at his watch. For the mere fact that Arthur's watch, like Poyser's clock, is fast leads to no true or effective exceptionalism; to the contrary, it engenders a relentless prospectivity, whereby Arthur can never live up to the real possibilities of the moment, because he has taken up residence in some fantastic future. This lesson pervades the last moments of the epilogue, as Arthur laments Hetty's death: "I could never do anything for her, Adam—she lived long enough for all the suffering—and I'd thought so of the time when I might do something for her" (539). Even after Hetty has been immersed in suffering, Arthur has held out hope that he might accomplish some kind of reparation once her sentence is served. But that meliorative moment never comes; the progressive consequences of the seduction have been crueler to Hetty than Arthur could have imagined, and every plan that Arthur has ever made—even the feeble, desperate plans he continues to make during the girl's seven-year sentence—comes to nothing. Hetty lives just long enough to suffer. Her time for solace is not at the end of the suffering, as Arthur would have wished, but in the midst of it, when Dinah is still drifting, still preaching, a cousin but not a neighbor, with no eye to the clock.

Sympathy and Interruption

The disruptive power of sympathy does not flow naturally from Irwine's liberalism, Seth's good nature, Adam's civic-mindedness, or even Dinah's concern. It comes and goes throughout the novel, manifest in transient moments of help and consolation, and—no longer a comfort but a source of anguish and regret—comes to settle on the outcast, the wandering squire. It resists the machinery of the social and interrogates the costs of epistemological certainty. Thus sympathy provides the same undercurrent against Eliotic realism that spontaneity provided against the regimentation of social work. Eliot's array of exceptional moments—moments that might as well be lifted out of the novels of Laurence Sterne or Ann Radcliffe—defy her evolutionary history, in which narrow ritual gives way to enlightenment, the loss of illusions, and a Wagnerian cultural awakening. It is certainly the case that this kind of evolution constitutes the main thrust of Eliot's narratives. The discrepancies of uninterrogated custom are supplanted by a purposive cultural movement; "holiday time" is replaced by work, commitment, and social incorporation, all of which are associated with a clearer and more integrated vision of the world.[48] But as we have seen, sympathy works through misperception, accident, and unconscripted time, providing a locus of disruption and doubt in the face of the ethical and epistemological mandates of progress.[49]

Essentially, I am proposing to give sympathy a new role in the well-established drama of Eliot's historical realism. This drama, in almost every critical account, follows a dialectical pattern of disruption and integration—a pattern famously theorized by Georg Lukács, who credited realism with the capacity both to expose the limitations of conventional narratives and to offer a "total" view of society and historical process.[50] Thus, in the first phase, the "real" represents a new horizon of freedom. Critics take *Adam Bede* as the paradigm case for a realism that turns away from form, transcending social and literary convention. In his classic schematization of *Adam Bede*'s realism, Ian Adam explains that Eliot's novel "conforms to Ian Watt's description of realism . . . as 'critical, anti-traditional, and innovating.'"[51] Anticipating George Levine's descriptions of the Victorian realists, Adam holds that realism denotes an epistemological attitude that is always trying to undermine conventions of representation.[52] This epistemological conception of realism accords well with the more specific historical argument made by many critics of *Adam Bede:* that the novel depicts a transition from an archaic to an industrialized society. The modern democratic state abandons the rigid forms of the past, replacing kinship bonds with affective ones, and forgoing aristocratic structures of authority in favor of unconstrained self-help. Eliot's campaign against convention is generally cast not as an attempt at epistemological subversion (as critics might find in Thackeray) but as an effort to replace a series of half-truths and particular views with an integrated picture.[53] Her concern to find the most expansive narrative possible is taken by many as an axiom: Henry Auster, for instance, argues that the problems Eliot thought important were "internal, permanent, and ultimate rather than external, circumstantial, and immediate."[54] Others see a much stronger tension operating between the disruption and integration that are endemic to Eliot's fiction. Barry Qualls sees Eliot's recourse to the "typical" as a way of resisting the freedom of the real: "Her commitment to a realist aesthetic . . . involved a commitment to the representation of particulars that threatened always to obliterate the 'typical,' to sever characters from the very traditions of memory and human feeling that were to 'bind' them and their actions into the human community."[55] Along these lines, many critics argue that Eliot tried to salvage elements from a stable past as a refuge against realism's threatening freedom. Goode, Graver, Carpenter, and Semmel all discuss the ways in which Eliot attempts to assimilate past and present within a continuous historical narrative, writing against historical rupture and narrative disintegration.

The dialectical contest between disruption and integration is usually temporalized, such that a period of stasis gives birth to a period of rupture, which leads ultimately to a new stability, more enduring than the first. The paradigms for this progressive narrative are many. It is often associated with Auguste Comte's depiction of a scientific age in which all speculative principles are held accountable to empirical facts, which, by a process of generalization, lead to new principles.[56] A rather different paradigm is millennialism, which saw the mutable forms and events of the present as preparing a new age that would transcend historical change.[57] Carpenter convincingly contrasts Eliot's apocalyptic hermeneutic with romantic representations of rupture, showing that in Eliot's "continuous histories," all events are ultimately related to beginnings and endings.[58] Other progressive models include Edmund Burke's organicism, Herbert Spencer's theories of natural law and adaptation, and Ferdinand Tönnies's theory of *Gemeinschaft* and *Gesellschaft;* all of these paradigms imagine an integrated society arising out of fragmentation and historical accident.[59] This same temporal structure is often seen to be reproduced within the actual narrative of *Adam Bede,* a book that begins with convention, introduces various threats of formal dissolution, disposes of these threats, and restores equanimity. According to Ian Gregor, the novel begins and ends in a pastoral world that is idealized and wholly conventional; the modern, tragic strain enters the novel in the form of Hetty's disillusionment but can never "reach" the pastoral world to complicate it.[60] Adam agrees with Gregor that the pastoral and the tragic are in tension with one another, but Adam sees the two as integrally related; the "leisurely" and "generous" pictorial realism of the early phase of the novel modulates into the "urgent" dramatic realism of the later parts.[61] Goode sees the seeming unassailability of the pastoral community as exactly the point: "[T]he struggle of the individual to adapt to the given medium, is precisely the basis of the moral fable. In the contrasting stories of Hetty and Adam we have an evolutionary drama of alienation and individuation which can only take place on a 'pastoral' stage."[62] The trajectory is described straightforwardly by McDonagh: "A crucial part of the early novels is in fact to chart a shift from the old to the new, but also to show how modern society can, ideally, be infused with the values of the old."[63]

But to temporalize this tension—to claim that *Adam Bede* progresses from harmony to disharmony to a restored harmony—is to miss the degree to which disruption and integration are tied up in one another. In fact, as the preceding pages attest, the novel no more shows the triumph of continuity against dispersion than it shows the opposite; the dominant temporal narratives could just as easily be reversed. For instance, let us revisit Sedgwick's claim that *Adam Bede*'s "apparently timeless" gender and familial roles become eroded and reorganized. The apparently timeless roles never really appear timeless within the space of the novel; rather than shoring up or tearing away the remaining fragments of a tradition, the inhabitants of Hayslope are occupied, as we have seen, with trying to create viable protocols and define themselves as a community. We might also question the more literary formulation: that the pastoral myth of Hayslope is interrupted by the contingencies of modern life. For old Hayslope can be seen as an "ordinary" world (unfamiliar to literature) of contingency and idiosyncrasy, while Arthur's seduction of Hetty suddenly enters the literary tradition, reenacting a hundred other conventional stories of this type. This is all to say that many of the novel's ethical problems are attendant upon its accession to conventional forms. *Form* is a key term in the great seventeenth chapter of the novel, where it is understood as a threat to sympathy (as in the epigraph). Against the misleading idealism of the novelist's forms, Eliot sets the inconsistencies of actual people. Her fear of the conventionalization of character strongly invokes the perceived dangers of institutionalized charity, which, wedded to its protocols, gradually made "inconsistency" its cardinal sin. The establishment of form, for Eliot, is always attended by disruption (as with Arthur's return in the final chapter), just as the obtrusion of exceptional moments is always met by the gathering together of form.[64]

This phenomenon is especially noticeable in *Adam Bede*'s chapter titles, which foreground the interplay between causal sequence and exceptional moment.[65] In a series of titles dominated by the definite article, there are three places (one in each volume) where the indefinite article enters, opening the narrative to formless possibilities. The first comes in the eighth chapter of the first book, "A Vocation." The chapter is part of the second phase of the narrative; having moved away from Adam and Dinah, Eliot introduces (in chapter 5) "The Rector," "The Hall Farm," and "The Dairy" in succession. But Dinah's ministry cannot be so easily assimilated or understood, and its identification as "a vocation" speaks to Irwine's difficulty in defining exactly what kind of vocation it is. The second occurrence of the indefinite article comes in the middle of the second volume, again after three chapters using the definite article to denote ordinary events in the community ("The Health-Drinking," "The Games," and "The Dance"). With "A Crisis" and "A Dilemma," the narrative loses step with the organic history of Hayslope and even with the seduction plot per se. For the crisis is one of response, of what attitude Arthur and Adam should take toward a situation that has to this point followed a chain of cause and effect. The introduction of the indefinite article is especially important in that the real crisis—Hetty's pregnancy—is unknown to both men, such that their sense of possibility is both a genuine ethical context for their decisions and a mistake that dooms their solutions to inadequacy. As if to emphasize the triumph of naturalist causation over formlessness, "A Dilemma" is followed by two uses of the definite article and then—at the end of the second volume and beginning of the third—by an extraordinary sequence of ten chapters, from "The Betrothal" to "The Verdict," using the definite article to plot the inexorable course of Hetty's crime and its consequences. And yet, even after the interruption of the second volume is buried under an avalanche of assimilative consequences and judgments, the indefinite article returns as if to herald a new disruption. This happens in chapter 48, "Another Meeting in the Wood," where a penitent Arthur reenters the life of the carpenter who had wished never to see him again. The article is both limited and unlimited; "another meeting" invokes Arthur's earlier meetings with Hetty and with Adam but, unlike "*the* other," leaves open the question as to whether or not there will be more meetings to follow. This chapter once again introduces into an integrative narrative the redemptive possibility of formlessness.

Nowhere, then, is there a halting of the evolutionary movement of history; disruption and integration are simultaneous, and Eliot's dialectic takes place within every articulation of form, every instantiation of community. The rigidity of social commitment—even of the most humanitarian kind—is as dangerous as the myopia of egoism. Assimilation requires distinction; it requires, in fact, the relative inscrutability of particulars. This is the general principle explained in Eliot's 1868 essay, "Notes on Form in Art": "Form, as an element of human experience, must begin with the perception of separateness ... [and] things must be recognized as separate wholes before they can be recognized as wholes composed of parts, or before these wholes again can be regarded as relatively parts of a larger whole."[66] According to Eliot's argument, real artistic form arises organically out of an "indissoluble" and separate whole; it must not be externally imposed. The "spontaneous unreflecting" expression ("Notes," 235) thus serves as not only a source but also a test case for any given set of conventions, which correspondingly become not just guidelines for behavior but also clues for extrapolation. For every static course contains and implies a prior moment of disruption—one in which alternative courses were possible. The fruits of reform are held accountable to the reformist impulse. In all her narratives of progress, Eliot shows the same mixture of pessimism and optimism that attached to even the strongest philanthropic reformers. For while Eliot and her contemporaries feared that the new, liberal forms of charity might forfeit the rewards of spontaneous giving, they had faith that even in the planned appointment, the extraordinary fact of sympathy—a sympathy that must struggle to overcome the resentments, complacencies, and antagonisms that plagued all encounters between rich and poor—would itself be grounds for perpetual surprise.

CHAPTER THREE

Why Settle?

Samuel Barnett, Octavia Hill, and the London Slums

In the crowded and unsanitary homes of the poor, Victorian charity found both its loudest call to arms and its best theater of engagement. To be sure, many forms of philanthropy were not centered on the home: Sunday schools, mothers' meetings, workingmen's clubs, charity hospitals, and children's outings, to name just a few. But philanthropists generally agreed that the most important way to reach poor families was in the rooms where they lived. This emphasis on the home derived in part from public fears of professional mendicants, unworthy applicants who preyed on the goodwill of their wealthy neighbors. Throughout the century, the middle classes became increasingly suspicious of vagrants and begging-letter writers, whose movements were hard to track and whose identities could not be verified.[1] Perhaps for this reason, home visits—which in the eighteenth and early nineteenth centuries had mainly been the province of landlords and clergymen—became enormously popular, both under the semiofficial auspices of the District Visiting Societies and the independent initiatives of groups such as the Bible-women and the Salvation Army.[2] Visiting the poor in their homes enabled volunteers to see (or to think they saw) petitioners as they really were; visitors could both identify the objects of their charity and monitor the effects of their contributions. Therefore, while the practice of home visiting is often accused of demonstrating middle-class arrogance, it can also be seen as a response to the deep insecurities that plagued charitable giving. A charity worker could find self-assurance and clarity of purpose in the rooms of the poor, an assurance that was paradoxically threatened when he was approached by panhandlers in his own street or delivered a begging-letter at his own breakfast table.

No wonder, then, that the home visit seemed at once a solution and a prod to the dilemmas of charity. On the one hand, visiting was legitimately understood to be a bold and radical form of giving. Visitors, usually though not always women; would make their way through the worst slums, uninvited and often unwelcome. Rather than write cheques for a subscription list, the visitor risked rejection and humiliation; rather than hand out alms that would be gratefully accepted, she offered the less reliable currency of her friendship and influence. And all agreed that the risk was worth it, as, more than with any other form of charity, the visit was seen to foster meaningful personal contact between rich and poor.[3] But, as discussed in the introduction to this volume, philanthropists feared that the home visit would be poisoned by any trace of condescension. Whereas condescension had once been a principle by which the superior and the subordinate revealed themselves to one another, it was now the opposite: just a whiff of condescension on the visitor's part would be an end to contact, another brick in the wall between rich and poor. And taking the most skeptical view of home visiting, one could argue that this sort of wall-building was inevitable—that it was even part of the visitor's unacknowledged agenda. Discussing the benefit of the attachment that formed between rich and poor as a result of home visiting, one writer explains, "Few among the rich are aware how easily they might thus surround themselves with an impregnable barrier of attachment,—a barrier which no political convulsion would be able to destroy."[4] This is an odd image, wherein the philanthropist bridges the gap between rich and poor to reinforce the barrier between them.

Charles Kingsley, too, suggests some such motive in a passage discussed earlier, in which he accuses the visiting lady of frequenting the cottages of the poor specifically because in that setting she can be superficial and in a sense untouchable, whereas if she is charitable within her own home and with her own servants, they might take liberties.[5] In this perspective, the visit serves as a kind of smokescreen, obscuring the visitor's interests and responsibilities. It is an opportunity for an uncoerced, disinterested charity, allowing the rich to confront the poor in circumstances where they would have little at stake.

This is certainly an ungenerous reading. At the same time, it seems to explain the tendency, in many visiting narratives, for the writer to erase all signs of his or her own presence on the scene. In the standard visiting narrative, the charity worker intervenes in a crisis for which she, importantly, bears no responsibility. The visitor is invisible as the scene of crisis unfolds. This pattern was firmly established by the slum exploration narrative, a genre that began in the sensational press but was soon adopted by serious journalists. Here is one such example taken from George Godwin's series of articles published in the 1853 *Builder:*

> There are fifteen houses in this narrow place. Let us take one at random, and examine the interior. We have, Asmodeus-like, removed the outer wall from the top to the bottom, that our readers may examine without fear, and at their leisure, the extraordinary and distressing scene it presents. . . . The ground-floor back presents a sad scene of distress;—the man, his wife, and some children earn a living by chopping fire-wood; the man had been ill and not able to rise for two days, he was lying on a quantity of wood-shavings, and was partly covered with an old black and ragged blanket; his skin did not appear as if it had been washed for weeks; he was very ill, and evidently in a state of fever; his wife was almost equally dirty. "We have no wood to chop," was the expression of their ultimate distress. The room was much dilapidated, and they had suffered greatly during the late severe weather, owing to the broken condition of the windows. The rent was 1s. 9d. per week: the window overlooks a back yard, the condition of which was shocking: the senses of these poor creatures have, however, become so deadened that they seem only to be susceptible of cold and hunger, and the grossest impurity of the atmosphere is in no manner cared for.[6]

The reporter's invisibility is striking. He removes the wall of the building "Asmodeus-like" and never indicates his own place within. While some of the information Godwin reports comes from external impressions ("his skin did not appear as if it had been washed"), other information must have come from conversation, yet no record is given of any such interaction. Rather than complain to Godwin, the family are portrayed as if speaking their suffering into the void: "'We have no wood to chop,' was the expression of their ultimate distress." Of course, Godwin is a reporter and not a missionary; he enters this home to report on it, not to fix it. But it is always with these acts of reporting that the visiting narrative begins: the problem is already established when the visitor comes onto the scene, and only as part of the solution does the visitor make himself felt.

With invisibility comes security, and visiting (unlike begging) was frequently portrayed as a sort of encounter in which the well-meaning middle-class charity worker would not be imposed upon. Even in the most sensationalistic narratives, the poor are rarely violent, resentful, or demanding toward the visitor. It is often the dumbness of the poor that is most eloquent. Andrew Mearns famously delivered just this kind of eloquence in *The Bitter Cry of Outcast London: An Inquiry into the Condition of the Abject Poor* (1883): "A mother . . . was propped up in a chair, looking terribly ill, but in front of her, in another chair, was the wash-tub, and the poor woman was making a feeble effort to wash and wring out some of the children's things. She was dying from dropsy, scarcely able to breathe and enduring untold agony, but to the very last striving to keep her little ones clean and tidy."[7] The cries of Mearns's outcasts are bitter in the ears of the reformer, not in the mouths of the poor. Mearns's poor make no protest, propose no change, take no measures. They suffer and they wait. It is important to Mearns that the sense of shame attaching to such scenes be generated by his readers rather than his subjects. The pathos of this scene comes from the fact that the woman behaves as the middle-class mother would and shows no awareness of her own dispossession. For the narrative to be fully affecting (and effective), the mother must not attempt to coerce her audience into sympathy, nor may she try to take the things she does not have.

When I talk about the invisibility of the visitor, I do not mean to say that visitors were emotionally detached or that they did not feel a deep and personal stake in the people they visited. I mean simply that the point of the visit was to tend to the needs—sometimes the desperate needs—of the visited. Charitable visits would as a matter of course reveal the day-to-day lives of the needy to those who wanted to help them,[8] while the day-to-day lives of the charity workers themselves were beside the point. It is in this sense that the visitor is invisible: she has entered the scene specifically to deal with affairs that are not her own. In fact, the force of the visit derives in part from the fact that she *has* put her own affairs aside for a space.[9]

This type of asymmetry was seen as a problem by the founders of the Charity Organisation Society (established in 1869), who believed that rich and poor should relate to one another as neighbors and, more importantly, as fellow-citizens. The society's mission, broadly formulated, was to end the existence of a dependent class, by preventing state or private relief from being distributed among the able-bodied poor.[10] Feeling that the philanthropy industry, through its indiscriminate distribution of alms, was hurting the very people it wished to help, the COS attempted to coordinate and unofficially to legislate the operations of all relief organizations. The COS was enormously influential, setting the terms for the public discourse of philanthropy; it was also well subsidized, boasting over a thousand subscribers by its tenth year.[11] The most enduring legacy of the COS was its methodical, professionalized casework, which was adopted subsequently by progressive reformers (including the COS-trained Beatrice Webb) who rejected the actual aims of the COS. In their visits to the poor, COS social workers made the same rounds that philanthropic visitors had made many times before but took pains to distinguish the purpose and effects of their investigations from the visiting practices of others.

The Charity Organisation Society attacked the aspects of visiting most closely aligned with condescension: the rich needed to stop thinking of the poor as charity cases, just as the poor needed to stop thinking of the rich as potential benefactors, and the relationship between rich and poor could be secured only by exorcising the specter of help and gratitude. The COS particularly objected to the spontaneity of charity. Visitors could not be susceptible to momentary impulses to help; their intervention had to be calculated. Charitable acts were to be evaluated not according to their motives (as in the discourse of condescension) but according to their effects. Perhaps most controversially, the COS claimed that private charities (including visiting societies) were uninterested in ending poverty but instead found the gap between rich and poor to be a useful one, as a way of allowing middle-class philanthropists to exercise their benevolence and keep the poor under their control.[12] Charity could never be successfully transacted between strangers, the COS argued; only those well acquainted with a family in crisis could suggest, and help effect, a real and lasting remedy. This claim, invalidating the work of the district and evangelical visiting societies, was at bottom an attack on the condescension act, which requires an observable and intractable authority gap between superior and subordinate.

The visit of the COS caseworker could be seen, then, as an attempt to restore what Kingsley said was missing from the ordinary home visit: a genuine, reciprocal connection between rich and poor, one in which members of both classes would learn to recognize each other as fellow beings with a practical stake in one another's welfare. Yet one could equally argue that with its systematic operations, the COS amplified the visitor's remoteness, masking the personality of the individual caseworker behind a carefully constructed protocol. In contrast to the "hearty, living, loving, personal" work that Kingsley espoused[13]—spontaneous, emotional, and idiosyncratic—the COS worker saw herself as part of a broader administrative process. Her mission was to help the poor function within a social system that included the schools, the marketplace, the relief boards, and the courts. Thus, the power of the visitor was everywhere and nowhere; she was a personification of the system, a ghost in the machine. Beatrice Webb abandoned this work when she decided it was ultimately all about surveillance, branding the COS caseworkers as a fleet of amateur detectives.[14]

Among those who felt that the charitable visitor was becoming more and more insulated from the people she visited, there arose a related but, I argue, contrary movement: the movement among the upper and middle classes to settle in the slums. This chapter focuses on two slum settlers: Samuel Barnett, who founded Toynbee Hall (the first and most famous university settlement); and Octavia Hill, who purchased buildings in poor neighborhoods and put them under the superintendence of middle-class landladies. Gertrude Himmelfarb emphasizes the link between settlement and home visitation, describing the work of Barnett and Hill as "an extreme form of visiting . . . with the social worker not only visiting but actually residing among the poor."[15] But if settling extends the scope of the visitor's intervention, it just as surely modifies the character of the encounter. In Toynbee Hall, Barnett conducted a social experiment whose subjects were rich and poor alike. He claimed that in contrast to other charity work, the settlement uniquely allowed the social elite to reveal themselves to the social underclass. Some decades earlier, Octavia Hill created, with her buildings, a forum in which the middle-class reformer would plant herself in the scene of destitution and become involved in the daily frustrations of her impoverished tenants, an involvement that necessarily embattled and exposed her. Hill and Barnett outlined a transformation in which the visitor was made permanent and permeable; as the social worker became a part of the organic life of a poor neighborhood, he or she could for the first time be seen and known. Thus, while settlement is often seen as a natural counterpart to home visiting—both claimed to address the separation between the classes—I argue that settlement was just as much a response to visiting: an antidote to the insulations and isolations endemic to the charitable visit. Both Barnett and Hill mounted challenges to the kind of charity that allowed and even forced the social worker to conceal herself within a system.

Looking-Glass Oxford

The proponents of home visiting believed the practice would build personal bridges between rich and poor and that the ever-growing antagonism between classes would dwindle once the adversaries got to know each other better. But such knowledge is not easily obtained, and as the volunteer worker cast her eyes around the rooms of her less fortunate neighbors, both she and they must at times have wondered how to get from scrutiny to intimacy. Samuel Barnett, a charity administrator and the vicar of St. Jude's parish in Whitechapel, became convinced that modern philanthropy was not a two-way street. In an essay entitled "Hospitalities," Barnett argues that philanthropic practices typically allow the rich to give in a way that insulates them from the poor: "They give, but they will not share; they send their money, but keep themselves and their homes behind servants, conventionalities, and high walls."[16] While Barnett's critique was in part directed against material assistance, the problem as he describes it extended to many forms of personal charity, including home visits. Even when a volunteer entered the homes of the poor, she kept her own home well protected and distant; even when she made personal contact, she was insulated by "conventionalities." Barnett further explains the problem with reference to the charity-funded popular entertainments: "They are gifts which do not rise to the level of sharing; they do not make at one giver and receiver; they do not reveal the thoughts and manners of [the giver's] home; they do not provoke a sense of common possession by interest in one another's possessions" (59). If the visitor was unable to share, it was because she could never really reveal herself—even her thoughts and manners—in another's home. In their effort to form a charity that could not be imposed upon, the visiting societies, in Barnett's view, had driven the common humanity of the visitor out of sight.

In fact, Barnett begins his Oxford address on university settlements with a critical comment about exactly the kind of charity represented by the COS: "'Scientific charity,' or the system which aims at creating respectability by methods of relief, has come to the judgment, and has been found wanting. . . . [T]he outcome of scientific charity is the working man too thrifty to pet his children and too respectable to be happy."[17] In other words, the Poor Law's strict criteria of respectability when combined with the visitor's surveillance and prescriptions were enough to demoralize even the most deserving poor. But Barnett was also, even primarily, concerned with the demoralization of the volunteers who, as they took part in "the usual parochial machinery of district visiting, mothers' meetings, clubs, &c.," were frustrated in their desire to "themselves bear the burdens of the poor" (167–68). While the visitor may have been witness to a great variety of social problems and may have worked tirelessly to offer new remedies, he could never properly share the burdens of poverty. Of course, the relative exclusion of the visitor from the actual difficulties of the poor was an important part of the COS program, and any real reliance of the poor on the social worker would have worked against its doctrine of self-help. But Barnett maintained that volunteers, if they were to keep their sense of purpose, had to be allowed to be themselves and to interact with the poor in a way that was neither temporary nor circumscribed by procedures.[18]

Barnett found an alternative in the idea of hospitality; only in my own home, Barnett maintained, can I be seen as I am. According to his wife and fellow worker Henrietta, Samuel Barnett counted it a religious duty to give parties, and indeed his argument takes on a mystical tone when he explains that around a neighbor's tea-table you get "the revelation of another being."[19] Barnett calls hospitality "the gift which most nearly rises to the level of sharing, the giver making himself one with the receiver, whom he takes into his own home. It is the means by which West End society holds itself together, and every season the army of the classes in possession is welded by dinners and parties. Host and guest have a peculiar relation. They have eaten salt together, and, if nothing higher is developed, the savage instinct remains to keep them from lifting up hostile hands" (53). In other words, it was not rational self-interest but savage hospitality that kept Knightsbridge from marching against Westminster. And this was not just a practice among the rich; according to Barnett, hospitality was used within every class to bind individuals together and strengthen their own political causes. Hospitality was how a class revealed itself *to* itself; by extension, it was the only way that different classes could know one another. All of this convinced Barnett, by the mid-1880s, that the rich, who had ventured into the slums, likewise needed to allow the poor into the domains of wealth and culture.

Out of this conviction came Toynbee Hall, a red brick manor in Whitechapel where university men would plant themselves—for decades in some cases—to showcase the life of the cultured classes. Toynbee Hall was established by Barnett in 1885 in the East End of London as a dwelling place for university men who wished to devote themselves to social work among the poor.[20] Within its boundaries, Toynbee Hall offered innumerable classes; sponsored men's and women's clubs; hosted dinners, entertainments, and public lectures; designed art exhibitions; encouraged cooperative labor; and served as a meeting place for trade unions.[21] But the particular activities of the settlement were less important than its general plan: "The first object, to which every other is subsidiary, is to make friends with the neighbourhood—to become part of its common life."[22] Barnett explains this intention in his initial proposal: "The Settlement would be common ground for all classes. In the lecture-room the knowledge gathered at the highest sources would, night after night, be freely given. In the conversation rooms the students would exchange ideas and form friendships. At the weekly receptions of 'all sorts and conditions of men' the residents would mingle freely in the crowd."[23] Besides the events within the hall, residents might take up any number of civic positions within the community at large; they could become school managers, poor-law guardians, club members, visitors to the sick, and members of cooperative and political associations.[24]

As Toynbee Hall melded into the common life of the neighborhood, the settlers would, as a matter of course, bring their brand of West End hospitality to Whitechapel. The settlers must go on living their own lives, Barnett insisted, and simply allow the poor in. He explains that the residents "have . . . at their hands the means of hospitality: they may ask two or three guests to their own rooms—asking them to drop in for an hour after work—to eat, drink, and smoke, as over the fire they chat about the affairs of the neighbourhood; and they may invite to the large common rooms a larger party of their friends, to meet at dinner, or supper, or for an evening's talk."[25] Barnett characteristically sees in this the germ of social revolution; he proclaims, "Tyrants have been well advised in preventing by curfew bells the evening chats, when men of ideas pass on their thoughts to men of action. The conditions of modern society, which separate thinkers and workers, prevent such chats; and a settlement which makes them possible is doing something to overthrow a tyranny more powerful than that of Norman conquerors."[26] Barnett's implication is that these cross-class confabs, which may have seemed like a quirky innovation, were actually the natural state of affairs, a state that had been suppressed by both the impersonal conditions of modernity and the scheming of tyrants.

In this way the settlers had two tasks, which Barnett believed to be compatible. They were to be very fully themselves, pursuing their own interests and bearing the marks of their class. At the same time, they were to be seamlessly integrated within the ordinary life of the neighborhood around Toynbee Hall. Barnett obsessively reiterated his premise that Toynbee Hall was not a mission, religious or otherwise: if the residents saw themselves as ministering to the poor, they would forfeit the kind of self-revelation possible among friends. Unlike the parochial machinery of philanthropy, the settlement would have no specific tasks; its whole point was not to do but to be. In fact, Barnett's great hope was that settlements would become so numerous that they would "cease to seem settlements" ("Hospitalities," 66), and later in life he observed that the settlements had too much emphasized *work* among the poor instead of *life* among the poor. Rather than reform the poor or educate the rich, Barnett was intent on creating a new and unified social body that shared the strengths of both classes. As Gorst explains in Arnoldian terms, "It is the object of University Settlements to bring together these two impotent factors [the laborer and the political philosopher], and to make out of them an efficient instrument for national progress. There is the latent interest and the latent power in the masses; there is the latent knowledge and the latent ability in the men and women of culture" ("Settlements," 15). Reform should become no longer the work of the middle classes, but of rich and poor alike. Whereas COS and District Visitors might have helped the poor bring their homes and affairs up to an approved standard, for the pioneers of the settlement there was no standard to draw upon. The settlement was not a tool for administration, nor would it preach conformity to a set of behavioral norms. It was a new dispensation whose history, Barnett says, was still in the making:

> This interchange of life between the University and the Settlement will keep up between the two a living relation. Each term will bring, not a set speech about the work of the Mission, but the many chats on the wonders of human life. The condition of the English people will come to be a fact more familiar than that of the Grecian or Roman, and the history of the College Settlement will be better known than that of the boat or the eleven. On the other side, thoughts and feelings which are now often spent in vain talks at debating societies will go up to town to refresh those who are spent by labour, or to find an outlet in action.[27]

The vagueness of Barnett's program—"interchange of life, thoughts and feelings" and, most cryptically, "outlet in action"—attests to his characteristically Arnoldian mistrust of machinery and protocol. As long as the mechanisms of philanthropy attempted to enforce prescribed practices, they would fail; the better hope was that settlements would bring about creative social changes that could be felt from the university curricula to the trade unions.

Despite Barnett's single-minded conviction that the Toynbee residents would fit into the neighborhood perfectly, there is something unsettling about his vision of settlement hospitality. For one thing, when Barnett spoke about the power that Toynbee Hall would have to gather and welcome men and women of all classes, he seemed to disregard the fact that he was essentially welcoming people to their own neighborhood; it is as if his men, having settled, would instantly become the backbone and conscience of the community. Seth Koven points out the oddness of the fact that settlement pioneers justified their enterprise as creating natural relationships between the classes, given that these natural relations required "a band of wealthy graduates to live in single-sex male communities in the heart of a London slum."[28] Far from adapting his vision to the customs and manners of East London, Barnett was proud that the activities at Toynbee Hall would be a kind of revelation to the depressed residents of Whitechapel. The settlement was to blend in but stand out, to settle in but never to settle down. The residents themselves were decidedly exceptional; as Oxford men, they had not yet affiliated themselves socially and professionally, and thus, as Koven puts it, they could be a disinterested class (239). So the purportedly natural environment of the settlement was a kind of supercharged reality; all of the machinery was designed, that is, to try to engineer an ordinary encounter between rich and poor in the most extraordinary of circumstances.

The ordinary and extraordinary merged in Barnett's primal scene of hospitality, the meeting in the resident's room: "Obviously very little can be said about the use made of private rooms. Residents who make friends in the neighbourhood entertain and are entertained. The intercourse which they enjoy, and the effect of that intercourse on character and action, are sacred from description. It is sufficient to say that those who live in settlements do ask to their rooms those whom they learn to know in clubs, in committees, or at meetings, and are in turn asked again."[29] This scene, at the center of the Toynbee experience, is sacrosanct; it can be extolled, but must not be represented. Barnett makes the same move elsewhere, evoking the scene and then drawing back: "The resident in a settlement, who has made his room his home, is able to entertain his friends with a power impossible in strange quarters. . . . It is sufficient to say that the power is used—the result must be imagined" ("Hospitalities," 62). It makes sense that Barnett would not want to describe these encounters, because no possible description would convey a success. If the encounter were extraordinary, then Toynbee Hall hospitality would have failed to create an environment where people of all classes could relate to each other in a perfectly ordinary way; in fact, it would provide exactly the kind of poignancy that the charity missions offered. Yet a truly ordinary interchange would be in some ways the least convincing thing of all, hardly the stuff of a new social awakening.

The goal, then, was to re-create something very much like the elite university but to hold present and visible the strange fact of re-creation. Toynbee Hall would be a looking-glass Oxford, a simulation of the real thing, which is impressive precisely because it ought not be there at all. Interestingly, and perhaps inevitably, this exercise in imitation would resolve into an interrogation of the university itself. Indeed, in most accounts of Toynbee Hall, the settlers, not their working-class neighbors, are the ones who seem to be the subjects of an experiment. Again and again, Barnett and later settlement leaders return to the question, how do the poor see us? In this respect, the whole project of revealing the self to others becomes also a call to turn one's scrutiny upon oneself, whether to probe or to preen. In one such moment, Barnett reports back on what he takes to be the public image of the university crowd: "[T]he Oxford or Cambridge man is still held to possess some peculiar knowledge,"[30] a belief that has led three of the most democratic boroughs to pick university professors as their representatives. Barnett refers to a workingman who commented of a Cambridge professor, "He speaks beautiful German, but of course those University gentlemen ought to" ("University," 170). And when a speaker is advertised, the poster, says Barnett, always includes his degree and college. Here Barnett is gently mocking the public's sense of awe regarding the university man, who has initials after his name and speaks in tongues. At the same time, he is reminding the university students what their capital is and where their influence comes from. In trying to market their talents and vocation to a curious public, the Oxford men must have been somewhat in awe of these very aspects of themselves; they, too, were caught up in the mystique of the thing. Indeed, by building a replica of the university, the settlers had a chance to fabricate the university's best self, to capture and reconstitute the university in exactly the image that best appealed to them—which in this case was an image inextricably bound up with Whitechapel.

With his doctrine of sincere self-revelation, Barnett could only hope that the stripped down, uncommissioned self of the settler would be a good sort of neighbor to the poor. Or put differently, he could only hope that the upper- and middle-class residents of Toynbee Hall, insofar as they *were* good neighbors, were able to be so in their own character, without concealing themselves behind the veil of a cause or mission. But could the university even be itself in East London? And if not, what would this reveal about the university's true character? This question may have worried Montagu Butler, the headmaster of Harrow, when he spoke at Oxford about the depressed conditions of life in the slums. Butler expressed the hope that "*here,* in this great home of eager thought and enlightened action and generous friendship, the bitter cry of outcast London may never seem intrusive or uninteresting, but that year by year her choicest sons may be arrested by it."[31] The troubles of poverty, Butler said, should be familiar in the university; they must not come to seem intrusive. What appears to have concerned Butler was the possibility that these things were incompatible—that the university was what it was exactly because it had turned away from the slum and that such an exclusion may have been essential to its identity. But if not—if the "choicest sons" of the university could continue to lead a life of eager thought and enlightened action even in the East End—it would count as a kind of proof that Oxford could survive, and even support, the demolition of privilege.

This hope is evident in the following story of Toynbee Hall hospitality, in which some university men do indeed maintain their character through an unlikely ordeal. It takes place in 1902 during a Toynbee Hall debate about foreign policy. According to William Bowman's later account, "There were half a dozen East Enders present . . . including a stranger who, although shabby, was rather better dressed than his colleagues. Afterwards, I learned that he was called Richter and, although we did not know it, was, in fact, Lenin."[32] If, as I have argued, one function of hospitality is to see what one looks like through another's eyes, Lenin is glad to oblige: he passionately denounces the British imperial policy and asserts furthermore that it is useless to talk about it in the East End, where nobody understands or cares about it. The response of the Toynbee men to Lenin's rage is to ratchet up their hospitality, and so Dean Robinson of Balliol House (an annex of Toynbee Hall) invites him to a Saturday tea. At this tea, we witness a push and pull between the dean's hospitality and Lenin's irascibility. From Lenin's critique of British politics there is no safe haven. For instance, the revolutionary explains that "Great Britain has become rich and indolent by robbing these countries [South Africa and India] of their possessions; but the day will come when they will rise up against you and clear you out, you will have to return to them their lands and you will have to live on your own industry or else starve. The Imperialist British Empire will dissolve" (Bowman, "Lenin," 338). The dean's response to this puts him in even deeper water: "That's not true . . . but it's too big a subject to discuss here today. What's your attitude to religion?" To this fastball pitched over the plate, Lenin replies, "I regard it as an opiate used by the capitalist classes to dope the people." Yet in the midst of these denunciations, Lenin responds powerfully to the dean's hospitalities. He eats a great deal, taking a special interest in the muffins, and after reaching a final impasse with the dean, announces that he has enjoyed himself. According to Bowman, Lenin "shook hands, thanked the Dean very sincerely for his hospitality, and went out. None of us realised that we had been entertaining the world's greatest revolutionary" (338).

No doubt, both sides felt a moral victory. Lenin had denounced the capitalist machine and had not conceded a single point to his adversaries. But just the same, Dean Robinson and his company won a concession from the revolutionary. While Lenin identifies the Toynbee men as part of the social problem, he also seems to accept the idea that Toynbee Hall is a place apart. His revolutionary discourse is framed by a narrative of socialization; he enters the presence of these men disgruntled, and leaves a civil and appreciative guest. Barnett would have been proud: that day a revolutionary Marxist witnessed genuine Oxford hospitality and liked what he saw well enough to shake hands afterwards, with no thought of pulling down the walls.

The rest of this chapter focuses on Octavia Hill, whose program of housing management, I argue, was a response to the same concerns about insulation and concealment that we have seen in Barnett. Like Barnett, Hill wished to fashion an environment in which the social worker could interact with the urban poor not as a visitor but as a neighbor, an environment to which would attach "a sense of common possession." The landlady would not, like the visitor, be a ghost in the machine; rather than hide her interests, she would broadcast them, urging compliance and, often enough, provoking dissent. Ultimately, Barnett's program of urban immersion and cultural dissemination was less radical—or at any rate less explosive—than Hill's plan, which essentially placed rich and poor in custody of the same property. In the clogged courts of an urban tenement, the idea of civic life took on a more fraught and urgent tone than it could have amid the sweetness and light of Toynbee Hall.

Joint Custody

Octavia Hill, celebrated landlady of the London slums, spent her whole adult career at the vanguard of the Charity Organisation Society. She was a founding member, and long after many of the early COS leaders had defected, Hill continued to serve on the society's central committee. The creation of the COS in 1869 came just three years after Hill had purchased her first building, Paradise Place. Therefore, Hill forged her general theories of philanthropy at the same time that she was establishing the basic operations of her buildings. Hill saw the principles of the COS—particularly its insistence on the independence of the poor—as central to her work in the slums. Correspondingly, historians have often cited Hill's housing work as an extension of COS principles and practice. Yet a social worker's visitation is much different from a landlady's supervision, and in Hill's case, the practical differences between the two kinds of work imply very different ideas of philanthropy. In the following pages, I question the easy association of Hill's housing work with COS ideology, even though it is an association encouraged by Hill herself.

Hill embarked on her first housing experiments as a personal project, not as a new kind of social work to be taken up by other volunteers. Throughout her adolescence and into her twenties, Hill had worked in close contact with poor families, a practice that was engendered by her parents' political activism, her involvement with the Christian socialists, and her own family's intermittent poverty.[33] At fourteen, Octavia supervised a workroom of pauper-girls at toy making. In her late teens she worked as secretary to the women's classes at the Working Men's College (where she would occasionally lecture), and shortly afterwards she joined with her sisters in creating a school for girls at Nottingham Place. In her mid-twenties, Hill, backed by John Ruskin, wished to build model houses that could be occupied by her poorer friends; when this proved unfeasible, she decided to purchase two existing buildings in Marylebone (where she lived) and bring them under her own management. Rather than select tenants among her friends as she had hoped, Hill would have to supervise the tenants already occupying the buildings. In the years that followed—the years leading up to the creation of the COS—Hill documented her successes and failures as a landlady in the slums. For the most part, she considered her work extremely salutary, and by the 1870s, she was promoting her system of management as one that could be widely implemented by others.[34] As she accrued public support, Hill extended the scope of her operations. For decades, her system grew in popularity, and many aspiring social workers (including Beatrice Webb) had their start as rent collectors in Octavia Hill's buildings.

Hill's work can best be placed at the intersection of the antimaterialist practices of the home visiting associations and the materialist—or "environmental," in Victorian terms—approach of the model dwelling companies. The mission of these companies was to build sanitary working-class dwellings that could be operated at a profit, thus becoming a viable financial prospect for socially minded investors.[35] The first of these companies was the Metropolitan Association for Improving the Dwellings of the Working Classes, formed in 1841; among the more successful companies to follow were Sidney Waterlow's Improved Industrial Dwellings Company and Shaftesbury's Artisan's, Labourer's and General Dwellings Company. Despite government subsidies, the rents in the model buildings were invariably higher than the families of casual laborers could afford, and it was typically the artisan class (or "working-class aristocracy") who occupied them.[36] Nevertheless, the model dwellings, like the Council flats of later decades, were always in demand.[37]

The model dwelling companies generally implemented rules and procedures that were paternalistic but impersonal. The Peabody Trust, for instance, strictly prohibited arrears of rent, required tenants to pay for any property damage in their rooms, and made tenants responsible for cleaning the passages and stairs in turn.[38] According to Anthony Wohl, the premier historian of Victorian working-class housing, the model blocks "answered perfectly to that conception of self-help which held that just the right dose of philanthropic paternalism was needed to get the poor to help themselves"; the efficacy of this paternalism was enhanced by the care with which model dwelling companies selected their tenants. The strict rules of the model buildings, along with their cell block design and their "formidable railings," made them an unappealing option to many poor families and middle-class onlookers.[39] Yet for the Victorians who were convinced that the only road to the spiritual improvement of the poor was through the physical improvement of their surroundings, the model buildings were a hopeful beginning. The authority represented by model dwelling companies inverted that represented by the philanthropic visitor: while visitors brought order to the homes of the poor through intervention, the model dwelling companies would prevent disorder and distress from ever entering their homes in the first place.

Hill united the close and constant personal contact of the visitor with a custodial rigidity very much akin to the rules of the model dwelling companies. Her premise was that poor families could gain economic security only if landlords brought their tenants under a stricter and more reliable management, especially regarding rent collection. Part of the rents would be invested in a repair fund, allowing tenants to use any money left over at the year's end for whatever appliances or improvements they wished; this, Hill said, encouraged tenants to keep their apartments in as good a state of repair as possible. Hill was famous for housing poorer tenants than the model dwelling associations did.[40] When she acquired a building, she would allow any family living in a single room to stay in one room—a policy strictly prohibited in all of the model buildings, which required every family to take at least two rooms. Hill always gave strict management priority over physical improvement, so her buildings would improve gradually over the course of months or even years. While Hill very rarely gave tenants help in the form of loans, she would employ out-of-work tenants to do repairs on the buildings. The girls were frequently hired to scrub the walls and stairs. She created work classes for the women, social clubs for the men, boys' and girls' evening classes, and supervised playgrounds for children, as well as encouraging Christmas parties and maypoles on May Day. On rent-collection nights she sat in an assembly room and held court; tenants would gather together in a great crowd.

In a way, Hill's methods of supervision—despite their popularity—never outgrew their origins in the local and the personal. Her emphasis on particular cases has often been labeled anachronistic; she is seen to have offered a simple, individualistic solution to a complex economic problem.[41] Wohl defends Hill against some of her critics, objecting to the manner in which she has been "abruptly dismissed . . . as an absurd anachronism."[42] He feels there is something quintessentially modern about Hill's approach: "It is easy to condemn her paternalistic attitudes, but most modern social workers would applaud her insistence that personal knowledge, combined with sympathy and understanding, are the essential ingredients for a better rapport with the urban poor" (*Eternal,* 190). Yet while he may not find Octavia Hill absurd or easily dismissed, Wohl finally cannot acquit her of her limited scope, which rang too much the voice of the past. "Miss Hill never seemed to have realized that the slums were not just minor aberrations nor cancers on an otherwise healthy body," Wohl explains; her advocacy of small dwellings "shows that she was grotesquely out of touch with the realities of working-class housing needs" (197, 194–95). In this way, Wohl too sees Hill as an anachronism whose real importance lay in her failures: "For while she did much individual good she also did general harm. . . . [H]er contribution was, after all, a negative one."[43] Wohl believes that at a time when Victorian housing reform was tentative about the prospect of municipal socialism, Hill's powerful but inadequate program usefully demonstrated the larger inadequacy of "philanthropic capitalism and individualistic efforts" ("Octavia," 131).

Hill's apparent anachronism actually attests to the way in which she straddled conflicting approaches to social work.[44] While she believed strongly in the COS's campaign against paternalism and for self-help, Hill attempted to achieve these aims through precisely the strategy that other reformers had rejected: a conflation of the economic and the personal.[45] As we have seen, other reformers struggled to disentangle these aspects of the relations between rich and poor. Many sought spaces for the personal—spaces such as the charitable visit—that would neither challenge nor impinge upon the economics of class interest; others looked primarily to material help through philanthropic investment schemes; and a growing number fought for an economic socialization that would undermine the mystifications of personal charity. Hill's housing work ran against all of these currents. She would attest at one moment to the intensity of the emotional bonds between landlady and tenant, and at the next moment she would insist on the punctual payment of rents. In her conflation of the economic and personal, Hill of course resembles the paternalist of old, yet her intentions were not paternalistic. Rather, she hoped that by making the landlady's custodial role conspicuous, she could both provide an avenue of personal relation and acknowledge the agency of the working-class tenant in determining what that relation should be. Unlike the charitable visit, the landlady's presence would bear none of the structural traces of condescension; by acknowledging her own interests and investments, she would obviate any sense of deference, gratitude, or self-congratulation.

Hill feared that charity in the pattern of the visiting narrative produced a distorted view of the real relations between the classes. Contact between rich and poor was not by itself a solution to the problems of poverty or class antagonism, especially a contact grounded in middle-class generosity. In her buildings, Hill attempted to create an environment where visits were *not* generous—where, in fact, they were the landlady's duty. Landlady and tenant shared responsibility for the crowded and unhealthy rooms that, in the visiting narratives, had stood witness to the failings of the poor. Destitution itself became, in some degree, the landlady's problem. Unlike the casual visitor, the landlady was culpable, vulnerable to the frustrated demands of her tenants; at the same time, she had a right to make demands of her own, even to insist on her own interests. Favors, gratitude, friendship: these things would come only after a reciprocal relationship had been established. Against every doctrine of mid-Victorian philanthropic reform, Hill's system of management entangled itself in the ordinary burdens of poverty, bringing the crisis home to the reformer.

The idea that the social worker would become a perpetual support for particular families ran counter to the COS mandate of limited intervention.

The COS prescribed middle-class intervention like a strong chemical; too much or too little, and any at all if taken at the wrong time, could be lethal. The charities were not to attend to the constitutionally dependent poor; those were the province of the Poor Law and the workhouse. But self-sustaining poverty—respectable poverty—was also out of bounds. The independent poor had to be left alone. The only people who could benefit from the intervention of a social worker were the temporarily unsettled, those independent poor who had been unexpectedly and unavoidably afflicted. Here, where the poor family was in danger of slipping into dependency, a worker might give aid and advice to help the family maintain an independent footing. For the COS, then, the intervention of the rich belonged to times of crisis and change and ended with the resumption of stability; the object of intervening was to make further interventions unnecessary. But while the COS was trying to limit and suppress the need for middle-class management of the independent poor, Hill was trying to institutionalize that management. The relationship between landlady and tenant was potentially permanent; its normal state was to be not crisis but security. The very idea of a volunteer landlady cut against the COS belief that middle-class philanthropy should turn its eye away from the properly functioning life of the working poor, as it was exactly this normal life that the landlady entered and inhabited.

The landlady's permanence at the scene of poverty gave her a power unavailable to the visitor, the power of constant and radical interference. Hill's determination to rule her buildings was explicit, her colonialist metaphors evident. Of one of her early possessions, Hill explains, "Such was the court in the winter of 1869. Truly a wild, lawless, desolate little kingdom to come to rule over."[46] She asks, "On what principles was I to rule these people?"[47] To the new landlady, the act of possession leads to a power-consciousness that might seem incompatible with any possibility of reciprocity:

> I think no one who has not experienced it can fully realise the almost awed sense of joy with which one enters upon such a possession as that above described, conscious of having the power to set it, even partially, in order. Hopes, indeed, there are which one dares scarcely hope; but at once one has power to say, "Break out a window there in that dark corner; let God's light and air in;" or, "Trap that foul drain, and shut the poisonous miasma out;" and one has moral power to say, by deeds which speak louder than words, "Where God gives me authority, this, which you in your own hearts know to be wrong, shall not go on. I would not set my conviction, however strong

> it might be, against your judgment of right; but when you are doing what I know your own conscience condemns, I, now that I have the power, will enforce right; but first I will try whether I cannot lead you, yourselves, to arise and cast out the sin—helping your wavering and sorely tried will by mine, which is untempted. (*Homes*, 26–27)

Suddenly the landlady reveals her authority—not just an authority to trap the drain but an authority to command her tenants against their will, if not their conscience.

The will to power suggested by such a passage may seem a forfeiture of Hill's more egalitarian ideals. And yet the landlady's power was an intractable fact of working-class life. Hill meant not to establish "rule" as a new principle but to challenge the sort of rule that operated by sporadic fits of license and repression. She would miss no opportunity to attack the ordinary run of slum landlords who, in her account, governed their tenants recklessly and capriciously.[48] Given the unevenness of such a rule, Hill was not surprised that tenants embraced her alternative: "They are accustomed to alternate violence of passion and toleration of vice. They expected a greater toleration, ignorant indulgence, and frequent almsgiving, but in spite of this have recognised as a blessing a rule which is very strict, but the demands of which they know, and a government that is true in word and deed" (19). Hill claimed that whereas "helping" would oppress her tenants, strict government would foster their independence (17–18).

The relationship between landlady and tenant could be constituted only mutually, by both parties; accordingly, Hill relied on a contractual model of rule to support her discourse of reciprocity. "[F]ulfilment of mutual duties," she explains to prospective landlords, "binds you and them together."[49] Hill demonstrates the contractual character of her rule with an anecdote about a tenant who refused to send his children to school:

> At last I gave him notice to leave because he refused to send them, and because he had taken three children to sleep in the room I had let for his own family only. The man was both angry and obstinate. . . . "The room was his; he took it, and if he paid rent he could do as he liked in it." "Very well," I said; "and the house is mine; I take it, and I must do what I think right in it; and I say that most landladies won't take in children at all, and we all know it is a good deal of loss and trouble; but I will risk these gladly if you will do what you can to teach the children to be good, and careful, and industrious; and if

> not, you know the rule, and you must go. If you prefer liberty, and dirt, and mess, take them; but if you choose to agree to live under as good a rule as I can make it, you can stay. You have your choice." Put in the light of a bargain the man was willing enough.[50]

This episode is characteristic of the way Hill enforced her rules. She gravitated toward the language of bargain, exchange, negotiation; rather than threaten, Hill dealt in contractual terms. This is not to understate her coercive power. As Hill was well aware, her tenants were often without options. Yet the idea of the contract is still significant, as it encouraged the tenant to weigh the advantages of the landlady's program against its disadvantages and to consider the landlady an obligated party.

With her constant recourse to negotiation, Hill created circumstances in which authority was no longer taken for granted. To Hill, the modern danger was not that landlords and tenants would forget their place, but the opposite: that landlords and tenants would fall into automatic authority structures that justified themselves through custom rather than reciprocal benefit. Hill may have admired the active responsibility of the traditional country landlord, but her own relational model must not be confused with an organicist paternalism; it is exactly to the presumption of authority that Hill objected. Both reciprocity and contractual rule work against this presumption of authority.

The idea of mutual obligation becomes most shocking when it leads Hill to endorse the tenant's dependency on the landlady. Consider the following story, which occurred on one of Hill's collection evenings: "A pale woman comes next, in great sorrow. Her husband, she tells us, has been arrested without cause. We believe this to be true; the man has always paid his way honestly, worked industriously, and lived decently. So my assistant goes round to the police-station at once to bail him, while I remain to collect the savings. 'Did he seem grateful?' I say to her on her return. 'He took it very quietly,' is her answer; 'he seemed to feel it quite natural that we should help him'" (*Homes,* 50). Looking at this anecdote—first published in the year of the Charity Organisation Society's creation—we must notice its sharp divergence from COS ideology. This exchange, which Hill considered a great triumph, illustrates most blatantly the presumption of the poor upon the rich. Above all else, the COS objected to favors from rich to poor, favors that would teach the poor that they could rely on future help and thus encourage them to fall into a habit of dependency. Yet this reliance is exactly what is celebrated here. The story makes a point of the fact that the husband is not even outwardly grateful; he feels it natural that the landlady should extricate him. His lack of gratitude would brand any act of charitable visiting a failure, but Hill counts it a success. Nor does the landlady herself seem at all confused as to her role; her intervention in the man's case is presented as a natural obligation toward a tenant who has paid his way. Sending to the police station and collecting the savings are kindred acts; they are precisely the two sides of the landlady's coin.

Provocations of a London Landlady

We have so far examined various structural aspects that distinguish Hill's housing management from the social work of her colleagues. These aspects—the culpability of the landlady, the contractual basis of the relationship between landlady and tenant, and the economy of mutual obligation—elevate the idea of reciprocity, an idea that had some currency in the wider world of philanthropy. The model housing companies, for instance, emphasized the economic benefits that well-planned philanthropic housing projects might confer upon investors, while various visiting associations discussed the moral benefits to both rich and poor of personal contact between the classes. Hill's first housing article opens with a vision of reciprocity that seems to be borrowed from both of these discourses: "The subject of dwellings for the poor is attracting so much attention, that an account of a small attempt to improve them may be interesting to many readers, especially as the plan adopted is one which has answered pecuniarily, and which, while it might be undertaken by private individuals without much risk, would bring them into close and healthy communication with their hard-working neighbours" (17). While many touted the reciprocal benefits of philanthropy, Hill believed that the very relationship between worker and client had to be at every point reciprocal. This was hardly the case in the model buildings, where the whole role of the management was to establish and enforce strict regulations over the tenants. Nor was it the case with home visiting, where the relationship hinged on the uncoerced initiative of the visitor. Because the relational framework between Hill's landlords and tenants was more fully reciprocal (if not more democratic) than those of casual philanthropy, Hill's program enabled a much wider range of possible relations than those described by most social workers. The exchanges that take place between Hill and her tenants in her *Homes of the London Poor* are alternately effusive and businesslike, generous and selfish, friendly and antagonistic. In other words, unlike other programs, Hill's system of management is not a doctrine of relation. There is no single pattern that the exchanges between landlady and tenant must necessarily follow; instead, the circumstances of reciprocity create opportunities for social experimentation, producing an array of possible relationships that largely transcend the behavioral roles of conventional charity.

In some cases, Hill relates to her tenants unproblematically as friends and equals.[51] In such relationships, an authority differential must never appear, must never even be felt. Her elaboration of this point is worth quoting at length:

> And, finally, I knew that I should learn to feel these people as my friends, and so should instinctively feel the same respect for their privacy and their independence, and should treat them with the same courtesy that I should show towards any other personal friends. There would be no interference, no entering their rooms uninvited, no offer of money or the necessaries of life. But when occasion presented itself, I should give them any help I could, such as I might offer without insult to other friends—sympathy in their distresses; advice, help, and counsel in their difficulties; introductions that might be of use to them; means of education; visits to the country; a loan of books; a bunch of flowers brought on purpose; an invitation to any entertainment, in a room built at the back of my own house, which would be likely to give them pleasure. I am convinced that one of the evils of much that is done for the poor springs from the want of delicacy felt, and courtesy shown, towards them, and that we cannot beneficially help them in any spirit different to that in which we help those who are better off. The help may differ in amount, because their needs are greater. It should not differ in kind. (42)

The most remarkable characteristic of this passage is the degree to which it acknowledges the landlady's advantages over her tenants but supposes these advantages to play no part in the character of the relationship itself. In the constitutive moment of the relationship, the landlady must forget the contingencies that separate her from her needy tenants, even though afterwards it is largely these contingencies that define their exchanges. In this formulation, Hill exposes one of the contradictions of many visiting narratives, in which visitors are asked to regard poor families as friends and, at the same time, to withhold gifts and favors. To base the relationship on the gift would, it was argued, preclude the possibility of real friendship—yet as Hill shows, to withhold gifts from a friend in need would do the same thing. The contractual foundation of the landlady's relationship with her tenants enables her to be charitable as friends, not benefactors, are charitable.

While personal intimacy can obtain for the rich a certain power to help, it can also earn them the right to do so, by removing the stain of authority from the class encounter. It entitles the rich "to be near with strong help should the hour of trial fall suddenly and heavily, and to give it with the hand and heart of a real old friend, who has filled many relations besides that of almsgiver, who has long ago given far more than material help, and has thus earned the right to give this lesser help even to the most independent spirits" (23–24). This is how the young Octavia Hill brought order to the toy-making workroom, according to C. Edmund Maurice; by sharing the girls' work, "she won them to obey as well as to love her."[52] Help from a friend is distinct from the condescension of an authority figure, particularly because it is so routine. Part of the resentment produced by condescension comes from the fact that charity, by definition, can be withheld, and that anyone who pleads for help must anticipate (and provisionally accept) the humiliation of being refused. But when one friend asks another for help, there is no possibility of refusal, so that the asking never compromises the asker.

Hill's wish to treat her tenants as her intimates in no way attenuates her desire to have her own way; in fact, she trades on her charismatic influence in a way that is both flattering to her tenants and highly coercive. Hill reminds her tenants often that she herself—her property, her judgment, and her approval—is involved in the various decisions they make about their own lifestyle:

> I have learned to know that people are ashamed to abuse a place they find cared for. They will add dirt to dirt till a place is pestilential, but the more they find done for it, the more they will respect it, till at last order and cleanliness prevail. It is this feeling of theirs, coupled with the fact that they do not like those whom they have learned to love, and whose standard is higher than their own, to see things which would grieve them, which has enabled us to accomplish nearly every reform of outward things that we have achieved; so that the surest way to have any place kept clean is to go through it often yourself. First I go at regular times, and then they clean to receive me, and have the pleasure of preparing for me, and seeing my satisfaction; then I go at unexpected times, to raise them to the power of having it always clean. (45)

The landlady's constant presence is the efficient cause of the tenants' reform. Whereas the district visitor might supply a poor family with various *means* of improvement—advice, money, and so forth—Hill supplies the *motive* as well.

There is no talk here of the industrious poor who simply need temporary assistance in their struggle upward. Hill is trying to create desires among her tenants. She is untroubled by the thought that they should act for her sake, nor does it bother her that their industry depends on her continual encouragement and surveillance.[53]

Even when she cannot bring her tenants to share her judgment or wishes, Hill frequently goads them to act for her sake. Here is a representative case:

> [T]wo women among my tenants fought; one received a dreadful kick, the other had hair torn from her head. They were parted by a lad who lived in the house. The women occupied adjoining rooms, they met in the passages, they used the same yard and wash-house, endless were the opportunities of collision while they were engaged with each other. For ten days I saw them repeatedly; I could in no way reconcile them—words of rage and recrimination were all that they uttered; while the hair, which had been carefully preserved by the victim, was continually exhibited to me as a sufficient justification for lasting anger. One was a cold, hard, self-satisfied, well-to-do woman; the other a nervous, affectionate, passionate, very poor Irishwoman. Now it happened that in speaking to the latter one evening, I mentioned my own grief at the quarrel; a look of extreme pain came over her face—it was a new idea to her that I should care. That, and no sense of the wrong of indulging an evil passion, touched her. The warm-hearted creature at once promised to shake hands with her adversary; but she had already taken out a summons against the other for assault, and did not consider she could afford to make up the quarrel because it implied losing the two shillings the summons had cost. I told her the loss was a mere nothing to her if weighed in the balance with peace, but that I would willingly pay it. It only needed that one of the combatants should make the first step towards reconciliation for the other—who, indeed, rather dreaded answering the summons—to meet her half-way. They are good neighbours now of some months' standing. (31)

It is instructive to examine the various stages of reconciliation with regard to the landlady's involvement. As the combatants turn the building into a battleground, they defend their behavior to the landlady, who is pressured at least to let the fighting continue and, even better, to take sides. One woman repeatedly exhibits the hair before Hill, as if the landlady were a county magistrate. All of this changes when Hill makes it known that, far from having the power to sanction or end the quarrel, she herself is a party to it, a fellow-sufferer. Hill displays no traces either of her missionary imperiousness nor of the philanthropic equanimity of the middle-class visitor; instead she puts her own feelings up as ransom in this battle that is not her own. It is significant that Hill approaches the poor, affectionate Irishwoman rather than the self-satisfied, well-to-do Englishwoman. In doing so, Hill makes herself a substitute for the latter (who appears to resemble her temperamentally), acting out the emotional capitulation that would never come from the combatant herself. Once Hill has won the emotional battle, she is glad to let the situation reconstitute itself as an economic problem, a matter of domestic management, in which she can intervene as easily as she does with the man who needs to be bailed out of jail.

Hill's tendency to make herself a party to quarrels often leads to antagonistic exchanges with her tenants. In such episodes, Hill unapologetically brandishes her own interests, but the very structure of the encounter creates a space for resentment, anger, and even threats on the tenant's part, a kind of behavior that (as we have seen) cannot be accommodated by the successful visiting narrative. The following narrative shows the extent to which Hill is willing to antagonize, and be antagonized by, her "subjects":

> More than one woman locked me in her room with her, the better to rave and storm. She would shake the rent in her pocket to tempt me with the sound of the money, and roar out "that never a farthing of it would she pay till her grate was set," or her floor was mended, as the case might be. Perfect silence would make her voice drop lower and lower, until at last she would stop, wondering that no violent answers were hurled back at her, and a pause would ensue. I felt that promises would be little believed in, and, besides, I wished to feel free to do as much, and only as much, as seemed best to me; so that my plan was to trust to my deeds to speak for themselves, and inspire confidence as time went on. In such a pause, therefore, I once said to a handsome, gipsylike Irishwoman, "How long have you lived here?" "More than four years," she replied, her voice swelling again at the remembrance of her wrongs; "and always was a good tenant, and paid my way, and never a thing done! And my grate," etc., etc., etc. "And how long have I had the houses?" "Well, I suppose since Monday week," in a gruff but somewhat mollified tone. "Very well, Mrs. L—, just think over quietly what has been done in the houses since then; and if you like to leave, and think you can suit yourself better, I am glad you should make yourself comfortable. Meantime,

> of course, while you stay you pay rent. I will call for it this evening if it doesn't suit you to pay now. Good morning." (44)

The general logic of this passage works much along the lines of visiting anecdotes in which the visitor is required to restrain her impulses to give help, in the face of the pleading poor. But Hill's account is quite different in crucial ways. To begin with, it is the poor tenant tempting the wealthy landlady with the money in her pocket, rather than the other way around. Additionally, it is not the impulse to charity that the landlady must suppress, but the impulse to violent speech, the usual province of the suffering poor. That Hill paints herself as a tempted subject is not an accident. In this encounter, the middle-class landlady is not a catalyst but a contender, with much to gain and much to lose. Here we might note the palpable difference between the passage above and the earlier passage from *The Builder*, in which the reporter removes the walls Asmodeus-like. Both passages are scenes of distress, but whereas Godwin's poor complain to no one in particular, Hill's tenant rails against the landlady. Hill, as it were, brings the crisis into the room. For the visitor, gaining the trust of the poor is a vehicle for progress, but for the landlady—as we can see in this anecdote—this trust is exactly what is at stake. Hill's triumph is not that she becomes unnecessary but that she has made a space for herself in her tenants' rooms.

All of these modes of relation attest to Hill's desire to make her buildings into functional, prosperous communities. Hill's concern for community differed markedly from the Charity Organisation Society's emphasis on the citizenship of the poor.[54] For COS leaders such as Loch and Bosanquet, the goal of social work was to help poor families consolidate their resources, insist on their self-respect, harden themselves against the pathologies of slum life, and transform their homes from shameful public exhibitions to private domestic enclaves like those of the middle classes.[55] But Hill, perhaps in part because she never lived in such a home, defied the individualism of her fellow workers. Ultimately, for all her hatred of economic dependency—and the campaign against socialization was one that Hill would fight to the end of her life—Hill's vision of working-class prosperity was a vision of corporate life. She thrilled to hear one tenant refer to another as "one of us" (*Homes*, 28). Hill thought the advantages of civil life came not from privacy but from exposure: "Think," she exclaims, "of what this mere fact of *being known* is to the poor!" (35). Hill's attraction to corporate life can be felt in her accounts of Freshwater Place: "I feel myself somewhat like an officer at the head of a well-controlled little regiment, or, more accurately, like a country proprietor with a moderate number of well-ordered tenants" (34). Hill did well to correct herself: she was a proprietor and not an officer; her tenants shared a building, not a campaign. But in her aims and her conviction, Hill really was more an officer than a proprietor, and her housing work was not after all so far from her days in the workroom of the Ladies' Guild, supervising pauper girls at their craft.

It is evident that neither the pauperizing charity of the middle classes nor the independent families of the COS could provide the "consciousness of corporate life" that Hill valued so highly (28). Any study of the Octavia Hill project as it related to other COS initiatives must recognize that this corporate consciousness—a special kind of dependency—was the foundation of Hill's housing work and in fact connects her work in the slums with her many other seemingly diffuse social contributions. This drive toward interdependency is evident in a story from Hill's childhood that her biographers have found compelling. Octavia would often take charge of games with her sisters, and in one such game, "they were all fastened by a cord tied round her waist, and she ran them down the meadow and leaped over the brook there, reached the bank safely, but forgot that her tail would assuredly not be beside her but drop into the water, which they did to her great surprise and remorse."[56] The biographers clearly mean this story to demonstrate Hill's overambition, her relative blindness to the deficiencies of others, and her genuine goodwill that surfaced when these deficiencies were revealed. But we might draw a further analogy: Hill's game, like her buildings, assumes that her followers perfectly share both her aims and her abilities. And if mishaps occur, it is because the affinity between leader and follower is not fully *enough* realized. Hill never cared to loosen the cord of dependency between rich and poor; even when she cut her tenants off, it was in an attempt to tie a knot that would hold tighter and last longer. In the mid-Victorian contest between a bountiful charity and a restrained one, few programs required so complete an identification between the volunteer worker and the working poor.

CHAPTER FOUR

Tennyson's Salvation Army

The slum settlers sought to enter into the organic life of the poorest neighborhoods and to reproduce a well-regulated middle-class life for the poor to share. This was an effort to solve the problem of condescension: by having a fuller contact with the poor than a typical charity worker could ever do in an occasional visit, the settler would reveal aspects of his or her authentic self that the mists of charitable condescension ordinarily concealed. There must be no causes, missions, or dogmas; these things created the static of official charity, and only in their absence could reform (or for Barnett, revolution) be achieved.

A related but sharply contrasting development—a mirror image of the settlement ideology—can be seen in what we might call charity by conscription. The goal of this type of charity was to recruit the poor into the cause of charity itself and in this way remove the divide between reformer and reformed. If the slum settlers submerged themselves within the ordinary lives of the poor, the missionary reformer would instead lift the poor and socially outcast into the realms of officialdom. This solution, no less than Barnett's, sought to bind the classes together through commonality, but whereas the settlement movement looked for commonality in ordinary life, proponents of conscription sought to sweep all the classes up in a great cause. This was, perhaps, the other way out of Barnett's dilemma. If, as he believed, the condescension of philanthropic missionaries served only to separate them from the people they wished to help, there were two options: to dispense with the mission (as the settlers attempted), or to make everyone a missionary. In the logic of conscription, the richest and poorest could link arms as fellow soldiers in the battle for a general social uplift.

This sort of missionary conscription was not to everyone's taste. Dickens, most prominently, was deeply skeptical of regeneration schemes in which the reformed became a reformer or otherwise touted himself as a pattern of behavior for his fellows. For Dickens, handing over leadership to the recently rescued was a sign that the rescue mission was not worth much. Such is the case with the temperance meeting in *The Pickwick Papers,* in which the newly temperate testify somewhat confusedly as to the way drink ruined their lives. H. Walker, an out-of-work tailor, speculates that his poverty owes either to drink "or the loss of his right hand; is not certain which, but thinks it very likely that, if he had drank nothing but water all his life, his fellow workman would never have stuck a rusty needle in him" (*Pickwick,* 459). Dickens's "The Perils of Certain English Prisoners" features a different sort of convert, a West Indian native named Christian George King. King embraces the language and the customs of the English colonists, who are delighted with his civilities—until he betrays them to a band of invading pirates. Equally unregenerate are the pupils of the ragged school described in *Our Mutual Friend,* children who, like Uriah Heep, learn to placate their social superiors by speaking in sanctimonious tones: "Young women old in the vices of the commonest and worst life, were expected to profess themselves enthralled by the good child's book, the Adventures of Little Margery," while "unwieldy young dredgers and hulking mud-larks were referred to the experiences of Thomas Twopence," a boy who is rewarded with three and sixpence for not robbing his benefactor (214–15). Such an education, says Dickens, only encourages these children in the clutching self-interest that has already been bred into them by a life of poverty: "Several swaggering sinners had written their own biographies in the same strain; it always appearing from the lessons of those very boastful persons, that you were to do good, not because it *was* good, but because you were to make a good thing of it" (215).

Dickens levels the same complaint against the "pet prisoners" at Pentonville, men who learn quickly, in Dickens's view, that a small amount of contrition can purchase them a great deal of comfort. The Pentonville prisoners, says Dickens, are trained to become infatuated with their own penitence and to believe that by virtue of repenting, they have entered a condition of spiritual privilege from which they may proceed to judge and perhaps improve their fellow men. Whereas many reformers might rejoice in the fact that the moral barrier has been removed between the criminal and the rest of society, Dickens insists that the barrier ought to be maintained, for the sake of the criminal and of repentance itself. If the criminal is "recruited" for the cause of his own reform, he begins to fetishize his own state of mind: "[A] strange absorbing selfishness—a spiritual egotism and vanity, real or assumed—is the first result. . . . *I* did this, *I* feel that, *I* confide in the mercy of Heaven being extended to *me*."[1] In his celebration of the reformation of his character, the prisoner loses interest in his crime and the real repercussions of his actions in the world. Rather than "make restitution," the criminal will "thank God for . . . imprisonment" and hope that others can have the privilege of sharing in his own sense of contrition before God ("Pet Prisoners," 402–3). Besides all of this, Dickens is suspicious of the "pattern penitence" that he observes, the way in which the prisoners' meditations adhere to a formula that was doubtless propagated by the clergymen who visited them. The whole process, he implies, is designed to create a pleasing spectacle, much like the spectacle of the poor pupils speaking like pious middle-class children. Rich and poor, law-abiding and criminal, Englishman and savage cannot simply join hands, pronounce themselves members of a single social crusade, and thereby erase their differences.

Nevertheless, for many Victorians, this was exactly the way forward. It was commonly believed that the disenfranchised ought to be recruited into the reform enterprise, and numerous charities from soup kitchens to mechanics' institutes were managed largely if not entirely by working-class volunteers.[2] Although many of the cooperative charities were modern innovations, the ideology of conscription had a significant pedigree, reaching back most notably to the Methodist movement, in which a worshipper's initial moment of conversion was also often the beginning of his or her public ministry.

David Hempton gives the example of John Edwards Risley, whose "career as a preacher, revivalist, city missioner, and patron of dying Methodist causes is a remarkable tribute to the enduring power of the message he first embraced as a teenager."[3] Risley, like many other Methodist preachers, was converted to the movement at the same time that he was converted to the faith; his own spiritual rescue was, from the first, a signal that he was to begin rescuing others. The same is true for the Salvation Army, which drew many of its preachers from among the wayward souls who attended the meetings. As Edward McKinley explains, "Once rescued, the new convert was immediately pressed into the war for souls, as a testifier and supporter if not as a soldier. 'We are a salvation people,' William Booth wrote in 1879; 'this is our specialty—getting saved and keeping saved and then getting somebody else saved.' The life of converts was given new meaning—the highest possible meaning: they were not only saved, but given the privilege of saving others."[4] Booth's synopsis implies a perfect continuity between the Salvationist's own conversion and his work to convert others; in fact, even the initial action of "getting saved" is seen as just one battle within the Salvationist's larger campaign. The Salvation Army, and other charitable missions that emphasized recruitment, offered a unique kind of promise to the destitute, who, by a single decision, could stop being "matters of concern" and join the ranks of the concerned.

Correspondingly, the work called for a new kind of public servant, one who either had literally risen from the ranks of the people he or she wanted to help or else could demonstrate his or her own frailty or kinship with the downtrodden. Ideally, there would be no difference between the agent and the object of charity, except that the charity worker had already joined the cause that was held out, shimmering, before both. If the worker successfully conveyed the sense that he or she had once been a soul in crisis—and that his or her present security was contingent—then the outcast might not feel singled out or insulted by an offer of help. For this kind of mutual identification to work, the charity worker had to show that he or she, too, had a private self that had been won over to the public cause. Paradoxically, then, an agent of charity might expect to be most effective in persuading the disenfranchised to take up a cause if the agent could display the traces of his or her own previous self, a self that had rejected help, resisted incorporation.

For missionaries who worked in this vein, it was often important to make frequent reference to their old, dangerous, sinful selves, the selves that had been won to Christ and that, except for the power of God's grace, would quickly relapse into dejection or depravity. This is nowhere better exemplified than by the rough and tumble male preachers and Hallelujah Lasses of the Salvation Army. Salvationist men, according to Pamela Walker, needed constantly to demonstrate to their audiences that their new religion did not compromise their manhood, as defined by working-class constructs of masculinity.[5] One might conjecture that these men told their stories of brawling, gambling, drinking, and womanizing not only to show what God's grace had rescued them from but also to establish a pedigree with their listeners. Walker describes a Salvationist preacher who carried himself like a street fighter, wrestling with the devil. In a sense, the preacher never leaves the moment of his conversion; again and again he stages his own struggle with sin in order to reach other men of low morals—and also to show that he is as good a brawler as ever, a dangerous man who is only barely held in check by the irresistible force of the gospel. Similarly, Salvation Army women, Walker argues, took on the "image of disorderly women" normally associated with prostitutes, both to put themselves forward as "public women" and to throw their own mission of purification into relief. Salvationist men and women seemed to claim a family relationship with bad behavior, selling their spiritual mission as a kind of natural recoil from sin, an enterprise that the sinful were especially suited for. This was not just a marketing tactic but a sincere conviction, very much in line with Salvationist holiness theology, which, according to Walker, ended not in "peace and repose" but in perpetual militancy.[6]

Condescension would be eradicated if two things were clear: that the outcast could in an instant be recruited to the army of God and that the missionary agent was at bottom a tough customer. The shortcomings of the agent could be flourished as a testament both to the worthiness of the cause and to the fact that the cause could be taken up by anyone. Therefore, the idea of conscription relied on the unsuitability of the agent of charity, the inevitable gap between the worker's private self and his or her public commission. The volunteer was as much in need as the outcast, and it was the cause of reform (whether spiritual or material) that had the power to raise them both. Of course, it would be a great exaggeration to say that in the course of recruitment, every missionary or volunteer worker represented him- or herself as a soul in crisis, a fragile human edifice in danger of imminent collapse. The point, instead, is that the work of charitable conscription relied on the recruiter's separability from the cause. The recruiter should be at the core a private person, both reflecting the glory and shouldering the burden of a noble public vocation. Indeed, the danger of recidivism—that the missionary or public servant could in a moment lose sight of his calling and fall back into a life of sin or selfishness—is in a sense the guarantee that the mission is truly universal, available to any who would take it up and by no means the secure possession of the right "kind" of person.

The figure of the compromised agent is in some ways fundamental, then, to a politics of inclusion, an image of society in which every individual is asked to be the bearer of a public mission. In fact, such a figure fits perfectly into the Victorian landscape of semiofficial public administration. In a society where the private citizen is expected to be infused with and guided by public feeling, it stands to reason that the public person (whether a civil servant, charity worker, or missionary) would be prone to house a private self in tension with his or her official purpose. Several studies have recently treated the centrality of voluntary association to Victorian political ideology. M. J. D. Roberts discusses the ways in which nineteenth-century "moral reform" in England was driven by the efforts of private citizens organized in diverse volunteer networks, while Lauren Goodlad explores how the Victorian model of liberal governance enfolded, even within the operations of the (limited) state bureaucracy, an ideal of individual voluntary initiative.[7] A voluntaristic ideology of public service invests confidence in the private citizen as a person with moral resources, practical ability, and civic enthusiasm; as Roberts explains, "[A] major reason why moral reformers usually retained a strong commitment to voluntary status . . . was that it helped them to retain a living sense of personal responsibility for those they perceived as 'less fortunate' than themselves—a sense which most of them envisaged as difficult to preserve if the work was entrusted to [a] professional or official agency."[8] But beneath this claim we can recognize the flip side of voluntarism: the suggestion that the private citizen has to struggle to make this responsibility his or her own. In a society where private feelings of enthusiasm are sufficient to conscript anyone into the cause of the public good, one must be ever vigilant against the feelings of despondency, reluctance, or inadequacy that could stand between the public servant and his or her commission.

This chapter investigates one of the most prominent literary portraits of civic voluntarism, Alfred Tennyson's *Idylls of the King*.[9] In particular, I consider the knights in Arthur's court, men who are both the agents and the objects of a national reform movement. Tennyson's knights are missionary zealots; at the same time, they are the ones most in need of rescue. Like Booth's "salvation people," they divide their efforts equally between "getting saved and keeping saved and then getting somebody else saved." While the knights' moral struggles are apparent enough, those struggles are often read as part of a broad existential conflict, signaling the inevitable failure of political or spiritual ideals.[10] But I would suggest that the knights' struggles are at least partially an effect of their vocation as missionary reformers—that their dilemmas, in other words, are the inevitable condition of their participation in the social process of conscription.

Tennyson's knights are rarely discussed as a distinct professional class; they have traditionally been read as the embodiments of various temperaments and spiritual conditions, and they are almost always understood in terms of their relationship to the sovereign. Tennyson himself inaugurated this reading in one of his many meditations on the meaning of his epic: "By King Arthur I always meant the soul, and by the Round Table the passions and capacities of a man."[11] Matthew Reynolds complicates this approach, saying that the "parabolic drift" of the poem requires us at times to consider the characters as "persons in their own right" and at other times "as elements of a larger being": "The *Idylls,* therefore, enquire into [the] idea . . . that a well-governed State is like a person, with the various sections of society assuming the roles of different faculties, organs, or limbs." Reynolds goes on to observe that in the earlier idylls "Arthur's subjects are good and happy in so far as they . . . recognize themselves to be constituents within the greater personality which is the State," whereas in the later idylls "the resemblance of State to person progressively fades."[12] Reynolds is surely correct that Tennyson vacillates between treating Arthur's knights as independent persons and making them extensions of the king's authority, but I would argue that this alternation is not simply a peculiarity of Tennyson's method. Rather, it is a sign that in the social system of the *Idylls,* the subjectivity of the king's agents is very much at issue.

Because the *Idylls* so consistently chronicle the anguish that attends those who defect from the court, it is natural to read them as enacting a basic conflict between attachment and separation. Linda Hughes and Michael Lund, for instance, see the 1859 *Idylls* as repeatedly staging a character's abandonment of the court and struggle at the margins: "The issue then becomes the degree to which the margin is an extension of the center or a free-floating domain without subordination or relation." In the face of this crisis of relation, Hughes and Lund argue, the cyclical structure of the poem's narrative (as it unfolds through its serial publication) ultimately reaffirms "the potential within Arthur's realm for renewal, growth, and expansion from a clear center," and thus the stability of the empire.[13] Ian McGuire offers a somewhat different interpretation of the knightly predicament, describing an Oedipal process that both requires the knights to obey and destroy the father and keeps them "suspended indefinitely between the renunciation of the mother and the discovery of the wifely substitute,"[14] a process that gives rise to the political contradictions of empire.

I would contend that for Arthur's knights, separation—even rebellion—is not an alternative to the kind of attachment they seek to attain, but an effect of it. The kind of attachment the poem envisions, a service grounded in missionary conscription, admits and even draws its strength from the idea that the agent can never be worthy of the cause, that the obedient knight and the recreant can change places in an instant. Thus the poem, even as it condemns the knights who rebel against the king's authority, portrays such rebellion as inevitable and interesting; in fact, in some cases Tennyson seems to sympathize most readily not with Arthur but with the alienated knight, whose private purposes chafe against the explicit requirements of his job. This tension between independent action and public duty is so deeply ingrained that it, and not obedience, is the defining characteristic of the government agents in Arthur's employ, and much of the *Idylls* concerns Arthur's efforts not to win control of the kingdom but to win back the hearts of his own knights.

This is the double edge of conscription, which offers a release from the pressures of condescension and deference but equally forfeits the security of a social system in which condescension can reconcile high and low. As Arthur's civil and military corps, the knights are public men, men who live and work as agents of the state. Their interior lives must be wholly synchronized with their public commission. By subsuming the self within the mission, the knight in principle is united to both his sovereign and his social inferiors by a common purpose and thus transcends the failures that plague the condescension narrative. And yet, as we have seen, the power of conscription depends on the superiority of the cause to the agent and also on a fundamentally private subjectivity that can come into and out of alignment with a shared vision of official welfare. By depicting a political culture in which even the best knights resist or revise the work that they are called upon to do, Tennyson suggests that in a society where no distinction is made between the agents and the objects of social work, the public servant must of necessity be poised to fall, a compromised subject whose outward efforts are plagued by private doubts.[15]

The Public Servant

Only once does Tennyson describe a scene of perfect concord between the king and his knights, and it is appropriately offered not as a tangible fact but as an impression. The incident is narrated by Queen Bellicent, who experienced it as a moment of conversion, the point when she became convinced of the king's legitimacy. Thus, the episode is less a plot event than a metaphysical vision, a deep revelation of who and what the king truly is. In the scene, the king and his knights share a kind of ecstatic communion:

> "But when he spake and cheer'd his Table Round
> With large, divine, and comfortable words,
> Beyond my tongue to tell thee—I beheld
> From eye to eye thro' all their Order flash
> A momentary likeness of the King:"
>
> ("The Coming of Arthur," lines 266–70)

Bellicent presents this impression as part of her argument for Arthur's pedigree, and the implication is that his very origin is bound up with his knights. Arthur's legitimacy is palpable in the exuberant loyalty of his followers; indeed, he is unthinkable without them. The knights, too, draw strength and purpose from their faith in him, so that their power is a proof of their fealty: "Thou dost not doubt me King," Arthur tells Lancelot; "So well thine arm hath wrought for me today" (125–26). In the golden age, soldier and sovereign act in perfect accord.[16] The poem explains that "Arthur and his knighthood for a space / Were all one will" (lines 514–15), subduing the "petty princedoms" and overcoming the "heathen hordes" (lines 516–18). There is no question of morale here, no rousing Crispin's Day speech to persuade the knights of their high purpose. Persuasion is for petty princes and heathen hordes, not for the sober, fanatical agents of the court. A king might as well persuade his own arm.

Almost from the first, Arthur's knights fail him precisely by breaking this communion. Arthur may have no self apart from his knights, but they most definitely do have independent selves, selves that were only recently conscripted into service.[17] The principal heroes of the 1859 *Idylls*, Geraint and Lancelot, go wrong when, after establishing reputations within the court, they try to strike out on their own as free agents. Their struggle is not a simple contest between loyalty and disloyalty but a more complex affair in which each knight attempts to deny the degree of his own alienation, to convince himself that he can fulfill a public mission while nourishing private causes for rebellion. Actually, both Lancelot and Geraint harbor fantasies that their independence from the court can make them even stronger soldiers in the king's cause. In these early poems, although Tennyson does not allow that anything productive can grow out of this kind of dissonance, he does set the stage for the *Idylls* of later years, in which the knight-conscript's rebellion is in some degree justified and even hallowed.

Lancelot, in particular, struggles to differentiate himself from Arthur while retaining the king's favor. Lancelot walks a fine line: his "guilty love" for Guinevere ("Lancelot and Elaine," line 244) makes him a renegade, yet even as he knowingly intrudes on the king's marriage, Lancelot tries to demonstrate at every point that he remains a loyal soldier. He is not satisfied to lead a double life; instead, he takes great pains to show that his private pursuits are consonant with his public character and can withstand scrutiny. When Guinevere fears for the scandal that Lancelot's attentions to her will bring, he rebukes her, arguing that their love has been acknowledged and authorized within the public world of the court:

> "But now my loyal worship is allowed
> Of all men: many a bard, without offence,
> Has linked our names together in his lay,
> Lancelot, the flower of bravery, Guinevere,
> The pearl of beauty: and our knights at feast
> Have pledged us in this union, while the King
> Would listen smiling."
>
> (lines 110–16)

In Lancelot's account, his worship of Guinevere is well understood by all; the private obsession is part of his public image. Indeed, Lancelot's argument hinges on the king's smiling approval. Lancelot does not gloat or take pleasure in any thought that he is tricking the king. Rather, he wants to imagine that the king sees and condones all. It is a fantasy of wholeness in which the errant self turns out, even at his worst, to have been a good servant all along. This fantasy of loyalty-in-rebellion explains why, after having intentionally missed the Diamond Jousts, Lancelot submits to Guinevere's stratagem: he will enter the tournament in disguise, and when he wins, will obtain even greater glory for having done so without the power of his name. The plan perfectly encapsulates Lancelot's conflicting impulses: the wish to distance himself further from his king and the wish to be forgiven for having already done so. Throughout the rest of the poem, Lancelot pursues these rival aims, riding out in disguise to win a crown of diamonds for Guinevere, yet constantly paying tribute to King Arthur as his superior. "I am not great," he protests to Lavaine; "There is the man" (lines 449–50). In Astolat, Lancelot can do nothing but sing Arthur's praises. By extolling his king, Lancelot seems to want to soften his sense of betrayal and also his dread of the consequences. He explains, for instance, that although Arthur is fierce in battle, he doesn't mind being thrown in the jousts by his own knights: "For if his own knight cast him down, he laughs / Saying, his knights are better men than he" (lines 312–13). This is an image of a king who will never go to war against his own knights, and the image nicely displaces the graver matter of Lancelot's betrayal with Guinevere; perhaps in that affair, too, the king will be contented to celebrate his knight's accomplishments even at his own expense.[18]

Lancelot imagines that he can work for Arthur and against him at the same time. But the poem does not support this possibility. The real problem is not Lancelot's love for Guinevere but his tendency to conceive of his own interests separately from the interests of the king and the nation, a tendency that, in the symbolic logic of "Lancelot and Elaine," amounts to sedition. Lancelot enters the poem poised to win the last of nine diamonds from Arthur, having won the oth ers previously. His campaign to garner all of the diamonds and present them to the queen is dubious, in that his rationale for doing so completely contravenes Arthur's rationale for giving the diamonds away. We read that Arthur first found the diamonds long before he was king; they had been the property of a "nameless king" (line 442) who died in civil war against his brother. After Arthur does gain sovereignty, he has this other crown stripped of its diamonds, announcing, "These jewels, whereupon I chanced / Divinely, are the kingdom's, not the King's— / For public use" (lines 58–60). Arthur views his kingship as a public affair whose glory and responsibility must be distributed among his followers. But Lancelot gathers and reassembles the diamonds, undoing the democratic machinery instated by the king; rather than participate in a broader public enterprise, Lancelot reconstructs the crown that Arthur has rejected, and does so for a private purpose. Symbolically, Lancelot takes up the mantle of the nameless king; his private pursuits mount a challenge to the civil authority that the king has delegated to his followers at large and consequently work to usurp the king's sovereignty itself.

Even as they alienate him from the king, Lancelot's private interests poison the deepest sources of the self; when he is not carrying out the king's agenda, Lancelot simply becomes a nonentity. The tournament, for instance, does not go as Lancelot expects. His plan, of course, is to win the day in disguise—without the benefit of his name—and thus, having established his formidable power as a free agent, to make his allegiance to Arthur even more impressive. What happens instead is that his confused kinsmen, deciding that the great prowess of this mysterious knight amounts to a threat against the established primacy of Lancelot, battle him in his own name: "a fury seized them all, / A fiery family passion for the name / Of Lancelot, and a glory one with theirs" (lines 474–76). In the struggle he is dealt a nearly lethal blow, and more significantly, his victory is meaningless, since he has spent the whole battle effectively dismantling the glory of his own ("Lancelot's") generalship, the same glory he had hoped to amplify. The victory of the alienated self over the conscripted self leaves no room for loyalty, glory, or allegiance. Lancelot recognizes this at the last minute and refuses the diamond, perhaps realizing that to win the whole crown of jewels from Arthur would deeply and finally undermine his ability to serve.

Lancelot's failure to incorporate himself within the king's cause is contrasted with the earlier two-part tale of Prince Geraint of Devon, a knight who, like Lancelot, puts aside his commission for a space but ultimately settles his personal dilemmas and resumes his public work. Geraint takes on two separate missions, one official and one personal. In his official mission, the prince sets out to teach some manners to a recreant knight who will not answer to the queen. As Prince Geraint seeks the offending knight, his public work flourishes; he performs a series of political acts in the king's name and ultimately brings justice to an oppressed valley. He wins himself a bride along the way and places her, too, at the queen's disposal. This mission would seem to have the Tennysonian stamp of approval, epitomizing the kind of selfless and high-minded courtesy that is possible in the days before Camelot is shot through with scandal. But after the prince returns to the court, his public mission gives way to a private compulsion. Hearing the gossip, Geraint finds that his personal scruples are too finely tuned to let him see his wife consorting with his one-time commissioner the queen, and he thus strikes out on his own, trying—utterly without success—to establish a better, gossip-free, rule over his own private kingdom. His marriage falls into jeopardy, and he and Enid embark on a kind of marital odyssey in which Geraint finally learns to trust his wife. Only when he has straightened out his private life is Geraint fit to return to public work; at that point, he is sought out by the king and once again pressed into the national service.[19] Unlike "Lancelot and Elaine," then, the pair of Geraint idylls seem to present a triumph of conscription and incorporation—though I argue in the chapter's next section that from the first, Geraint's relationship to his mission is more ambivalent than it would appear.

Geraint's story begins[20] full of public feeling and recalls a period when the prince's every action was done for the sake of his sovereign (in this case, the queen). In fact, if Tennyson's own vassalage to his monarch enters the *Idylls* anywhere, it is in "The Marriage of Geraint," which charts a prince's service to his queen and allows Guinevere for a space, like Victoria, to be a patroness both of military conquest and of bourgeois domesticity. Events are set in motion when the queen, riding out with Geraint, is insulted by a strange knight (Edyrn) who refuses to give his name. Geraint might with good reason have pursued this as a personal rather than an official matter, as the knight's attendant, an "irritable" dwarf, has lashed Geraint with his whip and drawn blood ("The Marriage of Geraint," lines 194–207). But with a kind of professional forbearance, Geraint overlooks the injury to himself and makes it his mission instead to avenge the insult to the queen. In contrast to the mystery knight, who hides his identity in an effort to evade the reach of the queen's jurisdiction, Geraint is all fealty, a man fully absorbed within his public role. He has even left his own arms behind, which means that for the purposes of the queen's mission, he is a blank slate. Before he can fight Edyrn, Geraint must arm himself, and the first part of his quest is concerned with his comical attempts to muster the right equipment. For a prince to go on a quest for armor seems an absurdity, but for Geraint and Guinevere, it is the charm of the whole mission; in the course of his duty to the queen, Geraint will be building commitments that will reconstitute his identity as a fully public person. Throughout the events that follow, Geraint repeatedly subdues his own vexations, and at no point does he forget either the gravity of his mission or the one who has commissioned him. Earl Yniol, who has his own list of grievances against Edyrn, can perceive that Geraint is interested only in serving the queen: thus, in the climactic battle scene, clever Yniol makes no mention of the wrongs that have been done to him and his daughter but instead cries, "Remember that great insult done the Queen" (line 571)—whereupon Geraint promptly cuts his opponent to pieces. Even in affairs of the heart, the prince acts entirely within the bounds of his mission; as he courts Enid, Geraint fulfills his queen's injunction to "light on all things that you love, / And live to wed with her whom you first love" (lines 226–27).

Geraint's resolutely public mission becomes rather awkward when he realizes that by attempting to defeat Edyrn in battle, he is interrupting a family story already in progress. Edyrn's situation is that of the prodigal son. Discontents within the family (his rejection by Enid) have led him to play the truant, adopting the name "the sparrow-hawk" and robbing Uncle Yniol of his possessions. The family feelings surge and rankle, as Edyrn holds an annual tournament to shame Enid ("Geraint and Enid," lines 838–44) and Yniol groans under a conviction that Edyrn lets him live only out of spite. In light of this universal despair about Edyrn, the story is ripe for a reunion in which the sparrow-hawk might see the error of his ways and rejoin the family. Instead, Prince Geraint interferes; he swoops down from above and collects Enid. Geraint is the queen's champion, and by the steady-state logic of the prodigal plot, Edyrn should become Enid's. But Geraint breaks the family story to pieces: instead of restoring the household, he settles affairs by recruiting both Enid and Edyrn to the national service, the same service he is committed to. Edyrn's incorporation is elegant and swift:

> And rising up, he rode to Arthur's court,
> And there the Queen forgave him easily.
> And being young, he changed and came to loathe
> His crime of traitor, slowly drew himself
> Bright from his old dark life, and fell at last
> In the great battle fighting for the King.
>
> ("The Marriage of Geraint," lines 591–96)

Edyrn's reconciliation with his uncle is not narrated, as it is beside the point. He is given not a personal but a political apotheosis, raised up by the queen's hand into the king's service.

Something similar takes place with Enid, the earl's daughter, who wishes she could present herself to Geraint and the queen in the splendid garments of her youth, not in the shabby dress she has worn since her family was ruined. But Geraint makes it clear that Enid, like Edyrn, must erase the traces of her old life. Just as the prince undertook his journey without arms, so too must Enid go without clothes and let herself be elevated by the raiment of the court. He explains to her mother,

> "I vowed that could I gain her, our fair Queen,
> No hand but hers, should make your Enid burst
> Sunlike from cloud—and likewise thought perhaps,
> That service done so graciously would bind
> The two together; fain I would the two
> Should love each other: how can Enid find
> A nobler friend?"
>
> (lines 787–93)

It is a disturbing sentiment, to be sure: the fact that Geraint believes that he has the prerogative to keep Enid in silks or rags, at his discretion, betrays unsettling patriarchal assumptions about marriage and foreshadows the relationship troubles that will plague the couple in days to come. Geraint's superiority is everywhere remarked on in Yniol's home, and Enid's mother is all too ready to see Geraint as a conqueror: "As this great Prince invaded us, and we, / Not beat him back, but welcomed him with joy" (lines 747–48). Yet it is also worth noting that Geraint's assertions here seem to arise more out of civic feeling than out of a desire for mastery. He is fairly relaxed about his own relationship with Enid and is much more concerned about her relationship with the queen. Geraint wants every aspect of Enid's emotional life to be tied to the court, and he tries to raise her sense of fealty above all other attachments, including her attachment to him. "No hand but" the queen's should bring Enid forward—not Enid's own hand, but not Geraint's either.

Geraint's return to Camelot, with his new wife in tow, ought to represent the perfect alignment of his private life and his public commission. As the new couple approach the court, they are embraced by the queen, who has mounted the tower three times in anticipation of their arrival. The moment is passionate, personal: it is everything the prince could have hoped for as a consummation of his loyalty. But things go amazingly wrong. When Geraint hears of the queen's sin, he instantly rejects the public life that he has worked so hard to win for himself and his wife and returns to his own kingdom. His withdrawal from Camelot is not simply a withdrawal from the court; even once he enters his own lands, Geraint turns his back on any sort of public feeling, concentrating only on Enid:

> He compassed her with sweet observances
> And worship, never leaving her, and grew
> Forgetful of his promise to the King,
> Forgetful of the falcon and the hunt,
> Forgetful of the tilt and tournament,
> Forgetful of his glory and his name,
> Forgetful of his princedom and its cares
>
> (lines 48–54)

In this passage, the promise to the king shades into the hunt, the tournament, and the knight's own glory: Geraint's abdication is therefore a move not against the king but against public life altogether.[21] The people's response is merciless, and the poem does not for a second entertain the idea that Geraint's inward turn has merit. As Enid says, "I cannot love my lord and not his name" (line 92).

Geraint's defection might seem a predictable effect of disillusionment: like the later Pelleas, Geraint has invested so great a faith in queen and court that the tarnishing of his official ideal sends him reeling into despair. Yet I argue that the problem precedes this disappointment—that in some sense, the queen's sins simply provide a justification and an avenue for an escape that Geraint has been contemplating all along. There is something inherent in the knight that will not allow him to be fully assimilated, such that, even at the height of his missionary enthusiasm, he is at odds with his mission. And it is this intrinsic separateness that causes Prince Geraint, conscript and missionary, to distance himself so urgently from the public home that would seem to be the best place for the citizen soldier.

Geraint and the Lure of Distance

Geraint's trouble coming home to Arthur's court suggests the possibility that he was never at home there to begin with.[22] And indeed, a second look shows that Geraint's quest in the queen's service—the high-water mark of his public zeal—is marred by an inauspicious beginning, one that shows him to be at odds with the rest of the king's knights. Geraint, like Guinevere, has overslept and missed the hunt; this is the reason he is present to see the insult to the queen. Having lost his chance to ride in the hunt, Geraint goes out to watch the others. He comes across not as a soldier but as a hanger-on, a man of fashion who is glad not to be wearing the standard issue. Geraint sports "neither hunting-dress / Nor weapon, save a golden-hilted brand" (lines 165–66); rather,

> A purple scarf, at either end whereof
> There swung an apple of the purest gold,
> Swayed round about him, as he galloped up
> To join them, glancing like a dragon-fly
> In summer suit and silks of holiday.
>
> ("The Marriage of Geraint," lines 169–73)

Thus, from the start, Prince Geraint is shown to be a kind of dandy, an insider-enthusiast whose refined tastes set him apart from the other knights. In fact, throughout his service to Guinevere, Geraint's brand of courtesy is tinged with the very decadence that later turns him against the queen and the court. His foppishness is clearly evident as he makes his way through the little town over which the sparrow-hawk is lord. Geraint quickly becomes frustrated that the local armorers, who are busy making weapons for their master, will pay no tribute to the great prince from Camelot. He expresses his outrage in an unexpectedly dandified kind of punning:[23]

> "A thousand pips eat up your sparrow-hawk!
> Tits, wrens, and all winged nothings peck him dead!
> Ye think the rustic cackle of your bourg
> The murmur of the world! What is it to me?"
>
> (lines 274–77)

Geraint is showing off here, and the armorer is "amazed" to see "one so gay in purple silks" (lines 283–84). In effect, Geraint's quest to police the queen's courtesy has revealed him to be an insufferable snob, and he attempts to dazzle and intimidate the provincials with his cosmopolitanism instead of asserting his official purpose. Indeed, when he conveys his frustration with the villagers to Yniol, Geraint complains that

> " . . . all unarmed I rode, and thought to find
> Arms in your town, where all the men are mad;
> They take the rustic murmur of their bourg
> For the great wave that echoes round the world;
> They would not hear me speak . . ."
>
> (lines 417–21)

Geraint equates the townspeople's provincialism with an inability to recognize himself as the representative of the wide world. In this way the prince's public mission might be seen to be attenuated by his own desire for recognition. While it is his position as the king's man that qualifies him to undertake this sort of field service, Geraint seems disposed to believe that he stands the best chance of being honored and revered when he operates at a distance from the court.

Geraint's mission on the queen's behalf sits unsteadily alongside a repressed private wish to address his own injury and resentment. He lights out on his quest "A little vext at losing of the hunt, / A little at the vile occasion" (lines 234–35). His desire to find and chastise the sparrow-hawk frequently throws him back upon himself, particularly at the banquet of Earl Yniol, where the drunken prince lurches back and forth between official explanations of his commission and inadvertent betrayals of his own emotion. As he indignantly recalls the dwarf's violence against the queen's handmaiden, Prince Geraint renews his vow to avenge the sparrow-hawk's insult to the queen. What Geraint does not mention is the blood that was drawn from his own cheek. That moment—the moment of his own injury—is one that Geraint feels intensely, but as an agent of the court he cannot acknowledge it. And yet the wound runs deep. In the earlier scene, when the dwarf cuts Geraint, the prince's first impulse is to charge upon dwarf and knight both and to vanquish them immediately. But he catches himself up in this act, as Tennyson explains:

> But he, from his exceeding manfulness
> And pure nobility of temperament,
> Wroth to be wroth at such a worm, refrained
> From even a word
>
> (lines 211–14)

Wroth to be wroth: even at the point of the offense, Geraint feels compromised by his impulse to address it. To chastise the refractory knight would be to acknowledge the insult to himself, an acknowledgement that the prince sees as incongruous with his high-minded professionalism. Geraint's mission, then, presents a particular challenge: the need to confront the offender without owning up to his own injury. The prince tries to suppress his immediate anger by putting distance between himself and his new enemy; he will begin his pursuit only after the sparrow-hawk is out of reach, and he will do so in the queen's name rather than his own. Yet as he closes in on his enemy, his self-absorbed petulance makes him unable to deal diplomatically with the people he meets along the way. He is less the queen's agent than the enforcer of his own vendetta.

Geraint's journey exposes his mixed motives, largely because his approach to the sparrow-hawk is mediated by others who bear their own grievances. The "buzz" about the sparrow-hawk makes it impossible for Geraint to manage his task as a simple piece of court business; instead, as the sparrow-hawk's complex history unfolds, precisely whose battles the prince is fighting becomes less and less clear. If he could have his way, Geraint would avoid hearing about the local grievances against the sparrow-hawk; he would prefer a simple, unmediated confrontation. To this end, he stops himself short while questioning Yniol about the mystery knight:

"This sparrow-hawk, what is he? tell me of him.
His name? but no, good faith, I will not have it:
For if he be the knight whom late I saw
Ride into that new fortress by your town,
White from the mason's hand, then have I sworn
From his own lips to have it—I am Geraint
Of Devon—"

(lines 404–10)

Geraint does not want to understand the sparrow-hawk's history or career, and the above passage goes a long way toward explaining why. Geraint sees the surrender of Edyrn's name as an affirmation of his own identity ("I am Geraint of Devon"); even the queen's command is temporarily bracketed as Geraint visualizes the moment of confrontation. The presence of any other actors in the scene—the interference of well-wishers or of parties with axes to grind—would change the terms of this encounter, threatening to withhold the moment of triumph from Geraint and to situate it instead as a communal victory over a local nuisance.

Because he is so deeply invested in this confrontation, Geraint's attempts to clothe his mission in the language of officialism cause him embarrassment. He jokingly agrees to join Yniol for dinner on the condition that "ye do not serve me sparrow-hawks" (line 304). But Yniol's response is quite serious:

. . . "Graver cause than yours is mine
To curse this hedgerow thief, the sparrow-hawk:
But in, go in; for save yourself desire it,
We will not touch upon him even in jest."

(lines 308–11)

The response is doubly threatening to Geraint, because it seems to accuse the prince of pursuing his own passions (that is, having a cause to curse the thief), and it suggests that Geraint's mission is less significant than the earl's "graver cause." Up to this point, Geraint has been able to make a show of his boredom; the sparrow-hawk has been a nuisance to Geraint largely because of his irrelevance. But Yniol's solemnization of the strange figure puts the prince in a difficult position. Geraint does not wish to admit that the sparrow-hawk affair is of any particular consequence to himself, yet by virtue of his aloofness, he seems to advertise himself as a man for hire, a possible ally in the restitution of the family fortune and town government. Geraint's unstable relationship to his mission causes him to become entangled in a commitment other than the one he has made to the queen.

In fact, even as Geraint tries to conscript Enid and Edyrn into public life (as we considered before), Earl Yniol handily incorporates Geraint into his own family saga, seeing the prince's arrival as a second chance for his lately disappointed daughter. Within Yniol's castle, Geraint is made to feel welcome, as Herbert Tucker notes.[24] When Geraint first hears Enid's voice in the castle court, he remarks, "Here, by God's grace, is the one voice for me" (line 344); he echoes this comment shortly: "Here by God's rood is the one maid for me" (line 368). Geraint may not realize how literally this is the case. Yniol has already considered him in the context of Enid's marriage prospects, as the earl proves by moving directly from an exposition about Geraint (lines 426–38) to the following comment: "O never yet had woman such a pair / Of suitors as this maiden" (lines 439–40). Not only is Geraint unable to set the terms of his own engagement with the family, but he is drawn into other engagements that were set in motion long before he ever caught a glimpse of either sparrow-hawk or beloved. As previously discussed, Geraint begins his mission armorless, a cipher waiting to establish proper social bonds. Enid, by contrast, is a girl with a past. If Geraint thinks that her Boethian song disdaining Fortune's wheel is a function of innocent inexperience, he misinterprets; her impassiveness is battle-worn.[25] Near the end of the idyll, Tennyson flashes to a moment of trauma in Enid's past:

> Before her birthday, three sad years ago,
> That night of fire, when Edyrn sacked their house,
> And scattered all they had to all the winds:
> For while the mother showed it [her dress], and the two
> Were turning and admiring it, the work
> To both appeared so costly, rose a cry
> That Edyrn's men were on them, and they fled
> With little save the jewels they had on
>
> (lines 633–40)

In his own involvements with Enid and Edyrn, Geraint can have little idea of the intensity of their prior relations. The fact that Yniol's ruined castle has a glorious past is inconvenient, as is the recovery of Enid's birthday dress. Enid's history needs to be reconstructed, and her obligations to Geraint must be her first ones, even to the detriment of her family, as we see when Enid "Dared not to glance at her good mother's face" (line 766).

Therefore, much as he would like to charge Edyrn's fortress directly, Geraint is met at every stage by diversions that would seem to interrupt his mission but in fact change it. Even to stay in Yniol's decaying castle is a kind of compromise, effectively giving Geraint a second point of origin and causing Camelot to recede. Similarly, Geraint's self-sufficiency is compromised by the local rules of confrontation: a knight cannot enter Edyrn's tournament without the accompaniment of a lady he loves (lines 480–81), and Enid thus becomes a critical stage on the path to the sparrow-hawk. Even before Geraint learns about this rule, he interpellates Enid into the mission:

> . . . then Geraint,
> For now the wine made summer in his veins,
> Let his eye rove in following, or rest
> On Enid at her lowly handmaid-work,
> Now here, now there, about the dusky hall;
> Then suddenly addrest the hoary Earl:
> "Fair host and Earl I pray your courtesy;
> This sparrow-hawk, what is he?"
>
> (lines 397–404)

It is as if Geraint's mission has become a conversation piece, or perhaps a way of situating himself within the foreign world of the earl's gothic history. But Geraint is involved in the history more fully than he understands. By the time he erupts onto the battlefield, Geraint has more or less given his commission over to his host: "Yniol's rusted arms / Were on his princely person, but through these / Princelike his bearing shone" (lines 543–45). At the moment Geraint becomes visible, he is in another man's armor, fighting another man's ancient battle.

Just as the idea of Enid interrupts Geraint's thoughts of battle at home, so too does it interrupt his thoughts of the queen's mission on the battlefield, or rather, divides them in two:

> "Then, Edyrn, son of Nudd," replied Geraint,
> "These two things shalt thou do, or else thou diest.
> First, thou thyself, with damsel and with dwarf,
> Shalt ride to Arthur's court, and coming there,

> Crave pardon for that insult done the Queen,
> And shalt abide her judgment on it; next,
> Thou shalt give back their earldom to thy kin.
> These two things shalt thou do, or thou shalt die."
>
> (lines 579–86)

The sense of there being two things (instead of one) is a trivializing one, partly due to the radical difference in the nature of the crimes Edyrn must atone for. By forcing Edyrn to yield his name and apology, Geraint is eliciting a symbolic gesture of fealty; in restoring an earldom to Edyrn's kin, Geraint is interfering in rural politics, performing a kind of local magistracy. Still, while it may seem as if Geraint is creating a parity between these functions, he is usefully segregating them. Perhaps, having sorted out the confusion at Sparrow-Hawk Junction, Geraint can return to the court, mission accomplished and a bride the richer.

But this turns out to be impossible, or at any rate unsustainable. Geraint gets the public marriage he looked for; Enid and Guinevere become fast friends, and the prince has a chance to experience the complete synthesis of family and career. But the division between the public servant and the private citizen is radical, and when he tries to unite them, it creates a short circuit:

> . . . and the Queen herself,
> Grateful to Prince Geraint for service done,
> Loved her [Enid], and often with her own white hands
> Arrayed and decked her, as the loveliest,
> Next after her own self, in all the court.
> And Enid loved the Queen, and with true heart
> Adored her, as the stateliest and the best
> And loveliest of all women upon earth.
> And seeing them so tender and so close,
> Long in their common love rejoiced Geraint.
>
> (lines 14–23)

All kinds of love are mentioned here, but what about Geraint and the queen? This missing match-up is an important one, because the state of affairs described at this point is the one that follows just a year after Geraint's mission. Whereas Geraint and the queen shared an idealized communion, now the prince can make his own presence felt to the queen only by putting Enid forth as his surrogate. Enid, then, in her mediating role, closes down the channel between commissioner and civil servant. This, and not Guinevere's sin, has produced the great change for Geraint. Consequently, Enid's rapport with Guinevere, which Geraint previously encouraged, now seems to him mysterious and unconstructive.

Of course, total alienation is no better an option for the good-hearted knight than total integration, and at the end of "Geraint and Enid," the prince does get pulled back into the fold in a wash of civic feeling. After Geraint has recovered his trust in Enid and the two have regained their marital composure, they are apprehended and welcomed first by Edyrn (now one of the king's great champions) and then by Arthur himself. Yet Geraint's reconciliation with his sovereign is limited; there is no restoration of the early missionary rapture. The king reveals that he felt Geraint's departure to be a reproach to him and that he has now decided to dedicate his efforts to "helping" Geraint establish order in the prince's lands. But the king also makes clear that his lieutenant in this mission is Edyrn, Geraint's erstwhile enemy, who has committed himself body and soul to the king's sacred service. These are words to chasten Geraint (once again), or at least the prince seems to take them that way, feeling that "His work was neither great nor wonderful" ("Geraint and Enid," line 920).[26] Geraint has a reunion, too, with the queen, and while he is better able to tolerate her concourse with Enid, it still makes him uncomfortable, and the couple depart the capital once again. Enid and Geraint settle down at a safe distance, keeping "the justice of the King" but establishing their own fame and their own legacy (lines 955–65). Like many of Arthur's other knights, Geraint seems to achieve his highest pitch of service in his last moments, "fighting for the blameless King." It is a "fair death" that crowns a "happy life" (lines 967–69). While the poem, then, seems convinced of the satisfactions of dying with the king, it seems also to suggest that a happy life is to some extent a life apart.

The Double Life of the Missionary Conscript

The knight's alienation from court and king provides the tragic consummation of "Lancelot and Elaine," while the Geraint idylls present this alienation as an uncomfortable necessity. Unlike the renegade knights of the later books, neither Lancelot nor Geraint questions the king's right to rule, but both are likewise unwilling or unable to follow the official script. The knight is always fighting two battles: to enforce the public good, and to suppress his own sense of separation from the king, who determines what the public good is. It thus happens that an adventure far away from the court can either activate or assuage the knight's doubts about his place within that court, since in those remote regions a knight could easily lose the thread of his commission.

The later-published books pursue the question of alienation even further, describing monstrous defections—Balin's descent into madness and Pelleas's turn to depravity—but also finding a kind of nobility in the knight's resistance to the sovereign, particularly in the account of Bedivere's dilemma in "The Passing of Arthur." The dividedness of the knight's conscience is portrayed no longer as a surprising or unusual failure but, at least in part, as a condition of his service. In the logic of these poems, the knight's identity partially depends on his alienation from the court; the knight is cast away, sent to affirm his mission in distant climes. Commission is separation.

"The Holy Grail" is a study of the knight's need to alienate himself from king and court, a need to locate the "best self" at a distance from, though still in relation to, the center of civic authority. In the *Idylls,* as in the work of Sir Thomas Malory, the Grail quest scatters Arthur's knights and heralds the dissolution of the court. The poem first names the Grail in response to a question the monk Ambrosius poses to Sir Percivale: "what drove thee from the Table Round, / My brother?" ("The Holy Grail," lines 28–29). With this question, Ambrosius has unwittingly gone to the heart of the Grail dilemma, echoing Arthur's description of the Grail as "A sign to maim this Order which I made" (line 297). The poem, like Arthur and Ambrosius, identifies the primary importance of the Grail quest as the breakup of the court; however, the poem does not wholly share Arthur's despondency over this event, suggesting that this scattering is to some extent necessary and salutary.

In his description of the court he left, Percivale makes it evident that the need to leave preceded the lure of the sacred cup. Conditions were not good in Camelot, and the Grail appeared, as it were, in the nick of time:

> "But the sweet vision of the Holy Grail
> Drove me from all vainglories, rivalries,
> And earthly heats that spring and sparkle out
> Among us in the jousts, while women watch
> Who wins, who falls; and waste the spiritual strength
> Within us, better offered up to Heaven."
>
> (lines 31–36)

The problems described in this passage are specifically problems that arise out of courtly life: rivalries, hatched in the king's jousts, that waste the energy the knight could expend on a higher purpose. The "earthly heats" the knight describes are largely endemic to his profession, whereas the better expenditures of spiritual strength are not specified and are not obviously consonant with the knight's public work. The first person to see the Grail, Percivale's sister, has also previously recoiled from the "scandal of the Court" and the "Sin against Arthur and the Table Round" (lines 78–79). She, like Percivale, is already in a state of alienation when the Grail appears, and her vision essentially authorizes her to dissolve a courtly confederacy that she has long understood to be ailing and unstable. The Grail, then, addresses a felt need for reform within the court, a call to reinvigorate a civil service that has not been sufficiently sustained by or responsive to the king's mission.[27] Ambrosius discusses the Grail with Percivale not as an ancient relic but as a kind of innovation, one that is as yet unfamiliar to the fusty old monks who "moulder—as to things without" (line 39). Thus, when Arthur describes the Grail quest as a tragic spiritual obsession that will undermine the earthly functions of the Round Table, he is not telling the whole story. As the poem presents it, the quest is also an attempt to recover morale, a practical (albeit risky) response to a practical problem.

Just as the court has declined, the relationship between Arthur and his knights has become troubled. At the very beginning of the poem, before the Grail is mentioned, Ambrosius discusses the nature of the connection between king and knight: "For good ye are and bad, and like to coins, / Some true, some light, but every one of you / Stamped with the image of the King" (lines 25–27). The figure of the coin partially recalls the passage in "The Coming of Arthur"—a poem that, with "The Holy Grail," debuted in 1869—where Arthur's likeness flashes "From eye to eye thro' all [the knights'] Order" ("The Coming of Arthur," lines 269–70). But the images are quite different. Whereas in "The Coming of Arthur" the likeness of the king is a sign of spiritual dedication and perfect communion, the meaning of Arthur's stamp is more ambiguous in "The Holy Grail." It is independent of conduct or worth, and it seems (as Ambrosius employs it) a mark more of origin than of mission or purpose. The king's image is no longer able to incorporate and transform the fundamental selfhood of every knight. Rather, the knight is a two-sided coin, a self that is divided between public commitment and private character. The king's image does not "secure" the knight any more than it challenges him, foregrounding the servant's failure to measure up. The poem shortly presents yet another representation of the king's image, this time in the form of a statue that towers over the hall at Camelot. Percivale mentions the statue as he is telling Ambrosius about the contention among the knights within during the king's absence. The statue inspires the "people in far fields," Percivale explains, who see it and cry "We have still a King" ("The Holy Grail," lines 238–45). But whereas the king's statue effectively calms and inspires the subjects working in the fields, it seems to be invisible to those within the castle, as if the knights' very closeness to the seat of the king's authority makes the meaning of that authority obscure. Whether in the statue above them or the image stamped on the other side of their brains, the king is too close to be an object of attraction or yearning.

Although Arthur believes the Grail quest is undertaken "in vain," the poem sees it as an enterprise in which the knights can and must come to terms with their separate and collective identity as public servants and fellow missionaries. One of the most ambiguous passages comes directly after the knights first apprehend the Grail:

> . . . every knight beheld his fellow's face,
> As in a glory, and all the knights arose,
> And staring each at other like dumb men
> Stood
>
> (lines 191–94)

Each knight's vision of the Grail instantly modulates into a vision of his fellow men, and the scene directly recapitulates the moment when the knights pass Arthur's likeness from person to person. But this is an alternative communion, separate from the king. While this could be read as a compromised or parodic substitution for the more genuine communion between Arthur and his knights, we find as the poem proceeds that this new communion has its own integrity. "The Holy Grail" shows a good deal of collaboration among Arthur's servants, something largely absent from the other poems. Galahad "believed in [the] belief" of Percivale's sister, and Percival "grew / One with [Galahad], to believe as he believed" (lines 165, 486–87); Percivale joins forces first with Galahad and then with Sir Bors; and Bors is stricken with grief as he watches Lancelot descend into madness. Indeed, Percivale observes that Bors

> ". . . well had been content
> Not to have seen, so Lancelot might have seen,
> The Holy Cup of healing; and, indeed,
> Being so clouded with his grief and love,
> Small heart was his after the Holy Quest"
>
> (lines 650–54)

For Percivale and Bors, the Grail quest gives way to demonstrations of love for and solidarity with their fellow seekers.

This aspect of the quest is what interests Ambrosius, who repeatedly asks Percivale questions about the social and professional dimensions of the mission. Ambrosius has nothing to say about the "miracles and marvels" that Percivale relates; such topics make his head swim. Though a monk, Ambrosius loves to "mingle with our folk" and wants to know about the people Percivale met on his journey (lines 540–63). Percivale is embarrassed by this digression into his social fortunes; he explains, with shame, that he did indeed meet a woman he once loved, but he departed from her wealth for the sake of the quest. The monk is overcome with pity and continues to press Percivale with social questions, asking whether he met his fellow workers along the way. When Percivale answers this question, Ambrosius wants to hear about the state of the court in the aftermath:

> "But when ye reached
> The city, found ye all your knights returned,
> Or was there sooth in Arthur's prophecy,
> Tell me, and what said each, and what the King?"
>
> (lines 704–7)

Ambrosius is mainly interested in the personal and professional shake-up the Grail quest creates among the king's constabulary, releasing the well-regulated knights of Arthur's court into an uncertain world where they must chart out their own trajectories. Percivale is sometimes embarrassed by the monk's questions, which draw him away from the religious narrative; he is far more inclined to recount his spiritual successes and failures, readily disclosing both his despair as his ghostly visions turn to dust, and his elation as he sees Galahad go off to the spiritual city. Percivale has trouble confronting the meaning of his quest in social terms, although the consequences of the quest (like its motives) are precisely social, turning him away from the court and into "the silent life" of the monastery.

I have noted the affinity between the unsteady civil servants of Arthur's regime, who both idealize and chafe against their official responsibilities, and the Salvation Army missionaries, who represented their converted state as one of perpetual spiritual warfare. "The Holy Grail" pushes the resemblance further, as it shows a cadre of Arthur's knights, en masse, creating a renegade missionary enterprise. While the Salvation Army was an army against sin, it was also an army against charity, or rather against the middle-class philanthropic establishment. By embracing various facets of working-class street culture, the Salvation Army fashioned itself an alternative to the repressive methods of mainstream evangelical missions, and it was likewise seen by other philanthropists as a renegade effort. In that sense, the Salvation Army might have seemed to the middle class like charity's unconscious, a kind of shadow-play in which Salvationists took sides with the poor in defiance against the doctrines of official welfare.[28] For Tennyson, the knighthood similarly functions as the rebellious unconscious of the court, the uncontrolled, passionate dimension of the king's just governance. The "defection" of the best knights from the court is not an accident; it is a predictable eruption in a volunteer army of zealots and idealists.

Of all of Arthur's knights, it is perhaps the violent Balin who best represents the embattled agent, the worker who is fiercely loyal to his king and at the same time prone to think himself unsuited to his work. Arthur sees Balin's "too fierce manhood" as a guarantee of his sincerity ("Balin and Balan," line 71) as well as a force that needs to be controlled. In fact, "Balin and Balan" opens some years after Balin's first great loss of temper, during which episode he struck a fellow knight, was dubbed "the savage" by Arthur, and nearly forfeited his place in the court. At the beginning of the idyll, Balin has weathered his years in exile, taking up a post with his brother beside a fountain and challenging every knight who rides past. Balin's strange plan is to reestablish his worth to Arthur by building up an anonymous reputation; though he no longer can announce himself as one of Arthur's knights, if he is able to generate a new glory on the fringes of Arthur's authority, he will become interesting and valuable again to Arthur. Balin's scheme strongly echoes Lancelot's attempt (in "Lancelot and Elaine") to recover the king's good graces anonymously.

But whereas Arthur reproaches Lancelot for "idly dallying with the truth" ("Lancelot and Elaine," line 587), Balin's similar stratagem is somehow acceptable, even pleasing, to the king: upon hearing of Balin's hidden campaign, Arthur instantly takes him back into service. Indeed, Balin's whole narrative arc differs significantly from Lancelot's. At the beginning of "Lancelot and Elaine," Lancelot is Arthur's greatest knight and by his own account has a perfect communion with the king. The drama of the poem rests in Lancelot's intentional abrogation of that communion, along with his attempt to restore it through a private, renegade action. But the first time we see Balin, he is already on the outskirts, trying to work his way back in. He enters the court as a reformed rebel, and Arthur's commission takes the form of a second chance: "Thy chair, a grief to all the brethren, stands / Vacant, but thou retake it, mine again!" ("Balin and Balan," lines 75–76). Not only does the poem countenance the idea that the fallen knight can return, but it takes the fall for granted. Balin's glory will rest on his ability to manage the antithetical forces of his own nature.

Balin's violence makes him unreliable, yet it is a testament to his intense commitment; he is a holy warrior, all the more zealous for his wildness and all the more dangerous for his zeal. His aversion to sin leads him not to any kind of high-minded placidity but to a state of perpetual warfare, one that takes its toll on his health and his sanity. The same passions that make Balin effective also threaten to undermine his loyalty; in this double bind, he strongly resembles some of the pugnacious Salvation Army preachers of the 1870s and '80s. "Balin and Balan" was published more than twenty-five years after "Lancelot and Elaine," and the years in between saw the emergence of these perpetually embattled soldiers for Christ, who proved the triumph of their conversion by convincing audiences of their explosive tendencies to sin. By recruiting Balin, Arthur has taken a page out of the Salvation Army playbook.

Balin's unsteadiness is given an emblem in his relationship to his own shield, which bears the king's stamp. Here Tennyson revives an image from "The Coming of Arthur," where the knights reflect the king in their faces, and "The Holy Grail," in which Ambrosius claims that each knight is a coin with the king's image stamped on one side. In "Balin and Balan," the stamp becomes literal. Arthur agrees to put the queen's crown-royal on Balin's shield for a particular purpose:

> "Thou shalt put the crown to use.
> The crown is but the shadow of the King,
> And this a shadow's shadow, let him have it,
> So this will help him of his violences!"
>
> ("Balin and Balan," 198–201)

As in "The Holy Grail," the image no longer signifies perfect communion; here, the king's presence is highly attenuated, manifest within a representation of the queen's crown, a shadow of a shadow of the king. Even more significantly, the king's image comes in as a corrective, a kind of therapy for Balin. It is not, in other words, foundational to the knight's identity or revelatory of his deep character; Balin does not bear the king's image at his core. Instead, the royal insignia is an acquired resource for Balin to use in the battle against his own violences. In Balin, nothing is deeper than conflict; there is no better state that he has fallen from. He is essentially unstable, and the king's stamp, like everything else that is noble about Balin (or the embattled Salvationist), is a testament primarily to the knight's great powers of repression.

Even with the safeguard, Balin cannot keep his cool. When he witnesses the queen speaking intimately with Lancelot, Balin rushes from the court, "mad for strange adventure" (line 284). Afterwards, when the scornful Sir Garlon insults the crown on his shield, Balin strikes him down. These acts overwhelm Balin with memories of his earlier savagery; he cries out, "My violences, my violences!" (line 429) and feels that he has made no progress. Arthur and brother Balan would likely agree with this prognosis; they have implored him to "move / To music with thine Order and the King" and "Let not thy moods prevail" (lines 73–74, 137). But is there really no difference? Balin's prior outburst had been a simple matter of temper and pride, but his outbursts within the idyll are grounded to an extent in his idealistic fervor and his conviction of the rightness of his cause. As if to make this case, Vivien comes singing through the woods; like a Hallelujah Lass, she commends the violent intensity of Balin's experience:

> "The fire of Heaven is lord of all things good,
> And starve not thou the fire within thy blood,
> But follow Vivien through the fiery flood!
> The fire of Heaven is not the flame of Hell!"
>
> (lines 446–49)

The last line, Vivien's refrain, bursts forward like a response to all of those who mistrust the boisterous enthusiasm of the Salvationist, and she offers it as consolation to Balin. The passion of righteousness must be inflamed, not stifled. A knight working in the service of Heaven cannot be expected to be orderly, and certainly not to rest contented within a fallen world.

By the poem's reckoning, Vivien is a deceiver (and certainly a victim of her own delusions). The fire of Heaven *is* the flame of hell: Balin's violences, rooted in an idealistic intolerance of all baseness, lead him to uncontrollable excesses, and he becomes the "Wood-devil" that he wishes to destroy. Balin is taught this lesson by his brother Balan, the controlled and controlling, who escaped the temptations that Balin has succumbed to and remains safe from the "madness" that does his brother in, a madness that grows out of Balin's sensibility to the worst things that are happening at court. But Balin's disillusionment, like Percivale's and his sister's in "The Holy Grail," is the inevitable fate of the high-minded. There is no answer for it, unless one is to say, like Balan, "Pure as our own true Mother is our Queen" (line 606)—to accept the official script as the language of one's own conscience and intellect. But the difference between public doctrine and private doubt, the same difference that allows the sinner to be swept up into the enthusiasm of a grand cause, also causes the volunteer to falter.

The double bind of the public servant is treated most compassionately in the poem's final book (and the earliest written), "The Passing of Arthur." The king commissions his last surviving companion, Sir Bedivere, to cast Excalibur into a wide lake, a task that Bedivere has great trouble fulfilling. It is a question not of loyalty but of perspective. Sir Bedivere is as eager as the king to salvage some consolation in the midst of the grand defeat of the Round Table, yet despite their shared purpose, he cannot view matters from the *position* of the king; he can only judge by his own lights. To Bedivere, the glory of the sword itself and its usefulness as a relic of a glorious time demand that it be preserved, and he cannot help but rebel against Arthur's command; indeed, Arthur treats Bedivere's hesitation with the gravity of treason, warning his last loyal knight that "if thou spare to fling Excalibur, / I will arise and slay thee with my hands" ("The Passing of Arthur," lines 299–300). Although Arthur may be right, we never know his reasons; Tennyson gives the incident from the knight's point of view and not the king's. It is not Arthur's vision but his voice that Bedivere finally has access to, and the knight can only hope that his actions embody a mandate that he can never quite claim as his own—just as the public servant can only hope that his agency conforms to the dictates of his Agency. Bedivere's tentativeness is not exactly failure, or at least not a failure to live up to his role: in hesitating, he is as much a knight as Arthur is a king.

In the late nineteenth century, it was Bedivere's story, not Arthur's, that stood at the center of the welfare narrative. The old question of how to reach the poor and the outcast was supplanted by questions of methodology: what must the reaching hand be like? Should it relinquish or clutch, coddle or strike? Under such scrutiny, the most confident agent might feel suddenly isolated. Whether working for the state or for a missionary society—whether traveling through the empire or navigating the city slums—the agent was in danger of being cut adrift, and the centers of piety and procedure were always, like Camelot, viewed through a mist.

After Conscription

Conscription is the way of progress in Tennyson, but it is a progress that moves along a razor's edge. The sinner is only ever an inch away from salvation; the missionary is only ever an inch away from perdition. And it is hard to resist returning here to the Salvation Army by way of George Bernard Shaw, whose Major Barbara renders the idea as follows: "There are neither good men nor scoundrels; there are just children of one Father; and the sooner they stop calling one another names the better. You neednt talk to me: I know them. I've had scores of them through my hands: scoundrels, criminals, infidels, philanthropists, missionaries, county councillors, all sorts. Theyre all just the same sort of sinner; and theres the same salvation ready for them all."[29] This is a reassuringly solid and businesslike expression of what is actually a rather unsettling vision of society. Barbara's words level all moral distinctions—between good men and scoundrels, between the faithful and the infidel, even between different sorts of sinners. For salvation to matter, the currency of ordinary morality must be cheapened and the difference between people must be blurred, so that, as in Tennyson, saint and sinner stand poised to change places. Thus Barbara reveals to the unregenerate thug Bill Walker that she, in her appointed time, has wrestled against her own salvation, as has the converted strong man of the Canning Town shelter, Todger Fairmile. Admitting herself to be a rebel and a moral infant, the Salvationist embraces the sinner with bewildering gusto; she once resisted her own rescue, and she will joyfully cheer you on as you try with all your might to withstand the force of God and conscience. She will laugh at you, and then with you, as you are brought to your knees, shattered, rescued, and commissioned.

But this triumphant irony is, from another perspective, destabilizing. The missionary may not speak with the derision of a philanthropist who condescends, but this is not because she better recognizes the personhood of the poor. Rather, it is because she is blind to all but the mission itself, before which all persons must give way. The cause is all that matters, such that the real world of people begins to lose its solidity; all are exchangeable counters in a struggle that is larger than life. Some such ideas are in the air at the West Ham shelter, where Rummy Mitchens, a poor woman fighting off starvation, cheerfully colludes by "pretendin to be a bad un." "Them Salvation lasses are good girls," she explains, "but the better you are, the worse they likes to think you were before they rescued you. Why shouldn't they av a bit o credit, poor loves? theyre worn to rags by their work. And where would they get the money to rescue us if we was to let on we're no worse than other people?" (70). Snobby Price will earn his ticket by pretending he used to beat his mother ("Not likely. She used to beat me"), and when Barbara and Snobby later return from an "experience meeting" down the road, Barbara complains that if Snobby had "given your poor mother just one more kick, we should have got the whole five shillings!" (71, 93). The missionary seeks to amplify both the convert's vice and his virtue and to see in both tendencies the familiar expressions of a cosmic struggle. Meanwhile, the new convert throws himself into the part of the reformed rascal; the profits are greater that way. Shaw's working-class penitents, like Dickens's Pentonville prisoners, blithely lay on the salvation talk to suit their own needs. And they equally (though unmeaningly) collude with the purposes of the state by adopting a stance of political passivity.

For Shaw, missionary causes do not change people or reconcile them to one another; they simply reproduce an official script. This may explain the play's obsession with foundlings, who ought to break the cycle of reproduction. Undershaft needs a foundling to run his cannon foundry—and not just someone without a family, as it turns out, but someone without a cultural or political home. He must be a man of perfect principle, but the principle must be of his own creation: "There is only one true morality for every man," Undershaft explains, "but every man has not the same true morality" (63). And in a grand irony, England's whole population of foundlings—who ought to be an unassimilated class, expert in stubborn survival—have been the victims of liberal recruitment and indoctrination: "Every blessed foundling nowadays is snapped up in his infancy by Barnardo homes, or School Board officers, or Boards of Guardians; and if he shews the least ability he is fastened on by schoolmasters; trained to win scholarships like a racehorse; crammed with secondhand ideas; drilled and disciplined in docility and what they call good taste; and lamed for life so that he is fit for nothing but teaching" (115). The modern foundling reveals the dead end of conscription. Energetically nurtured by an establishment that gives him no scope for resentment or complaint, the foundling becomes a guardian and apostle of that establishment. He is a living advertisement, the quality product of a public job well done. If the foundling is not two-faced like Rummy Mitchens or Snobby Price (or for that matter Uriah Heep and the Pentonville prisoners), it is only because no second face exists; the king has stamped both sides of the coin.

It is not surprising that Shaw the socialist would denounce the Salvation Army, along with the other organized philanthropies of his day, as docility machines. But it is rather startling that the antithesis the play puts forward—the plan to reinvigorate the working man in the face of failed liberal conscription schemes—is basically traditional English condescension. Undershaft represents this approach, contending that any meaningful form of social uplift requires distinctions of rank and influence: "We . . . must stand together above the common people: how else can we help their children to climb up beside us?" (92). And in the munitions works and the adjoining town of Perivale St. Andrews, Undershaft has re-created a social world in which every person knows his or her place. In contrast to the chaotic parity that the missionary conscript might purchase by performing dizzying somersaults of salvation, Undershaft offers calm respectability. In the town are two Methodist chapels, a nursing home, libraries and schools, and a pension fund (121, 126). Undershaft is received as the lord of the manor: rather than giving orders, he simply says to the man in the High Explosives Sheds, "Well, Jones, is the baby doing well? and has Mrs. Jones made a good recovery?" (122). All is secured by condescension. Indeed, even the faults of condescension—the corrupting sense of power and control that sent Dickens, Hill, and Tennyson looking for other solutions—are here recast as virtues. Jones does not much mind taking orders from Undershaft because he, in turn, can snub and bully the people beneath him, and so all the way down the ladder (122).

One must add that this is hardly Shaw's utopia: Undershaft's peaceable kingdom is engineered, as much as the Salvation Army, to make the workers productive and keep them in check. It is not an answer but an antithesis, laden with its own contradictions, including the fact that the industrial baron can only claim a rather fragile supremacy when he has purchased it by putting explosives into the hands of the millions. But if the munitions plant is not the final answer to the West Ham Mission, it remains significant as a surprising combination of forces: modern technologies of destruction, a Nietzschean determination to live without illusions, and old-fashioned English condescension. Shaw seems to imply that in an unequal society, condescension is the most honest kind of relation available. And if ultimately, through the resentment it causes, condescension (like Undershaft's five thousand pounds)[30] undermines the very system that produced it, so much the better.

Epilogue

Were the Victorians condescending? *They* say they were, and ask us only to believe them. Before we ever had a chance to take offense, the Victorians had already developed a withering critique of their own condescension. They knew it was not conciliatory, far from it; it was a goad to rebellion and rupture. They knew it had to go.

We are very ready to believe that they were condescending, but we are less prepared to believe that they were doing anything about it. So much of our progress, so much even of our critical distance, is a reaction against the blithe, unworried intractability of Victorian condescension. Our revolution depends on their being stuck. We need them, as it were, to condescend to us.

Virginia Woolf recognized this urgency and used it to color her portrait—at once a critique and a defense—of the Victorian lady philanthropist. With little regard for custom or habit, Woolf's ladies offer their gift of condescension in bewildered frustration, looking around them for another way and finding none. But they are the only ones hurt by their failure; no modern young person is likely to be put out by the condescension of a Victorian, and indeed, it may be that the condescension of one's Victorian precursors is most welcome, the very thing that makes full-throated rebellion possible. In fact, while condescension itself is no longer dangerous, it could be problematic *not* to be condescended to by an imposing figure from the past. For what if the Victorians had fixed the problem, had taught themselves to know better? How then to rebel?

In Woolf's *To the Lighthouse,* Charles Tansley stands vigilant against the condescension of his Victorian hostess and ever prepares a crushing response. When Mrs. Ramsay asks whether he writes many letters, he answers curtly, because "he was not going to be condescended to by these silly women."[1] Lily Briscoe (though herself disgusted by such condescensions) reluctantly follows Mrs. Ramsay's lead, and Tansley decides she means to put him down: "She was laughing at him. He was in his old flannel trousers. He had no others" (86). In response to these slights, Tansley "felt it necessary to assert himself" (86). But it is not such a painful necessity. In Tansley's eyes, the Ramsays' frivolous attentions are proof of his own superiority, and upon hearing an especially superficial remark, Tansley "pounced on this fresh instance with joy, making a note which, one of these days, he would read aloud, to one or two friends" (90). When Mrs. Ramsay prods Tansley about his seaworthiness, her condescension gives him what he wants, a chance to assert himself and to detest his interlocutor:

> Mr. Tansley . . . said only that he had never been sick in his life. But in that one sentence lay compact, like gunpowder, that his grandfather was a fisherman; his father a chemist; that he had worked his way up entirely himself; that he was proud of it; that he was Charles Tansley—a fact that nobody there seemed to realise; but one of these days every single person would know it. He scowled ahead of him. He could almost pity these mild cultivated people, who would be blown sky high, like bales of wool and barrels of apples, one of these days by the gunpowder that was in him. (91–92)

This is, of course, the reaction Mrs. Ramsay means to elicit: recognizing and pitying Tansley's sense of inferiority, she sees that his resentment will be a relief to him. He is plainly enough waiting for a chance to reject some offering of the Ramsays, and Mrs. Ramsay's condescension is a boon to him, valuable for its worthlessness.

But Tansley also wants Mrs. Ramsay's condescension, not just to hate it but also to have it. He wants the recognition it confers. As she walks Tansley into town, Mrs. Ramsay discusses another man's fortunes with him, and he suddenly feels distinguished. When she asks if he had been taken to circuses as a child, Tansley lights up, "as if she asked the very thing he wanted; had been longing all these days to say, how they did not go to circuses" (11–12). Tansley excitedly retails the privations of his childhood and youth, glad suddenly to be seen as a man who lacks. The nobility of his struggle—all of his efforts to raise himself—can be understood only by someone who regards him in his comparative poverty, who knows what he has come up from, what he is still (in his success) perpetually coming up from. Once diminished, he can be raised: "still he went on talking, about settlements, and teaching, and working men, and helping our own class, and lectures, till she gathered that he had got back entire self-confidence" (12). He is proud to be with Mrs. Ramsay; he receives her condescension with grateful gallantry and a measure of vassalage. He "felt the wind and the cyclamen and the violets for he was walking with a beautiful woman. He had hold of her bag" (14). Tansley is once more moved to assertion by Mrs. Ramsay, not because she has put him down but because she has brought him out. Her condescension serves Tansley well, making itself available both for his taking and for his scorn.

Still, if Tansley is relieved to encounter a condescending Victorian lady, Mrs. Ramsay cannot share his relief. It is she, not Tansley, who regrets her condescension; it is she, and not her explosive petitioner, who understands its value and its cost. She takes a more structural (though equally self-centered) view than Tansley does of the "insoluble questions" of social difference, pondering first her own attempts to win respect from those of high family,

> but more profoundly, she ruminated the other problem, of rich and poor, and the things she saw with her own eyes, weekly, daily, here or in London, when she visited this widow, or that struggling wife in person with a bag on her arm, and a note-book and pencil with which she wrote down in columns carefully ruled for the purpose wages and spendings, employment and unemployment, in the hope that thus she would cease to be a private woman whose charity was half a sop to her own indignation, half a relief to her own curiosity, and become what with her untrained mind she greatly admired, an investigator, elucidating the social problem. (9)

Aware that her charity work can so easily degenerate into self-satisfaction, Mrs. Ramsay does not withdraw from the field of battle: instead she tries to reform her method, to accept the failures of her condescension as a part of the very problem. She must risk condescending, because to refuse utterly to condescend would be to refuse to engage, as Lily considers refusing to "say something nice" to Mr. Tansley. Lily's verdict on her own (and on Mrs. Ramsay's) condescension is bracing: "She would never know him. He would never know her" (92). But this kind of knowledge is elusive by any measure. By continuing to visit the widow and the struggling wife, Mrs. Ramsay chooses not to retreat from the situations that evoke her condescension but to try to face it down with her notebook and pencil. This is not foolishness; it is an effort to be transformed, to "cease to be" one thing and to "become" something other.

In *The Years,* Woolf deals more directly with the dilemmas of the career philanthropist. Like Mrs. Ramsay, Eleanor Pargiter is drawn up short by her own charity. In the eleven years (1880–91) that stretch between the novel's first two chapters, Eleanor graduates from collecting rents, possibly in one of Octavia Hill's buildings, to managing buildings of her own and sitting on committees. But from the beginning, her career in philanthropy throws her back upon herself. Her sister Milly is amused by stories of the poor and the infirm, but Eleanor compulsively compares their lives with her own. "The poor enjoy themselves more than we do": it is not an observation but a fantasy, one that invests the dying Mrs. Levy with the warmth that Eleanor is unable to feel for her own dying mother. A decade later, as a thoroughgoing Organization Woman, Eleanor continues to puzzle through the chaos of her own motives and the motives of her colleagues. In a committee meeting, a picture of the Princess of Wales looks down upon the company, echoing Eleanor's scrutiny of their various unsettled lives. We find that Miss Sims is sensitive to condescension, Mrs. Lazenby shows off her family connections, and Mr. Judd envies people of consequence. On her own terms, Eleanor is capable and resolved, taking an imperious tone in her building inspection with Mr. Duffus. But when she immediately afterwards visits her sister Delia in a lurid, decrepit city square, she loses her self-possession and, despite her own experience, finds her sister's squalid life among the poor inconceivable. At bottom, Eleanor has only mastered her own program; outside of Rigby cottages, the encounter between wealth and poverty is as threatening as ever, and Eleanor's philanthropic exertions degenerate into confusion.

Yet for Woolf, confusion is not the end of the story but a continual starting-over. Eleanor's habitual uncertainty—"And what were atoms, and how did they stick together?"[2]—sets off a chain reaction of bewilderment, in which selves are probed and identities are destabilized. Sara, caught up in the *Antigone,* and her sister Maggie, coming in dazed from the ballroom, ask one another, "What's 'I'?" (134). Peggy, a doctor, wonders "what is this moment; and what are we?" (317). The intellectual, the sociable, the professional, the artistic: all of these sensibilities produce, in Woolf's younger generation, a frightening loss of boundaries, the great modernist revelation. But Eleanor Pargiter, Victorian pioneer of the same boundlessness, is neither an artist nor a socialite; she is a charity worker in the city. Woolf picks philanthropy as a prototypical practice in which the machinery of the social grinds against itself, until one's place in the system becomes conspicuous and fragile. Thus, Eleanor's spiritual expansion begins with a stumble, a habit of uncomfortable improvisations in infelicitous circumstances.

Scholars of Victorian charity will continue to thread our way through a labyrinth of motives that at once attract and repel us, that make us hopeful and suspicious. As we do so, we do well to remember that this dilemma is not of our own invention and that the critical power that we draw from our ambivalence on these matters is exactly the power that fashioned the rich complexity of nineteenth-century representations of charity. It is the power that animates Eleanor Pargiter, who finds that charity, ever creating a rift between intention and effect, can make the giving subject seem strange to herself. The hazard of condescension—that in coming down, one might be exposed—heralds a new liberation. As they pursued a failing charity into the realms of confusion and struggle, the Victorians proved that they, too, knew how to get lost.

Notes

Introduction: Charity and Condescension

1. Seth Koven notes this doubleness and states his intention "to recapture the altogether messier mingling of good intentions and blinkered prejudices that informed [the 'comfortable classes''] vision of the poor and of themselves." Koven, *Slumming* (Princeton: Princeton University Press, 2004), 3.

2. Although we have little direct testimony, Anne Summers believes there is reason to infer that the visited poor "resented condescension" and that the persistence of house-to-house visiting embodied a kind of "wishful thinking" whereby ladies of a higher class tried to preserve the satisfactions and tangible benefits of a clientage relationship. Summers, "A Home from Home: Women's Philanthropic Work in the Nineteenth Century," in *Fit Work for Women*, ed. Sandra Burman (London: Croom Helm, 1979), 43–46. Deborah Epstein Nord takes the visitor's intrusiveness for granted: "[H]owever paternalistic—or maternalistic—an element of bourgeois life this visiting was, and however presumptuous and invasive was the bourgeois woman's counsel, the visitor herself could benefit." Nord, *Walking the Victorian Streets: Women, Representation, and the City* (Ithaca, NY: Cornell University Press, 1995), 210. Martha Vicinus shares this opinion: "The class condescension that had characterized nineteenth-century philanthropy was being replaced by an equally invidious distinction, professional expertise." Vicinus, *Independent Women: Work and Community for Single Women, 1850–1920* (London: Virago, 1985), 23. Lynn Hollen Lees discusses the inability of the charitable classes to see beyond their own moral presumptions, stating that relief was meant to convey a stigma, though workers did not take it that way. Lees, "The Survival of the Unfit: Welfare Policies and Family Maintenance in Nineteenth-Century London," in *The Uses of Charity: The Poor on Relief in the Nineteenth-Century Metropolis*, ed. Peter Mandler (Philadelphia: University of Pennsylvania Press, 1990), 68–69. Likewise, Ellen Ross considers the gap between the spirit in which charity was offered and the spirit in which it was received; because this difference could prove a

shock or disappointment for the idealistic volunteer, the poor accepted the offerings of the rich with carefully orchestrated performances. Ross, "Hungry Children: Housewives and London Charity, 1870–1918," in Mandler, *Uses of Charity*, 167. And Brian Harrison posits that philanthropists would not have been bothered by whatever ignorance they displayed of working-class life. Harrison, "Philanthropy and the Victorians," *Victorian Studies* 9, no. 4 (1966): 371.

3. In this vein, Frank Prochaska notes that, alongside the rigidity of fictional visitors like Mrs. Pardiggle and Miss Clack, we should keep in mind "the softer more sympathetic benevolence of Agnes Gray, or old Alice in *Mary Barton*, or of the May girls in *The Daisy Chain*." While acknowledging the inevitable desire of middle-class philanthropists to propound their own "manners and morals," Prochaska argues that charity work often arose as "a response to the complaints and aspirations of the needy" and that it is more accurately seen as cooperative than antagonistic. Prochaska, *Women and Philanthropy in Nineteenth-Century England* (Oxford, UK: Clarendon, 1980), 117–18, 370–71. Gertrude Himmelfarb says that historians who accuse Victorian philanthropists of pursuing a narcissistic, self-serving agenda may themselves be standing on shaky ground: "The COS [Charity Organisation Society] may well have been guilty of imposing their values upon the poor. But later historians may be doing so as well, attributing to the poor a contempt for 'bourgeois' culture more congenial to intellectuals than to workers aspiring to that culture and to the material and social benefits associated with it." Himmelfarb, *Poverty and Compassion: The Moral Imagination of the Late Victorians* (New York: Knopf, 1991), 201.

4. Joseph Addison, *The Works of the Right Honourable Joseph Addison*, vol. 2 (London: Cadell and Davies, 1811), 339; Fanny Burney, *Evelina* (New York: Norton, 1965), 331.

5. For a classic study of the conflict between paternalism and liberal progress, see Raymond Williams, *Culture and Society, 1780–1950* (New York: Harper and Row, 1966). The character of liberal governance, and in particular the relationship between the liberal state and other centers of authority in Victorian society, has been a matter of much critical debate; see, for instance, Peter Mandler, *Aristocratic Government in the Age of Reform: Whigs and Liberals, 1830–1852* (New York: Oxford University Press, 1990); Mary Poovey, *Making a Social Body: British Cultural Formation, 1830–1864* (Chicago: University of Chicago Press, 1995); Lauren Goodlad, *Victorian Literature and the Victorian State: Character and Governance in a Liberal Society* (Baltimore, MD: Johns Hopkins University Press, 2003); and Peter Mandler, ed., *Liberty and Authority in Victorian Britain* (New York: Oxford University Press, 2006).

6. It is probably fair to assume that Mrs. Pardiggle was in the minds of many critics of philanthropic condescension. An 1864 article in the *New Monthly Magazine* claims that visiting ladies of the Mrs. Pardiggle type were often seen in the literature of the day; it cites Anne Brontë's Misses Murray and Thackeray's Lady Southdown, along with many examples taken from memoirs and magazines. Sir Nathaniel [Francis Jacox], "Mrs. Pardiggle: Typically Considered," *New Monthly Magazine*, June 1864, 174–77. When I say that philanthropists themselves were among the most severe critics of philanthropic condescension, I do not mean to imply that they were the *only* such critics or that the charitable establishment did not have its detractors on the "outside." One of the latter was Sir James Fitzjames Stephen, who objected to the way philanthropy unreasonably asserted

its own importance by deriding more common (and more useful) social pursuits. Stephen believed that philanthropy requires its practitioner to set himself up as the "guide and superior" of others, and thus, "He is more exposed than almost any other person to the danger of becoming pedantic and petty, and of trying to realize his own crude conceptions of what people ought to be and to do, instead of learning how slight and narrow those conceptions are." Stephen, "Doing Good," *Saturday Review*, 17 December 1859, 734.

7. Vicinus sees such cautions as a sign that philanthropists felt ambivalent about their work: "The frequency with which club leaders warned against condescension and rudeness and the strident tone of many annual reports indicate strains beneath the optimistic busyness of so many outings, clubs, and societies" (*Independent Women*, 238). Himmelfarb also notes these cautions against condescension but reads them as a testament to philanthropists' scientific self-awareness: "From the beginning the COS was sensitive to the charges of condescension and intrusion, of letting loose among the poor a gaggle of Mrs. Pardiggles" (*Poverty and Compassion*, 195).

8. Louisa Twining, *Deaconesses for the Church of England* (London: Bell and Daldy, 1860), 9–10.

9. For the purposes of this study, I will not dwell on the divergences between material/economic charity and religious charity; while there were some efforts (especially later in the nineteenth century) to separate these, they more often went together, and the charitable visitor had to equally contend with the problem of condescension whether she offered money, advice, prayer, or even sympathy. For a midcentury attempt to segregate spiritual and material charity within a single mission, see my essay on Ellen Ranyard's Bible-women: Daniel Siegel, "Charity through Dissociation: The Task of the Bible-Woman," in *Gender and Victorian Reform*, ed. Anita Rose (Newcastle upon Tyne: Cambridge Scholars Publishing, 2008), 2–11.

10. *Essays on the Principles of Charitable Institutions* (London: Longman, Rees, Orme, Brown, Green, and Longman, 1836), 202–3, 211.

11. Charles Kingsley, "The Country Parish," in *Lectures to Ladies on Practical Subjects*, ed. F. D. Maurice (Cambridge: Macmillan, 1855), 63.

12. Kingsley's is one of the essays that constitute *Lectures to Ladies on Practical Subjects*, a series of male-authored discourses on female philanthropy. Dorice Elliott offers a compelling analysis of the *Lectures to Ladies* and other guides for female visitors (such as the *District Visitor's Manual*), which served, she argues, to control the conditions under which women were permitted to operate within the male realm of professional public work. Elliott, *The Angel Out of the House: Philanthropy and Gender in Nineteenth-Century England* (Charlottesville: University Press of Virginia, 2002).

13. Twining, *Deaconesses*, 8.

14. Kingsley, "Country Parish," 54.

15. *Essays on the Principles of Charitable Institutions*, 210.

16. General Society for Promoting District Visiting, *The District Visitor's Manual* (London: John W. Parker, 1840), 80.

17. Ibid., 81.

18. *Essays on the Principles of Charitable Institutions*, 208–10.

19. J. L. Davies, "District Visiting," in Maurice, *Lectures to Ladies*, 122–23.

20. This is Himmelfarb's term, taken from Beatrice Webb. Himmelfarb characterizes the Time-Spirit as "a trust in science and a commitment to mankind"; she sees this trust and commitment as underlying the remarkable voluntary efforts that Victorians made to ameliorate the problem of poverty, efforts that she views as fundamentally consonant with one another (*Poverty and Compassion*, 181). I would argue that the incredible variety of Victorian charities and the competing Victorian approaches to philanthropy attest both to the serious social commitment of Victorians and to a growing uncertainty about the meaning and effects of charity.

21. Samuel Richardson, *Clarissa; or, The History of a Young Lady* (New York: Penguin, 1985), 274, 71.

22. Jane Austen, *Emma* (New York: Penguin, 1987), 239.

23. Sir Walter Scott, *Guy Mannering* (New York: Penguin, 2003), 252.

24. George Eliot, *Scenes of Clerical Life* (New York: Penguin, 1998), 148.

25. Anthony Trollope, *Can You Forgive Her?* (Oxford: Oxford University Press, 1977), 2:403.

26. Charlotte Brontë, *Shirley* (New York: Penguin, 1985), 446. Emphasis in original.

27. Sir Walter Scott, *Ivanhoe* (New York: Penguin, 1986), 150–51.

28. Anthony Trollope, *The Warden* (Oxford: Oxford University Press, 1991), 242; Trollope, *Orley Farm* (Oxford: Oxford University Press, 1991), 1:43; Trollope, *Can You Forgive Her?* 1:326.

29. Elizabeth Gaskell, *Mary Barton* (New York: Penguin, 1996), 352, 231.

30. Elizabeth Gaskell, *Cranford* (New York: Penguin, 2005), 76, 90, 156.

31. Elizabeth Gaskell, *North and South* (New York: Penguin, 1970), 141, 414. *North and South* is an especially rich novel as relates to the charitable visiting discussed earlier in this chapter. Elliott argues that in her visits to the home of Nicholas Higgins, Margaret Hale revises the conventional office of the Lady Bountiful to suit a modern social sphere (*Angel Out of the House*, 135–58).

32. Elizabeth Gaskell, *Wives and Daughters* (New York: Penguin, 1987), 37.

33. Sir Walter Scott, *The Antiquary* (London: J. M. Dent, 1975), 285.

34. Pardiggle's defiance bears out a claim of Harrison's: "Working people disliked being visited in their homes by philanthropists who often displayed great ignorance about the problems they faced. Even had they been conscious of their ignorance, many philanthropists would not have been perturbed by it. For their aim was not to accept working-class attitudes; on the contrary, philanthropists were in the forefront of the nineteenth-century attack on popular culture" ("Philanthropy and the Victorians," 371).

35. Raymond Williams makes this point: "In certain periods of relative stability the conventions are themselves stable and may be seen as no more than formal, the 'rules' of a particular art. In other periods the variation and indeed uncertainty of conventions have to be related to changes, divisions, and conflicts in the society. . . . For it is of the essence of a convention that it ratifies an assumption or a point of view, so that the work can be made and received." Williams, *Marxism and Literature* (Oxford: Oxford University Press, 1977), 179.

36. This view is best elaborated in Georg Simmel's account of the development of social forms. This development begins in a way compatible with Williams: "On the basis

of practical conditions and necessities, our intelligence, will, creativity, and feeling work on the materials that we wish to wrest from life. In accord with our purposes, we give these materials certain forms and only in these forms operate and use them as elements of our lives." At this point, Simmel turns away from the materialist argument: "But it happens that these materials, these forces and interests, in a peculiar manner remove themselves from the service of life that originally produced and employed them. . . . They come to play freely in themselves and for their own sake; they produce or make use of materials that exclusively serve their own operation or realization." Simmel, *The Sociology of Georg Simmel*, ed. Kurt Wolff (Glencoe, IL: Free Press, 1950), 41–42.

37. Stuart Hall, "The Problem of Ideology: Marxism without Guarantees," in *Stuart Hall: Critical Dialogues in Cultural Studies*, ed. Kuan-Hsing Chen and David Morley (London: Routledge, 1996), 24–45.

38. In isolating the form of the condescension act from its social determinants, we perform an analytical function essential to the critical apprehension of social phenomena. This structuralist practice has dominated anthropology, deriving from the foundational work of Émile Durkheim, Marcel Mauss, and Claude Lévi-Strauss. It has also been a major thread in sociology, owing mainly to Georg Simmel, who posited that all social phenomena are a composite of two elements: "an interest, a purpose, or a motive" which make up the "content," and "a form or mode of interaction among individuals through which, or in the shape of which, that content attains social reality." Simmel, *On Individuality and Social Forms: Selected Writings*, ed. D. E. Levine (Chicago: University of Chicago Press, 1971), 24. Describing an abstract form of interaction is a crucial procedural step even for a historical materialist study. In his study of working-class respectability, Peter Bailey gives a specific motive for paying attention to the forms of behavior: because of conditions arising from urban anonymity, Bailey contends, there is every reason to imagine that respectable behavior had a life of its own; by instead creating classificatory types of agent, historians have mistakenly presupposed "a continuity in casting where there may only have been a continuity in performance." Bailey, "'Will the Real Bill Banks Please Stand Up?' Towards a Role Analysis of Mid-Victorian Working-Class Respectability," *Journal of Social History* 12, no. 3 (1978): 339. The union of structuralism and historical materialism in literary studies has been best accomplished by Fredric Jameson in *The Political Unconscious: Narrative as a Socially Symbolic Act* (Ithaca, NY: Cornell University Press, 1981). Jameson's dialectical method requires a temporary separation between structure and content. The work of art is first described as completely as possible in terms of a series of social and narrative codes. This structuralist description, however, is always inadequate; it is, then, precisely where we find a break in the structural circuit that ideology (the political unconscious) becomes visible. Jameson's work represents a definitive return of morphology to the center of comparative studies of social and narrative process. Following Mauss, Simmel, and Jameson, I consider questions of morphology crucial to a historical apprehension of the condescension act.

39. Simmel, *On Individuality*, 26.

40. Marcel Mauss, *The Gift: Forms and Functions of Exchange in Archaic Societies*, trans. Ian Cunnison (New York: Norton, 1967). Mauss's study is significant both as a pioneering work of structural social analysis and as an influential meditation on the meaning of exchange outside of a capitalist framework.

41. In her study of *Cranford,* Jill Rappoport considers a Victorian attempt—motivated by the economic straits of women—to replace a market economy with an economy of sympathetic exchange. In opposition to the masculinized Victorian marketplace, Rappoport sees gift exchange as offering an alternative economy for women, one in which circulation knits the community together. Rappoport, *Giving Women: Alliance and Exchange in Victorian Culture* (New York: Oxford University Press, forthcoming).

42. Jacques Godbout, *The World of the Gift* (Montreal: McGill-Queen's University Press, 1998), 13.

43. Mauss, *The Gift,* 10.

44. Claude Lévi-Strauss, *The Elementary Structures of Kinship,* ed. Rodney Needham, trans. James Harle Bell and Richard Von Sturmer (Boston: Beacon Press, 1969), 59.

45. For a similar approach to the phenomenon of deference, see Howard Newby, "The Deferential Dialectic," *Comparative Studies in Society and History* 17 (1975): 145–46.

46. Mandler, "Poverty and Charity in the Nineteenth-Century Metropolis: An Introduction," in *Uses of Charity,* 1.

47. What is given and what is received must intersect somehow within the condescension encounter. As cited above, Mandler contends that there was a gap between "the forms in which charity was offered" and "the forms in which it was needed" (ibid., 1). Mandler's thesis would suggest that class condescension could never produce real sociation, since Victorian class encounters provided no intersection of motives or understanding. Yet the Victorian interest in condescension—whether an embrace of or revulsion from it—suggests otherwise. In these encounters with no object of exchange, relation is still transacted; whether that relation is adversarial or conciliatory, it still has substance.

48. Simmel accordingly explains that authority and domination are social processes that presuppose freedom on the part of the subordinate (*On Individuality,* 96–98).

49. Maria Edgeworth, *Patronage* (London: Pandora, 1986), 549.

50. See, for instance, Malinowski, *Argonauts of the Western Pacific.*

51. Ralph Waldo Emerson, "Gifts," in *Emerson: Essays and Lectures* (New York: Library of America, 1983), 536.

52. Audrey Jaffe sees exactly this kind of transaction attaching to exchanges of sympathy: "The scene of sympathy in effect effaces both its participants, substituting for them images, or fantasies, of social and cultural identity." Jaffe, *Scenes of Sympathy: Identity and Representation in Victorian Fiction* (Ithaca, NY: Cornell University Press, 2000), 4.

53. Marshall Sahlins, *Stone Age Economics* (Chicago: Aldine, 1972), 191–92.

54. Charles Kingsley, *Yeast: A Problem* (London: Dent, 1976), 144.

55. George Eliot, *Romola* (New York: Penguin, 1981), 61.

56. Thomas Hardy, *Far from the Madding Crowd* (New York: Norton, 1986), 101.

57. Mauss, *Gift,* 4.

58. Mary Elizabeth Braddon, *Lady Audley's Secret* (Oxford: Oxford University Press, 1987), 109.

59. Robert Louis Stevenson, *Dr. Jekyll and Mr. Hyde and Other Stories* (New York: Penguin, 1979), 92.

60. Mary Shelley, *Frankenstein; or, The Modern Prometheus* (Chicago: University of Chicago Press, 1982), 165.

61. Godbout, *World of the Gift*, 46.

62. Jacques Derrida, *Given Time: I, Counterfeit Money* (Chicago: University of Chicago Press, 1992), 40.

63. Judith Walkowitz, *City of Dreadful Delight: Narratives of Sexual Danger in Late-Victorian London* (Chicago: University of Chicago Press, 1992); Nord, *Walking the Victorian Streets;* Elliott, *Angel Out of the House;* Rappoport, *Giving Women;* Koven, *Slumming.*

64. Goodlad, *Victorian Literature*, 14. Here Goodlad takes issue with Mary Poovey's argument that philanthropic initiatives complemented other reforms, including the New Poor Law, in forging a new disciplinary regime.

65. See Miriam Bailin, "'Dismal Pleasure': Victorian Sentimentality and the Pathos of the Parvenu," *ELH* 66, no. 4 (1999): 1015–32; Jaffe, *Scenes of Sympathy;* Mary Lenard, *Preaching Pity: Dickens, Gaskell, and Sentimentalism in Victorian Culture* (New York: Peter Lang, 1999); Ellen Argyros, *Without Any Check of Proud Reserve: Sympathy and Its Limits in George Eliot's Novels* (New York: Peter Lang, 1999); Daniel Bivona and Roger B. Henkle, *The Imagination of Class: Masculinity and the Victorian Urban Poor* (Columbus: Ohio State University Press, 2006); Amit S. Rai, *Rule of Sympathy: Sentiment, Race and Power, 1750–1850* (Basingstoke, UK: Palgrave, 2002); and Brigid Lowe, *Victorian Fiction and the Insights of Sympathy: An Alternative to the Hermeneutics of Suspicion* (London: Anthem, 2007). Several social historians have tried to integrate the sociological concept of role into their studies of authority relations in Victorian England. Bailey questions the tendency of social historians to treat certain behavioral protocols of working-class respectability as demonstrating an ideology or a "permanent code of values"; such methodological assumptions, Bailey argues, fasten "the working-class respectable into a characterological strait-jacket." Bailey calls for a situational analysis of class encounters, one that understands respectability as a chosen social role rather than a "normative mode." He accordingly reads specific interactions as demonstrating an "instrumental or calculative deployment" of expected behavior. Bailey, "Will the Real Bill Banks," 337–38, 343. Mandler applies Bailey's suggestions to the study of Victorian charity, citing the "ritual conformity" of the poor. Mandler, "Poverty and Charity," 23.

66. Jameson, *Political Unconscious;* Nancy Armstrong, *Desire and Domestic Fiction* (New York: Oxford University Press, 1987); Rosemarie Bodenheimer, *The Politics of Story in Victorian Fiction* (Ithaca, NY: Cornell University Press, 1988); Jaffe, *Scenes of Sympathy;* Poovey, *Making a Social Body;* Elliott, *Angel Out of the House;* Goodlad, *Victorian Literature.*

67. In several books, Prochaska has explored the reasons that Victorians gave charity, particularly stressing factors that show the limitations of the social control thesis (the local character of charity, the fact that charitable giving did not track with other social and economic developments, the central role of working-class philanthropy, and above all the deeply ingrained Christian belief that held charity to be a primary religious duty). See Frank Prochaska, *Christianity and Social Service in Modern Britain: The Disinherited Spirit* (Oxford: Oxford University Press, 2006); Prochaska, *The Voluntary Impulse: Philanthropy in Modern Britain* (London: Faber and Faber, 1988); and Prochaska, *Women and Philanthropy.* In "Philanthropy and the Victorians," Harrison analyzes the diversity of rationales

that drove Victorians to give, while Himmelfarb (in *Poverty and Compassion*) shows that philanthropy was at the heart of the mid-Victorian Time-Spirit. For studies of the relationship between volunteer charity and the state, see Robert Humphreys, *Poor Relief and Charity, 1869–1945: The London Charity Organisation Society* (Houndmills, UK: Palgrave, 2001); Robert Humphreys, *Sin, Organized Charity, and the Poor Law in Victorian England* (London: St. Martin's Press, 1995); Martin Daunton, ed., *Charity, Self-Interest and Welfare in the English Past* (London: University College, 1996); Alan Kidd, *State, Society and the Poor in Nineteenth-Century England* (New York: St. Martin's Press, 1999); and M. J. D. Roberts, *Making English Morals: Voluntary Association and Moral Reform in England, 1787–1886* (Cambridge: Cambridge University Press, 2004).

68. See, for instance, Mandler, "Poverty and Charity"; and Lynn Holland Lees, *The Solidarities of Strangers: The English Poor Laws and the People, 1700–1948* (New York: Cambridge University Press, 1998).

69. There are notable exceptions. Goodlad, for instance, argues that a Foucauldian disciplinary paradigm does not recognize Victorian England's idealization of liberal self-governance and decentralized social agency (*Victorian Literature*, 7). And Lowe contends that New Historicist accounts of Victorian sympathy lead to perversely defeatist conclusions—defeatist because they reject from the outset the possibility that sympathy has any "positive potential," and perverse because they reserve all real power of ideological challenge for the critic (*Victorian Fiction*, 2–14).

70. For some studies of Octavia Hill, see Anthony Wohl, *The Eternal Slum* (London: Edward Arnold, 1977); Wohl, "Octavia Hill and the Homes of the London Poor," *Journal of British Studies* 10 (1971): 105–31; Jane Lewis, *Women and Social Action in Victorian and Edwardian England* (Stanford: Stanford University Press, 1991); and Diana Maltz, "Beauty at Home or Not? Octavia Hill and the Aesthetics of Tenement Reform," in *Homes and Homelessness in the Victorian Imagination*, ed. H. M. Daleski and Murray Baumgarten (New York: AMS Press, 1998), 187–211. Home visiting was one of the pillars of Prochaska's 1980 study of women and philanthropy and since then has been taken up in many social histories of charity; women's missions and settlements are the subject of Vicinus's detailed study, *Independent Women*. For a cultural history of the Salvation Army, see Pamela Walker, *Pulling the Devil's Kingdom Down: The Salvation Army in Victorian Britain* (Berkeley: University of California Press, 2001).

71. Frank Prochaska, "Philanthropy," in *The Cambridge Social History of Britain 1750–1950*, vol. 3, ed. F. M. L. Thompson (Cambridge: Cambridge University Press, 1990), 362–70. Prochaska explains, "The charity of the poor to the poor has hardly been touched, for it fits uncomfortably with the conception of philanthropy as middle class and patronizing" (*Voluntary Impulse*, xiv). This conception, as embodied in the failed condescension scene, is (I hope I have shown) common to us and to the Victorians. It is the subject of my study, and so I necessarily give it precedence; by doing so, however, I mean to demonstrate the prevalence of concerns about condescension, not to insist that charity was in reality condescending or that the charity from rich to poor was more important than working-class charity.

72. Colin Jones, "Some Recent Trends in the History of Charity," in Daunton, *Charity, Self-Interest*, 57.

73. In the same chapter of *Bleak House* in which he introduces Mrs. Pardiggle, Dickens offers a different paradigm of charity, where one poor woman, Liz, gives comfort to her bereaved friend Jenny. Esther reflects, "I thought it very touching to see these two women, coarse and shabby and beaten, so united; to see what they could be to one another; to see how they felt for one another, how the heart of each to each was softened by the hard trials of their lives" (134–35). Clearly, there is no condescension here, and part of Esther's puzzle is how she, being who she is, might offer a kind of charity as productive as Liz's.

Chapter One
Help Wanting: The Exhaustion of a Dickensian Ideal

1. The passage that follows is one of the most commonly cited episodes of Dickens's later journalism; see, for instance, David Pascoe's introduction to *Charles Dickens: Selected Journalism, 1850–1870* (New York: Penguin, 1997) and Daleski and Baumgarten's introduction to *Homes and Homelessness in the Victorian Imagination.* Dickens's source is Mark 14:51–52, where a young follower of Jesus flees the arresting soldiers in Gethsemane; we might also hear echoes of Matthew 17:14–20, where Jesus casts the devil out of a lunatic. Dickens finds himself not in the role of one who can cure and redeem but—as Pascoe points out—in the role of the arresting officer.

2. Dickens, *The Uncommercial Traveller and Reprinted Pieces,* 133.

3. The threat inherent in sympathy is discussed by Jaffe, who argues that sympathetic encounters between rich and poor create a "phantasmatic opposition between images of cultural ideality and degradation" (*Scenes of Sympathy,* 8).

4. Dickens's attitudes toward philanthropy have often been invoked in studies of his life and works, particularly with reference to Urania Cottage and the ragged school movement. However, there has been little Dickens scholarship that takes philanthropy as its primary subject. The notable exception is Norris Pope's *Dickens and Charity* (New York: Columbia University Press, 1978), a useful reference work that is nonetheless limited by its exclusive focus on evangelical reform.

5. Beatrice Webb, *My Apprenticeship* (London: Longmans, Green and Co., 1926), 176–77.

6. See Lees's "Survival of the Unfit" for a discussion of the ways in which charitable donations to an individual were often used to support other (sometimes "undeserving") members of the recipient's family.

7. Pam Morris compellingly argues that the return to an illicit past signifies the impulse of those at the margins "to unmask, even violate, the object of desire—genteel respectability." According to Morris, Dickens's later novels cast doubt not only on respectability but also on the entire project of securing that responsibility through a break with the past: "This involves a pattern of doomed circular flight, in which illicit love and illegitimacy centre increasingly upon the impossibility of escape from one's past, from shame, guilt, and the physical force of sexual desire. Again and again in these novels the hegemonic myth of causal progress is challenged, as origins assert their physical claims, and men and women are forced to recognize the impossibility of flight from the bondage of their own flesh into the frozen safety of genteel posturing." Morris, *Dickens's Class Consciousness: A Marginal View* (London: Macmillan, 1991), 12–13. Andrew Sanders has also

written about the influence of Dickens's "novelty"—his rise in class—on his social imagination. See Sanders, *Dickens and the Spirit of the Age* (Oxford, UK: Clarendon, 1999).

8. Dickens conveys a part of his premise in a letter to Forster: "Of course my point is that bad and good are inextricably linked in remembrance, and that you could not choose the enjoyment of recollecting only the good." *Letters of Charles Dickens: The Pilgrim Edition* (Oxford, UK: Clarendon, 1965), 5:443.

9. In fact, the reciprocity cycle extends beyond the story's thematics to its very structure. The narrative is divided in three parts: "The Gift Bestowed" (where Redlaw is made to forget his sorrow), "The Gift Diffused" (where Redlaw passes his forgetfulness on to others), and "The Gift Reversed" (where memory is universally restored). The strange terms—bestowed, diffused, reversed—show the sense in which Redlaw's fantasy (as it is realized by the ghost) distorts the principles of gift exchange. Redlaw never "receives" the gift of forgetfulness, because once it is upon him he is a different man; likewise, he does not "reciprocate" the gift but passes it on inadvertently through diffusion.

10. In *Given Time*, Derrida agrees: "*At the limit, the gift as gift ought not appear as gift: either to the donee or to the donor*" (14; emphasis in original). He further explains, "The simple consciousness of the gift right away sends itself back the gratifying image of goodness or generosity, of the giving-being who, knowing itself to be such, recognizes itself in a circular, specular fashion, in a sort of auto-recognition, self-approval, and narcissistic gratitude" (23).

11. Bruce Robbins and Kathleen Blake provide cogent readings of the problem of social "effectiveness" in *Bleak House*. Robbins focuses on the novel's discourse of professionalism, claiming that while the professions have generally been held to value *system* over *ethics*, they are in fact the embodiment of an agency that attempts to become analytically aware of social processes. "Through the intermediaries of Comte, Spencer, and Durkheim, a common attention to the disparity between the morality of individual actions and their eventual social value or function provides a historical link between Dickens and Foucault." Robbins, "Telescopic Philanthropy," in *Nation and Narration*, ed. Homi Bhabha (New York: Routledge, 1990), 223. Like Robbins, Blake rejects the notion that in the novel, individual ethics transcends social analysis or systemic action; against the Foucauldian "disparity" between individual actions and social value, however, Blake argues that *Bleak House*'s attack against social abuses falls in line with classical (that is, Benthamite) political economy, an affiliation that has been obscured by critical suspicions of Victorian liberalism. Blake, "*Bleak House*, Political Economy, Victorian Studies," *Victorian Literature and Culture* 25, no. 1 (1997): 1–21.

12. David Suchoff, *Critical Theory and the Novel: Mass Society and Cultural Criticism in Dickens, Melville, and Kafka* (Madison: University of Wisconsin Press, 1994), 81–82.

13. George Holoch's analysis of mystification is foundational to subsequent studies of society in *Little Dorrit*. Holoch argues that mystification is the process whereby characters claim an identity that is separate from the material sources of their social status. Mystification is alternately transparent, as in William Dorrit's case, and disguised, as in the case of Arthur Clennam, whose very acts of self-assertion continue to act out the economic drama of his family history. Holoch, "Consciousness and Society in *Little Dorrit*," *Victorian Studies* 21, no. 3 (1978): 335–51.

14. Ibid., 336.

15. Anny Sadrin puts the critique most crisply: "The great paradox of the patriarchal system that Dickens dramatizes here is that it magnifies a relationship that does not exist. The fatherhood of the fathers is exalted everywhere, but the fathers are not fatherly. They ooze benevolence, and they tyrannize." Sadrin, *Parentage and Inheritance in the Novels of Charles Dickens* (Cambridge: Cambridge University Press, 1994), 84.

16. Holoch correctly calls Arthur's code "a barely secularized version of his mother's" ("Consciousness and Society," 341).

17. The crucial discussion of liberal guilt in *Little Dorrit* belongs to Lionel Trilling, who sees this novel as the one in which the pressures of society are most fully carved out upon the will of the individual. Trilling, "*Little Dorrit*," in *Dickens: A Collection of Critical Essays*, ed. Martin Price (Englewood Cliffs, NJ: Prentice-Hall, 1967), 147–57.

18. Catherine Waters deftly discusses "the ideological function of the family in the novel's analysis of social and economic transformation." Waters, *Dickens and the Politics of the Family* (Cambridge: Cambridge University Press, 1997), 89.

19. His intervention in Arthur's plight is expounded in comic detail: "With no other attendant than Mother, Mr. Meagles went upon his pilgrimage, and encountered a number of adventures. Not the least of his difficulties was, that he never knew what was said to him, and that he pursued his inquiries among people who never knew what he said to them. Still, with an unshaken confidence that the English tongue was somehow the mother tongue of the whole world, only the people were too stupid to know it, Mr. Meagles harangued innkeepers in the most voluble manner, entered into loud explanations of the most complicated sort, and utterly renounced replies in the native language of the respondents, on the ground that they were 'all bosh.' Sometimes interpreters were called in; whom Mr. Meagles addressed in such idiomatic terms of speech, as instantly to extinguish and shut up—which made the matter worse. On a balance of the account, however, it may be doubted whether he lost much; for, although he found no property, he found so many debts and various associations of discredit with the proper name, which was the only word he made intelligible, that he was almost everywhere overwhelmed with injurious accusations. On no fewer than four occasions the police were called in to receive denunciations of Mr. Meagles as a Knight of Industry, a good-for-nothing, and a thief, all of which opprobrious language he bore with the best temper (having no idea what it meant), and was in the most ignominious manner escorted to steam-boats and public carriages, to be got rid of, talking all the while, like a cheerful and fluent Briton as he was, with Mother under his arm" (*Little Dorrit*, 806–7).

20. One such petitioner presents to him an "entirely novel description of Pump" (*Little Dorrit*, 332).

21. So resolved is Mr. Meagles on his handshake that he forces it: "[Miss Wade] would not have put out her hand, it seemed, but that Mr. Meagles put out his so straight before her, that she could not pass it" (*Little Dorrit*, 25).

22. That mustard seed has caused Mr. Meagles a good deal of trouble among many critics, who pronounce him a snob. So he is, although Dickens meant to show nothing especially insidious about Meagles himself but, instead, a much larger problem attached to social patronage generally.

23. Peter Mandler posits that the poor of Victorian London routinely developed the skill of telling philanthropists what they wanted to hear while using the charity of the

rich toward ends that they would not typically have condoned or understood ("Poverty and Charity" 23).

24. William Myers correspondingly claims that Mr. Meagles's "failure with Tattycoram points to a complete breakdown, in terms of sympathy, understanding and charity, between the classes"; in this failure, Myers argues, the novel's author and readers are inevitably implicated. Myers, "The Radicalism of *Little Dorrit*," in *Literature and Politics in the Nineteenth Century*, ed. John Lucas (London: Methuen, 1971), 85.

25. Waters demonstrates how Tatty's return, and her reappropriation within the Meagles household as a "family member," disguises the economic character of her relationship with the Meagleses. Because Tatty's appropriation is thus "smoothed over," Waters claims, Pet's "commercial value" to the family becomes visible (*Dickens and the Politics*, 100–101).

26. J. Hillis Miller, *Charles Dickens: The World of His Novels* (Cambridge, MA: Harvard University Press, 1958), 239. "The tragedy of *Little Dorrit*, then, is the tragedy of childhood distorted, betrayed, forgotten, buried so far down that it no longer seems to exist." According to Miller, Amy is able "to carry the innocence and spontaneous love of childhood into adult life" (239, 241).

27. Avrom Fleishman, "Master and Servant in *Little Dorrit*," *SEL: Studies in English Literature, 1500–1900* 14, no. 4 (1974): 581.

28. Jeff Nunokawa, *The Afterlife of Property: Domestic Security and the Victorian Novel* (Princeton: Princeton University Press, 1994), 32–34.

29. Waters, *Dickens and the Politics*, 91.

30. This position is well articulated by Myers: "Without explanation [Amy] is introduced into a totally unredeemed world as a rebuke both to smug quietism and [to] the distortions of revolutionary anger. She is at the center, in other words, of a literary rather than a practical appreciation of intransigent political and human problems; through her they are felt and judged; but she is not an instrument of change, a solution to the novel's problems" ("Radicalism of *Little Dorrit*," 102–3).

31. Dianne Sadoff, "Storytelling and the Figure of the Father in *Little Dorrit*," *PMLA* 95, no. 2 (1980): 240; Suchoff, *Critical Theory*, 58.

32. In this, Dorrit should be compared to Mr. Meagles, who at first feels Pet's presence as a consolation but cannot finally keep her fixed in his image of her.

33. Suchoff, *Critical Theory*, 61.

34. "Little Dorrit becomes a dialectical image for the infantilizing force of conventional Victorian expectations on a woman who, like the novel, retains her socially critical and imaginative power" (ibid., 58).

35. The young Amy Dorrit, most pointedly in her dialogues with the turnkey, is best compared to the otherworldly Paul Dombey.

36. Suchoff believes that the "facts" of Amy's life as a prison child are manifest in Clennam's constructions of her as a moral ideal: "[Clennam's] praise of Little Dorrit's virtue is exaggerated to the point of becoming lurid, encouraging readers to seek the social history that lies beneath his fetish and its social mask" (*Critical Theory*, 59).

37. "If the story of a son relates the search for a father's authority, the story of a daughter tells of incestuous structures of desire" (Sadoff, "Storytelling," 240).

38. Amy fulfills this role most completely in her final dialogue with Mrs. Clennam.

39. This is a modification of Nunokawa's claim that property is tainted by the fact of its acquisition (*Afterlife of Property*, 19); not only acquisition but also donation confers a taint.

Chapter Two
Preacher's Vigil, Landlord's Watch: Charity by the Clock in Adam Bede

1. George Eliot, *Adam Bede* (New York: Penguin, 1985), 181.

2. Amanda Anderson's *The Powers of Distance: Cosmopolitanism and the Cultivation of Detachment* (Princeton: Princeton University Press, 2001) definitively examines the "cultivation of detachment" among Victorian social analysts. Anderson argues that even as George Eliot critiques abstract theoretical stances that are ungrounded in direct experience, she also sees the "wide view" as "requisite to a comprehensive understanding of social life" (13).

3. Daniel Cottom discusses Eliot's sympathy as embodying the emergence of a wider perspective (associated with the public) out of the "circumstances of individual feeling" (associated with the private): "What is negotiated in the balancing act maintained in Eliot's writing is a division between private and public worlds that would submit the private to the public and yet would preserve within that submission an impression of the sacrifice it entailed." Cottom argues that for Eliot, the public is held accountable to the private, such that "the public ends of society . . . may be expected to flow from private resolutions and a domestic scale of commitments." Cottom, *Social Figures: George Eliot, Social History, and Literary Representation* (Minneapolis: University of Minnesota Press, 1987), 186, 187, 185.

4. This social trajectory is not the less historically forward-looking for its appeals to an idealized, preindustrial past; see Suzanne Graver, *George Eliot and Community: A Study in Social Theory and Fictional Form* (Berkeley: University of California Press, 1984), 3, 80.

5. Barbara Hardy, *The Novels of George Eliot* (London: Athlone, 1959), 43.

6. Bernard Paris, *Experiments in Life: George Eliot's Quest for Values* (Detroit, MI: Wayne State University Press, 1965), 128.

7. In this vein, Dorothea Barrett discusses Eliot's struggle between the personal, passionate self and the transcendent, public vocation. Barrett, *Vocation and Desire: George Eliot's Heroines* (London: Routledge, 1989), 16. Bernard Semmel claims that for Eliot, historical traditions "would make it possible for an individual to transcend selfish egoism and to feel a deep sympathetic concern, first toward his kin and then toward the extended family of the nation." Semmel, *George Eliot and the Politics of National Inheritance* (New York: Oxford University Press, 1994), 6. Josephine McDonagh contends that in Eliot's early novels, ties of affection and sympathy lay the foundation for "modern forms of social organization." McDonagh, "The Early Novels," in *The Cambridge Companion to George Eliot*, ed. George Levine (Cambridge: Cambridge University Press, 2001), 55. For Cottom, too, middle-class sympathy discovers the "unity of the public world," but it does so through the construction of a "private arena" in which the broader movements of public commitment can be enacted and controlled (*Social Figures*, 192).

8. Graver, *George Eliot and Community*, 99.

9. Ibid., 34. Graver's conclusion is that Eliot's true ideal of community draws on modern, individualistic aspects of culture as a way of addressing the limitations of *Gemeinschaft*.

10. This impossibility of translating sympathy into an ordinary mode of relation has relevance both to Suzy Anger's discussion of Eliot's "ethical intuitionism" and James Eli Adams's association of sympathy with inarticulateness. Anger, "George Eliot and Philosophy," in Levine, *Cambridge Companion*, 81; Adams, "Gyp's Tale: On Sympathy, Silence, and Realism in *Adam Bede*," *Dickens Studies Annual: Essays on Victorian Fiction* 20 (1991): 227–28.

11. *Hints on District Visiting Societies: A Plan for Their Formation, and Suggestions to Visitors* (London: Longman, Rees, Orme, Brown, Green, and Longman, 1836), 48, 14.

12. Mary Bayly, *Ragged Homes, and How to Mend Them* (Philadelphia: American Sunday School Union, 1859), 141.

13. Webb, *My Apprenticeship*, 252.

14. The regimentation of middle-class philanthropy has long been understood as exacerbating the cruelty of the New Poor Law by attempting to eradicate all outdoor relief, even that which might have flowed through unofficial channels. The Charity Organisation Society (COS) worked closely with the relief boards, increasing the degree of surveillance applied to any family petitioning for help and enforcing middle-class standards of respectability. This is, at any rate, the standard narrative of the politics of Victorian charity, although social historians of the past two decades have done much to complicate the picture. Peter Mandler (in *Uses of Charity*) and Lynn Lees (in *Solidarities of Strangers*), among others, have investigated the cultural networks through which the poor turned middle-class charity to their own ends. Alan Kidd has persuasively argued (in "Philanthropy and the 'Social-History Paradigm,'" *Social History* 21, no. 2 [1996]: 180–92) that neither the "personal kindness" account nor the "social control" thesis describes the intricate socioeconomic function of charity, and Lauren Goodlad (in *Victorian Literature*) claims that liberal voluntarism (like that which drove the COS) needs to be distinguished from, and very consciously distinguished itself from, the workings of a centralized bureaucracy.

15. Helen Bosanquet, *Rich and Poor* (London: Macmillan, 1896), 7.

16. So alleges Sir Charles Trevelyan in three letters to the *Times* on London pauperism (1870). Trevelyan claims that because the indigent poor were neither working nor seeking work, they could "spend the whole of their time in devising and carrying out schemes for plundering society." Trevelyan, "London Pauperism," *London Times*, 2 June 1870, p. 6B; 4 June 1870, p. 7B; 6 June 1870, p. 6C.

17. Gareth Stedman Jones discusses the new generation of liberals (in the 1860s) who believed in the evolutionary mobility of the working classes, classes that could, with thrift and industry, rise to the level of the middle class. Jones, *Outcast London: A Study in the Relationship between Classes in Victorian Society* (Oxford, UK: Clarendon, 1971), 9–10.

18. Himmelfarb, *Poverty and Compassion*, 191.

19. C. S. Loch, *Charity and Social Life* (London: Macmillan and Co., 1910), 27.

20. Along these lines, Stedman Jones invokes Brooke Lambert's sermon at Oxford, which argued that "[t]he moral of Christ's life ... is his repression of his powers of benevolence." Jones, *Outcast London*, 247.

21. Bosanquet, *Rich and Poor,* 75.

22. Eliot, *Romola,* 429.

23. Eliot, *Adam Bede,* 383.

24. Eliot, *Scenes of Clerical Life,* 70.

25. See note 64.

26. Ian Gregor and Brian Nicholas, *The Moral and the Story* (London: Faber and Faber, 1962), 15–16.

27. See John Goode, "*Adam Bede,*" in *Critical Essays on George Eliot,* ed. Barbara Hardy (London: Routledge and Kegan Paul, 1970), 19–41; Ian Adam, "The Structure of Realisms in *Adam Bede,*" *Nineteenth-Century Fiction* 30, no. 2 (1975): 127–49; Eve Kosofsky Sedgwick, *Between Men: English Literature and Male Homosocial Desire* (New York: Columbia University Press, 1985), 138. Sedgwick sees this transition as part of a social history of the middle-class family: "The basic historical trajectory of *Adam Bede* is to move the novel's normative vision of family from the Poysers' relatively integrated farm to the Bedes' highly specified nuclear household. *As part of this transition,* the normative female role must change from Mrs. Poyser's to one like Mrs. Bede's" (140).

28. See Mary Jean Corbett, "Representing the Rural: The Critique of Loamshire in *Adam Bede,*" *Studies in the Novel* 20, no. 3 (1988): 288–301; and Mark Warren McLaughlin, "*Adam Bede*: History, Narrative, Culture," *VIJ: Victorians Institute Journal* 22 (1994): 55–83.

29. E. P. Thompson argues that much of the appeal of Wesley's Lutheran theology among the poor came from the fact that, as against the election doctrine of middle-class Calvinists, Wesley emphasized the sinfulness of rich and poor alike and stressed the necessity of submission and obedience; in some sense, the poor could win spiritual comfort by giving up the temporal battle to the rich. Thompson, *The Making of the English Working Class* (New York: Vintage, 1963), 362–63.

30. Christine L. Krueger describes Dinah's sermon as participating in the women preachers' "two principal discursive strategies . . . the ethos of prophecy and the ethos of simplicity." Krueger, *The Reader's Repentance: Women Preachers, Women Writers, and Nineteenth-Century Social Discourse* (Chicago: University of Chicago Press, 1992), 60. Both of these strategies, I contend, rely strongly on the intimation of God's nearness.

31. Mason Harris demonstrates the extent of Eliot's indictment of paternalism in the novel, not just through the "stingy Squire" but more pointedly through "the amiable grandson Arthur." Harris, "Arthur's Misuse of the Imagination: Sentimental Benevolence and Wordsworthian Realism in *Adam Bede,*" *English Studies in Canada* 4 (1978): 41–42.

32. Of course, the tragedy of the novel, from the communal point of view, is that the estate eventually descends to Arthur only after the young squire has forfeited his right and ability to govern.

33. Elisabeth Jay, *The Religion of the Heart: Anglican Evangelicalism and the Nineteenth-Century Novel* (New York: Oxford University Press, 1975), 93. Jay disputes the commonly held association of premillennial theology with quietism, citing the Earl of Shaftesbury as a formidable counterexample.

34. Here I am borrowing the language the narrator uses with reference to the Methodist belief in the apparition of Jesus (Eliot, *Adam Bede,* 31).

35. B. Hardy, *Novels of George Eliot,* 32–46.

36. This parallel is foregrounded in chapter 30, "The Delivery of the Letter," in which two letters are actually delivered: the first from Arthur, apprising Hetty of his departure; and the other from Dinah, describing (among other things) the necessity for her absence and the possibility of further travels. Mary Wilson Carpenter discusses this interesting conjunction: "The writer of Hetty's letter is her lover of the past, while the writer of the letter Adam reads will be his lover in the future, suggesting the crossing or intersection of narrative past and future in these two letters." Carpenter, *George Eliot and the Landscape of Time: Narrative Form and Protestant Apocalyptic History* (Chapel Hill: University of North Carolina Press, 1986), 39.

37. Goode identifies Arthur's casual ethics with the utilitarian doctrine of expediency, an ethical system that Goode argues was anathema to Eliot (and to her close associate Herbert Spencer) because it tried to perpetuate social practices that were out of step with natural law. Goode, "*Adam Bede*," 26. An even more important association, though, is the antinomian doctrine in which Arthur shows so little interest in Irwine's study. Valentine Cunningham aptly mentions the relevance of antinomianism to Arthur's ethical lapses. Cunningham, *Everywhere Spoken Against: Dissent in the Victorian Novel* (Oxford, UK: Clarendon, 1975), 149–50.

38. Goode, "*Adam Bede*," 23–24.

39. The traditional understanding of Methodism as a vehicle for working-class solidarity and dissidence was influentially attacked by E. P. Thompson (in *Making*, 360–65), who sees the Methodist work discipline as almost universally serving the purposes of the industrial manufacturer. Subsequent critics have tried to recover the radicalism inherent in the early generations of the Methodist ministry. Elisabeth Jay (in *Religion of the Heart*, 43) contrasts the disruptiveness of Methodism with the respectability of Anglican evangelicalism, while Christine Krueger (in *Reader's Repentance*, 21) expounds on the politically ambiguous status of the women preachers.

40. Christopher Herbert mistakenly describes this contrast as one between Dinah's Calvinistic religion, which is "aberrant" and "euphorically ferocious," and her natural kindness. Herbert, "Preachers and the Schemes of Nature in *Adam Bede*," *Nineteenth-Century Fiction* 29, no. 4 (1975): 414–16. It is more appropriate to see a tension between disruption and conciliation as inhering both in her doctrine and in her character.

41. Gregor and Nicholas, *Moral*, 23; Barrett, *Vocation and Desire*, 26.

42. Barrett, *Vocation and Desire*, 45–47.

43. Mason Harris accordingly argues that Hetty's infanticide is an expression of the very shame-morality that underwrites the Poysers' respectability. Harris, "Infanticide and Respectability: Hetty Sorrel as Abandoned Child in *Adam Bede*," *English Studies in Canada* 9, no. 2 (1983): 55. Hetty's dread of charity stems from a pride that is not merely egotistical but is completely bound up in a sense of class identification: "Hetty had the pride not only of a proud nature but of a proud class—the class that pays the most poor-rates, and most shudders at the idea of profiting by a poor-rate" (Eliot, *Adam Bede*, 374).

44. Herbert, "Preachers," 419, 413.

45. Adams, "Gyp's Tale," 232–33.

46. Krueger argues that the Wesleyan idea of the "extraordinary call" gave Eliot a kind of excuse for her own intellectualism without forcing her to argue that *all* women

might eschew the "socialization" of "early marriage and motherhood" (*Reader's Repentance*, 235–36).

47. Sedgwick focuses on this delegation as a symbolic transmission of class authority (*Between Men*, 157). Kristin Brady sees the final reconciliation between Arthur and Adam as closing the rift in patriarchy that had been opened earlier in the novel: "It is fitting, therefore, that the Epilogue of *Adam Bede* should focus not only on the marriage of Adam and Dinah, but also on the revival of the male friendship between Adam and his own patron in the class system, Arthur Donnithorne: with this reconciliation, the male power structure has been fully restored." Brady, *George Eliot* (London: Macmillan, 1992), 92.

48. Graver associates "holiday time" most often (though not exclusively) with *Gemeinschaft*, describing the holiday world as ideal and poeticized, as against the workaday realism of ordinary life (*George Eliot and Community*, 82–87).

49. Insofar as Eliot's moments of sympathy resist a liberal model of rational exchange, they forgo the political aims of other Victorian scenes of sympathy (to borrow Audrey Jaffe's phrase), scenes that tend toward the regulation of public life under the strains of market capitalism. Such scenes, Jaffe contends, mediate between idealized and degraded images of the self, both challenging and enabling the middle-class subject to articulate his or her "place" in society (*Scenes of Sympathy*, 8–10). Miriam Bailin makes a related case for Victorian sentimentality, which "registers and provides solace for the anxieties which beset class advancement and decline within an increasingly stratified social terrain" ("Dismal Pleasure," 1016). For Bailin and Jaffe, Victorian sympathy responded to capitalist imperatives of competition and social mobility. It almost goes without saying that the charity industry served a comparable regulatory purpose. One need not denounce philanthropy as "social control"—a critical view that has been consistently challenged over the last decade—to agree that it worked in tandem with other structures of public governance, political participation, and economic distribution. In other words, whether Victorian philanthropy ultimately aided or injured the poor, it at any rate adapted itself to function efficiently within a modern system of capitalist exchange. But Eliot's moments of exceptional sympathy work differently: not only are they often transacted between people in similar class positions (Dinah and Hetty, for instance), but, as this chapter shows, they tend not to place the subject but to dislocate him or her. These moments abrogate the principles of participation and citizenship that define the struggle for identity within the capitalist state and are thus effectively cut off from any broader regime of philanthropy or socialization.

50. See Harry Shaw, *Narrating Reality: Austen, Scott, Eliot* (Ithaca, NY: Cornell University Press, 1999) for a discussion of realist claims to totality.

51. Adam, "Structure of Realisms," 128.

52. Adam claims, for instance, that "the author denies not merely literary conventions but also her own, in the defeat of expectations created for us by her own characters." Ibid.

53. A constant challenge to this trend is everywhere in the work of J. Hillis Miller, who sees Eliot's various invocations of formal unity and historical totality not only as incomplete endeavors but also as a deliberate campaign of self-defeat in which every illusion of organic history is dismantled. Miller, "Narrative and History," *ELH* 41, no. 3 (1974): 466, 468. Most recent criticism of Eliot, as my argument suggests, recognizes the force of epistemological disruption in Eliot but sees such disruption as a problem Eliot tries to solve. I would say,

with Miller, that disruption is an intractable aspect of Eliot's "continuous" narratives, but I see the recurrence of disruptive moments as growing specifically out of concerns about the possibility of meaningful association under the analytical regime of the social sciences.

54. Henry Auster, *Local Habitations: Regionalism in the Early Novels of George Eliot* (Cambridge, MA: Harvard University Press, 1970), 29.

55. Barry Qualls, "George Eliot and Religion," in Levine, *Cambridge Companion*, 124.

56. Thakur Prasad, *Comtism in the Novels of George Eliot* (Lucknow: Hindustani Book Depot, 1968), 6.

57. Jay (in *Religion of the Heart*, 89) shows that Mary Ann Evans's own millennial expectations were, in 1838, strongly tied to her expectations of political revolution throughout the world. Krueger cites Deirdre David's claim that for Eliot the millennium was "outside history, outside time"; Krueger sees this transcendence as justifying the exceptionalism of women's prophetic preaching (*Reader's Repentance*, 236).

58. Carpenter, *George Eliot*, 22–23.

59. It is not Tönnies but Eliot who, according to Graver's powerful study *George Eliot and Community*, attempts to create a social model that integrates the best qualities of *Gemeinschaft* and *Gesellschaft* (16).

60. Gregor and Nicholas, *Moral*, 24–25.

61. Adam, "Structure of Realisms," 129–31.

62. Goode, "*Adam Bede*," 22–23.

63. McDonagh, "Early Novels," 44.

64. Neil McCaw remarks on Eliot's awareness of the challenge that particulars offer the totalities put forward by Victorian historiography: "Comtean Positivism envisaged history as a human totality in which the idiosyncrasies and particularities of human identity are silenced. . . . As a consequence difference and dissimilarity were erased, leaving issues of nationalism and ethnicity unresolved. The whole thrust of Comte's philosophy amounts to a denial of difference, an ironing smooth of the historical metanarrative that worked to remove metaphysics and spirituality from the processes of interpretation." McCaw, *George Eliot and Victorian Historiography: Imagining the National Past* (New York: St. Martin's Press, 2000), 5–6.

65. Adam remarks on the predominance of the definite article throughout the novel's descriptive passages, which denotes an "inclusive" tendency toward "particulars" ("Structure of Realisms," 135). I would build on Adam's claim by seeing the definite article as not just *including* particulars but *mobilizing* them in the service of a particular organizational scheme. In other words, the definite article fixes an object's function, while the indefinite article suggests various possibilities.

66. George Eliot, "Notes on Form in Art," in *Selected Essays, Poems, and Other Writings* (New York: Penguin, 1990), 232.

Chapter Three
Why Settle? Samuel Barnett, Octavia Hill, and the London Slums

1. See M. J. D. Roberts, "Reshaping the Gift Relationship: The London Mendicity Society and the Suppression of Begging in England, 1818–1869," *International Review of*

Social History 36, no. 2 (1991): 201–31. See also Sir Charles Trevelyan's 1870 series of letters to the *Times* on London pauperism. As Gareth Stedman Jones argues in *Outcast London*, visiting allowed philanthropists to distinguish the "residuum" of society from the civic-minded working class (10–11).

2. In "A Home from Home," Anne Summers provides an account of the rise of clerical visiting and the inheritance of this practice by middle-class women. For the most comprehensive discussion of Victorian home visiting, see Prochaska, *Women and Philanthropy*.

3. Again, as in the introduction, I am concentrating here on middle-class visiting. While I recognize that the working classes, too, participated a great deal in the enterprise of charitable visiting, this study centers on the iconic power (along with the iconic failure) of certain images of charity, including that of the well-to-do visitor inside the homes of the poor.

4. *Essays on the Principles of Charitable Institutions*, 216–17.

5. Kingsley, "Country Parish," 53–54.

6. Godwin, "The Homes of the London Poor," *The Builder* (1853): 201–2.

7. Andrew Mearns, *The Bitter Cry of Outcast London: An Inquiry into the Condition of the Abject Poor*, ed. Anthony Wohl (New York: Humanities Press, 1970), 17.

8. Of course, according to many historians, the visited poor were inevitably "performing" for philanthropists, so one might reasonably question whether or not poor families were precisely revealing themselves to visitors. But however we answer that question, the fact remains that the visit depended at least on the illusion that the lives of the poor were being uncovered and examined.

9. "[District visitors] rise from their sumptuous fare, and quit their splendid dwellings, and lay aside the garment of proud pre-eminence, which separates them from all familiar intercourse with the destitute, and, clothing themselves with humility and kindness, exert their powers and privileges in ministering to those who know less, and have less of mental, and moral, and religious, and temporal treasures than themselves." General Society, *District Visitor's Manual*, 24.

10. C. S. Loch, *Charity Organisation*, 3rd ed. (London: S. Sonnenschein, 1905), 5–6.

11. Prochaska, *Women and Philanthropy*, 242.

12. Bosanquet, *Rich and Poor*, 138–39.

13. Kingsley, "Country Parish," 54.

14. Webb, *My Apprenticeship*, 196.

15. Himmelfarb, *Poverty and Compassion*, 202.

16. Samuel Barnett, "Hospitalities," in *The Universities and the Social Problem*, ed. John Knapp (London: Rivington, 1895), 54.

17. Samuel Barnett, "University Settlements," in Samuel Barnett and Henrietta Barnett, *Practicable Socialism*, 2nd ed. (London: Longmans, Green, and Co., 1895), 165.

18. Himmelfarb accordingly observes that Toynbee Hall may seem to have "served the interests of the residents better than those of the community" and goes on to argue that the settlement's communal function depended precisely on the opportunity it gave the poor to witness the elevated lives of the cultured classes (*Poverty and Compassion*, 240). This point of view is borne out by Sir John Gorst: "[The] teachers themselves have in all cases learnt more than they have taught. Their own views of life have been enlarged, their

own errors and prejudices have been corrected, and fresh qualities of the human character for love and admiration have been revealed to them. The class heresies, which the separation of the rich from the neighbourhood of the poor has engendered, have been to some extent removed." Gorst, "'Settlements' in England and America," in Knapp, *Universities*, 12–13. No matter whose interests were better served, it is certain that settlements were promoted as being mutually beneficial to settlers and their poor neighbors.

19. Barnett, "Hospitalities," 59.

20. Early accounts of Toynbee Hall and the settlement movement can be found in Samuel Barnett and Henrietta Barnett, *Practicable Socialism;* Knapp, *Universities;* and Henrietta Barnett, "The Beginning of Toynbee Hall: A Reminiscence," *Nineteenth Century* 53 (1903): 306–14. For further studies, see Standish Meachem, *Toynbee Hall and Social Reform, 1880–1914: The Search for Community* (New Haven, CT: Yale University Press, 1987); Asa Briggs and Anne Macartney, *Toynbee Hall: The First Hundred Years* (London: Routledge and Kegan Paul, 1984); Vicinus, *Independent Women;* Himmelfarb, *Poverty and Compassion;* and Koven, *Slumming.*

21. Gorst, "Settlements," 17–23; Meachem, *Toynbee Hall*, 66–67.

22. Gorst, "Settlements," 10.

23. Barnett, "University Settlements," 170.

24. Barnett, "Hospitalities," 62–63; Barnett, "University Settlements," 171.

25. Barnett, "Hospitalities," 60–61.

26. Ibid., 61–62. Barnett's revolutionary rhetoric alone makes clear how far his aspirations for Toynbee Hall were from the establishmentarianism of the COS.

27. Barnett, "University Settlements," 172.

28. Koven, *Slumming*, 248.

29. Barnett, "Hospitalities," 61.

30. Barnett, "University Settlements," 170.

31. Quoted in Briggs and Macartney, *Toynbee Hall*, 2.

32. William Bowman, "Lenin in London," *Contemporary Review* (June 1957): 336. This story is cited in Briggs and Macartney, *Toynbee Hall*, 54–55.

33. Hill's parents were James Hill, a radical editor, and Caroline Southwood Smith, an educational reformer and daughter of the famous London doctor.

34. These purchases and the publicity of her system of management constituted Hill's most important social contribution, but in the years that followed she continued to gain momentum as a social activist. Hill helped lead the Charity Organisation Society, founded the Open Air Movement, established the National Trust, and sat on the New Poor Law Commission.

35. The Torrens and Cross Acts (1866, 1875) made public funds available for clearance and rebuilding schemes, thus creating, according to Anthony Wohl, an inconspicuous form of municipal subsidy (*Eternal Slum*, 144–45).

36. This phenomenon was acceptable to many reformers, who would have agreed with Waterlow that "in housing 30,000 of the upper working classes [the IIDC] was freeing their former rooms for occupation by those beneath them." Ibid., 151.

37. For more on Victorian working-class housing, see ibid.; John Burnett, *A Social History of Housing, 1815–1985* (London: Methuen, 1986); and Martin Daunton, *House and*

Home in the Victorian City: Working-Class Housing, 1850–1914 (London: Edward Arnold, 1983). Jones discusses working-class hostility to the "paternal vigilance" of the model dwellings (*Outcast London*, 187).

38. Wohl, *Eternal Slum*, 159–60.

39. Ibid., 164, 160.

40. Because Hill never constructed new buildings but simply managed and renovated existing ones, her outlay was minimal. Still, according to Wohl (ibid., 182), the poor housed by Hill would have fallen into Booth's classes C and D (intermittent and small regular earners) rather than classes A and B, the poorest classes. The model dwelling companies, by contrast, typically housed Booth's class E, regular earners above the poverty line. Charles Booth was a Victorian sociologist whose survey of London redefined the public understanding of poverty within the metropolis. Booth identified eight economic classes, the first four of which (A through D) he considered to be below the poverty line.

41. Jones is among the historians who have branded Hill's schemes impractical (*Outcast London*, 194–96).

42. Wohl, *Eternal Slum*, 179.

43. Wohl, "Octavia Hill," 130–31.

44. Various historians have been unsatisfied with the traditional view of a nineteenth-century "progress" away from individualist solutions to social problems and toward state solutions. In fact, the Benthamite approach to reform that pervaded much early-Victorian social thought emphasized public policy measures; it was really in the 1860s and 1870s that private charity came into full prominence as an alternative to official measures.

45. Jones argues that the economic relationship between landlord and tenant was far less direct than that between employer and worker. This is so; the fortunes of landlord and tenant were not as completely interdependent as those of labor and capital. Nevertheless, the tenant-landlord relationship was certainly a commercial one, distinguishing it from the other incarnations of personal charity.

46. Octavia Hill, *Homes of the London Poor*, 2nd ed. (London: Macmillan, 1883), 41.

47. Ibid. Her answer: "To endeavour to be so unfailingly just and patient, that they should learn to trust the rule that was over them" (41). This answer attests to a contractual view of rule that is the subject of the paragraphs following.

48. Hill's criticism of the slum landlord's recklessness mirrors her criticism of reckless philanthropy.

49. Octavia Hill, "The Importance of Aiding the Poor without Almsgiving," *Transactions of the National Association for the Promotion of Social Sciences* (1869): 593.

50. Hill, *Homes*, 21.

51. This, at any rate, is the portrait that Hill paints in her account. I cannot say whether Hill's tenants shared her sense of their relationship with her; what I mean to show, instead, is that for Hill, the idea of settlement opened up a whole range of relational possibilities that could not have emerged from home visiting.

52. C. Edmund Maurice, *Life of Octavia Hill, as Told in Her Letters* (London: Macmillan, 1913), 18.

53. The process described above is repeatedly borne out in stories such as the following: "One tenant—a silent, strong, uncringing woman, living with her seven children

and her husband in one room—was certain 'there were many things she could get for the children to eat which would do them more good than another room.' I was perfectly silent. A half-pleading, half-asserting voice said: 'Don't you see I'm right, miss?' 'No,' I said; 'indeed I do not. I have been brought up to know the value of abundant good air; but of course you must do as you think best—only I am sorry.' Not a word more passed; but in a few weeks a second room was again to let, and the woman volunteered: 'She thought she'd better strive to get the rent; good air was very important, wasn't it?'" (Hill, *Homes*, 21).

54. See, for instance, C. S. Loch's *Charity Organisation*. Loch begins his appeal claiming that "[t]he State wants citizens. It cannot afford to have any outcast or excluded classes, citizens that are not citizens. . . . It must do its utmost to change the dependent sections of the community into independent" (4).

55. Karen Chase and Michael Levenson present a vivid portrait of the "provocation" that the crowded courts of the slums offered to the privileged classes, for whom the satisfactions of home depended on the walled privacy it afforded. Chase and Levenson, *The Spectacle of Intimacy: A Public Life for the Victorian Family* (Princeton: Princeton University Press, 2000), 148–49.

56. Gillian Darley, *Octavia Hill: A Life* (London: Constable, 1990), 34.

Chapter Four: Tennyson's Salvation Army

1. Charles Dickens, "Pet Prisoners," in *Selected Journalism, 1850–1870* (New York: Penguin, 1997), 400.

2. Prochaska, "Philanthropy," 362–70.

3. David Hempton, *Methodism: Empire of the Spirit* (New Haven, CT: Yale University Press, 2005), 62.

4. Edward McKinley, *Marching to Glory: The History of the Salvation Army in the United States of America, 1880–1990* (San Francisco: Harper and Row, 1980), 33. From the beginning, the Christian Mission (later to become the Salvation Army) recognized that its success depended on its general membership taking up the reins of the mission. According to Pamela Walker, "the Christian Mission was little more than its converts. They built the movement as well as filled its halls. . . . [W]hile the clergy found it difficult to bridge the chasm of class and culture that divided them from their flock, the Mission's converts could not help but address family, friends, and work mates when they preached in the streets. Indeed, the Mission urged converts to speak to everyone they knew about salvation" (*Pulling the Devil's Kingdom Down*, 60). An article in *Macmillan's* quotes General Booth as calling on the Salvation Army to "seize the slaves of sin, and not only set them free, and turn them into the children of God, but, as far as is possible in each case, to make them soul winners." Quoted in M. A. Lewis, "The Salvation Army," *Macmillan's* (September 1882): 404.

5. Walker, *Pulling the Devil's Kingdom Down*, 120.

6. Ibid., 134, 75. Olive Anderson understands the militarism of the Salvation Army and similar organizations partly as subjecting the charity worker to a disciplinary regimen intended to contain and direct his or her enthusiasm. Anderson, "The Growth of Christian Militarism in Mid-Victorian Britain," *English Historical Review* 86, no. 338 (1971): 66–67. John Peck sees something of a displacement: he suggests that Christian militarism

is an attempt to revive the "military code of the Wellington era" in response to the Indian Mutiny. Peck, *War, the Army and Victorian Literature* (Houndmills, UK: Macmillan, 1998), 72–73. In both accounts, this missionary militarism is an attempt to control something wild within the public servant—to rein in and refocus the energies of the enthusiast.

7. Roberts, *Making English Morals;* Goodlad, *Victorian Literature.*

8. Roberts, *Making English Morals,* 2.

9. Highly suggestive in this regard is Tennyson's early plan for the *Idylls,* in which the Round Table is said to represent "liberal institutions." Hallam Tennyson, *Alfred Lord Tennyson: A Memoir* (London: Macmillan, 1899), 521.

10. In *The Fall of Camelot,* John Rosenberg presents the most important analysis along these lines, claiming that the *Idylls* offer no stable image of the ideal life but rather that they stage the dilemmas that issue when humans try to create a coherent moral vision in the face of a fundamentally ambiguous reality. With this claim, Rosenberg takes issue with a critical tradition that treats Tennyson's epic as establishing a clear opposition between valued and devalued terms, as in Jerome Buckley's classic reading in *Tennyson: The Growth of a Poet* (Cambridge: Cambridge University Press, 1967). Rosenberg's interpretation is an important influence on the present argument, both in his insight that the binary oppositions of the poem actually coexist (and cannot be disentangled) within the perspectives of the poem's various characters, and in his emphasis on the thematics of failure. However, I believe that the knights' double vision is not just an existential condition but a function of their political role, and my concern is in the specifically social determinants, and indeed the social value, of the serial failures that the knights display. John Rosenberg, *The Fall of Camelot: A Study of Tennyson's "Idylls of the King"* (Cambridge, MA: Harvard University Press, 1973).

11. Quoted in the notes to *Idylls of the King,* in *Tennyson: A Selected Edition,* ed. Christopher Ricks (Berkeley: University of California Press, 1989), 672.

12. Matthew Reynolds, *The Realms of Verse, 1830–1870: English Poetry in a Time of Nation-Building* (Oxford: Oxford University Press, 2001), 252, 253–54, 255–56. Reynolds's discussion of the poem's parabolic drift refers to a comment in Hallam Tennyson's memoir: "[I]n later years [my father] often said, 'They have taken my hobby, and ridden it too hard, and have explained some things too allegorically, although there is an allegorical or perhaps rather a parabolic drift in the poem'" (*Alfred Lord Tennyson,* 523).

13. Linda K. Hughes and Michael Lund, *The Victorian Serial* (Charlottesville: University Press of Virginia, 1991), 132, 128.

14. Ian McGuire, "Epistemology and Empire in *Idylls of the King,*" *Victorian Poetry* 30, no. 3/4 (1992): 387–88.

15. Here Tennyson's epic opens into the territory of the novel, a generic conjunction deftly explored by Herbert Tucker in *Epic: Britain's Heroic Muse, 1790–1910* (Oxford: Oxford University Press, 2008), 385–461. One point in Tucker's analysis is of particular interest here: discussing Tennyson's *Idylls* as embracing "narration" over the Liberal "parliamentary" discourse of the early 1830s, Tucker points out that the epic of the 1860s had the hard job of telling a national story that could speak to a populace divided between "a newly enfranchised people and an established public elite, with an empire to care for in the bargain" (393). In this way, Tennyson's poem itself can be seen as a tool of conscription, and

the knight's dilemma in the face of national service appears to reflect the reading nation's dilemma over its relationship to literature (that is, as the bearer of communal messages or as the nourisher of private lives).

16. Cecily Devereux finds a political analogue to this model of reciprocity in the ideological construction of Canada as an equal partner with England in the greater imperial project, an idea that resonates strongly with the notion of missionary conscription treated in this chapter. Devereux, "Canada and the Epilogue to the *Idylls*: 'The Imperial Connection' in 1873," *Victorian Poetry* 36, no. 2 (1998): 223–41.

17. The communal character of Tennyson's Camelot might well be described by a passage from Railton's account of the early years of the Salvation Army: "A number of more or less harmonious but differing elements were at work together, and it would have puzzled anyone to say at any given moment which of these elements would eventually prevail." Quoted in Walker, *Pulling the Devil's Kingdom Down*, 51. Walker discusses this tension between the democratic tendencies produced by a structure in which every member was a leader, and William Booth's autocratic attempts to reorganize the Christian Mission into an army that would act in concert; this tension, as I argue, is present and fundamental in Tennyson's Camelot.

18. Erik Gray, though, argues that Lancelot does not have any particular illusions; in what Gray calls the "paradox of conscious error," Lancelot demonstrates, with deflated rhetoric, that he knows full well how weak his position is. Gray, "Getting It Wrong in 'The Lady of Shalott,'" *Victorian Poetry* 47, no. 1 (2009): 54.

19. Reynolds describes the trajectory similarly, claiming that Geraint represents devotion, spinning out of control but finally returning to his "proper, subsidiary role in Arthur's court" (*Realms of Verse*, 256). I recognize that for the purposes of this argument, I am conflating Geraint's service to the queen with his service to the king, describing both of these as his "public mission." Linda K. Hughes gives a precedent for this conflation, seeing Guinevere as mediating Geraint's relationship with his king. Hughes, "Victors and Victims: Tennyson's 'Enid' as Postcolonial Text," *Victorian Poetry* 31, no. 4 (1993): 422.

20. Here I follow the sequence of the story itself, not the narrative, which begins (like the other *Idylls*) in medias res, when Geraint's public feeling has ebbed and his private troubles have begun to preoccupy him.

21. This is not to say that Geraint's defection does not involve him in acts that have public consequences. Matthew Bevis characterizes Geraint's departure as an imperialistic campaign that allows the knight to "avoid the civil unrest created by rumours about the Queen at home." Bevis, "Tennyson's Civil Tongue," *Tennyson Research Bulletin* 7 (1999): 117. Bevis contends that such imperialist acts are contradictorily seen as both an alternative to and a reflection of political problems within the state. Most significant to my argument is the fact (discussed by Bevis) that Geraint's conquest is a renegade mission, outside of the king's discipline. In this respect, Geraint's excesses after he departs the court would suggest that the public worker, once he turns away from his commission, can only really pursue a private agenda, a conflation that is made clear by Linda Hughes's exploration of Geraint's dominion over Enid in postcolonial terms.

22. I depart, here, from a more usual reading in which Geraint's alienation stems from a late-breaking disillusionment with the queen and that his flight with Enid arises

out of a newfound sexual/conjugal panic. See, for instance, Ingrid Ranum's essay, which compellingly describes Geraint's removal of Enid as conforming to "the domestic doctrine of nineteenth-century Evangelicals" who see the home as a place from which sin can be excluded. Ranum, "An Adventure in Modern Marriage: Domestic Development in Tennyson's *Geraint and Enid* and *The Marriage of Geraint*," *Victorian Poetry* 47, no. 1 (2009): 251.

23. Herbert Tucker considers Geraint's dandification in relation to the novelistic aspects of Tennyson's poem. Tucker, "Trials of Fiction: Novel and Epic in the Geraint and Enid Episodes from *Idylls of the King*," *Victorian Poetry* 30, no. 3/4 (1992): 448–49.

24. Ibid., 446–47.

25. Tucker discusses Enid's uneasy portrayal of Dame Philosophy, explaining the psychological condition of her stoicism: "The freedom from love and hate vaunted in Enid's stoical song has evidently been purchased at [a] high price: her stance of detached contemplation takes as its primal topic her own worthlessness" (ibid., 448–49).

26. Bevis remarks on the uncanny nature of Arthur's rebuke to Geraint, which presumes, but leaves rather vague, a distinction between Geraint's wrong militaristic methods and the king's right ones ("Tennyson's Civil Tongue," 118).

27. Tucker sees, in Tennyson's "psycho-social understanding" of this state of affairs, the typical workings of the Victorian novel; he points out that Percivale is put in motion by "a cloistered nun's sexual sublimation" (*Epic*, 452).

28. "Finally, the Mission and later the Army negotiated cultural and class distinctions in ways that middle-class evangelicals and social reformers rarely agreed with or understood. The rules that governed social reformer Octavia Hill's dwellings, the prerequisites for assistance outlined by the Charity Organisation Society, the behavior expected at the clubs organized for working-class children by churches or settlement workers, the lessons taught at mothers' meetings, all began with the assumption that the values and aspirations of the urban working class led to poverty and disorder. Middle-class philanthropists, social reformers, and clergy regarded their own educational attainments as self-evidently superior; even if their working-class charges could not fully achieve the same standards, they were nevertheless a laudable objective. The Christian Mission, in contrast, was composed of working-class men and women intent on saving souls. Their means and objectives emerged out of their particular theological understanding, class, and community life." Walker, *Pulling the Devil's Kingdom Down*, 99.

29. Bernard Shaw, *Major Barbara* (New York: Meredith Corporation, 1971), 64.

30. Undershaft claims that his donation of five thousand pounds to the Salvation Army is deeply disinterested, since any organization that preaches peace and goodwill toward men cannot be good for the war profits (ibid., 103).

Epilogue

1. Virginia Woolf, *To the Lighthouse* (Orlando, FL: Harcourt Brace, 1981), 85.

2. Virginia Woolf, *The Years* (Oxford: Oxford University Press, 1992), 48.

Bibliography

Adam, Ian. "The Structure of Realisms in *Adam Bede.*" *Nineteenth-Century Fiction* 30, no. 2 (1975): 127–49.

Adams, James Eli. "Gyp's Tale: On Sympathy, Silence, and Realism in *Adam Bede.*" *Dickens Studies Annual: Essays on Victorian Fiction* 20 (1991): 227–42.

Addison, Joseph. *The Works of the Right Honourable Joseph Addison.* 6 vols. London: Cadell and Davies, 1811.

Anderson, Amanda. *The Powers of Distance: Cosmopolitanism and the Cultivation of Detachment.* Princeton: Princeton University Press, 2001.

Anderson, Olive. "The Growth of Christian Militarism in Mid-Victorian Britain." *English Historical Review* 86, no. 338 (1971): 46–72.

Anger, Suzy. "George Eliot and Philosophy." In Levine, *Cambridge Companion,* 76–97.

Argyros, Ellen. *Without Any Check of Proud Reserve: Sympathy and Its Limits in George Eliot's Novels.* New York: Peter Lang, 1999.

Armstrong, Nancy. *Desire and Domestic Fiction.* New York: Oxford University Press, 1987.

Austen, Jane. *Emma.* 1816. New York: Penguin, 1987.

Auster, Henry. *Local Habitations: Regionalism in the Early Novels of George Eliot.* Cambridge, MA: Harvard University Press, 1970.

Bailey, Peter. "'Will the Real Bill Banks Please Stand Up?' Towards a Role Analysis of Mid-Victorian Working-Class Respectability." *Journal of Social History* 12, no. 3 (1978): 336–53.

Bailin, Miriam. "'Dismal Pleasure': Victorian Sentimentality and the Pathos of the Parvenu." *ELH* 66, no. 4 (1999): 1015–32.

Barnett, Henrietta. "The Beginning of Toynbee Hall: A Reminiscence." *Nineteenth Century* 53 (1903): 306–14.

Barnett, Samuel. "Hospitalities." In Knapp, *Universities,* 51–66.

———. "University Settlements." In Barnett and Barnett, *Practicable Socialism,* 165–74.

Barnett, Samuel, and Henrietta Barnett. *Practicable Socialism.* 2nd ed. London: Longmans, Green, and Co., 1895.

Barrett, Dorothea. *Vocation and Desire: George Eliot's Heroines*. London: Routledge, 1989.

Bayly, Mary. *Ragged Homes, and How to Mend Them*. Philadelphia: American Sunday School Union, 1859.

Bevis, Matthew. "Tennyson's Civil Tongue." *Tennyson Research Bulletin* 7 (1999): 113–25.

Bivona, Daniel, and Roger B. Henkle. *The Imagination of Class: Masculinity and the Victorian Urban Poor*. Columbus: Ohio State University Press, 2006.

Blake, Kathleen. "*Bleak House*, Political Economy, Victorian Studies." *Victorian Literature and Culture* 25, no. 1 (1997): 1–21.

Bodenheimer, Rosemarie. *The Politics of Story in Victorian Fiction*. Ithaca, NY: Cornell University Press, 1988.

Bosanquet, Helen. *Rich and Poor*. London: Macmillan, 1896.

Bowman, William. "Lenin in London." *Contemporary Review* (June 1957): 336–38.

Braddon, Mary Elizabeth. *Lady Audley's Secret*. 1861–62. Oxford: Oxford University Press, 1987.

Brady, Kristin. *George Eliot*. London: Macmillan, 1992.

Briggs, Asa, and Anne Macartney. *Toynbee Hall: The First Hundred Years*. London: Routledge and Kegan Paul, 1984.

Brontë, Charlotte. *Shirley*. 1849. New York: Penguin, 1985.

Buckley, Jerome. *Tennyson: The Growth of a Poet*. Cambridge: Cambridge University Press, 1967.

Burnett, John. *A Social History of Housing, 1815–1985*. London: Methuen, 1986.

Burney, Fanny. *Evelina*. 1778. New York: Norton, 1965.

Carpenter, Mary Wilson. *George Eliot and the Landscape of Time: Narrative Form and Protestant Apocalyptic History*. Chapel Hill: University of North Carolina Press, 1986.

Chase, Karen, and Michael Levenson. *The Spectacle of Intimacy: A Public Life for the Victorian Family*. Princeton: Princeton University Press, 2000.

Corbett, Mary Jean. "Representing the Rural: The Critique of Loamshire in *Adam Bede*." *Studies in the Novel* 20, no. 3 (1988): 288–301.

Cottom, Daniel. *Social Figures: George Eliot, Social History, and Literary Representation*. Minneapolis: University of Minnesota Press, 1987.

Cunningham, Valentine. *Everywhere Spoken Against: Dissent in the Victorian Novel*. Oxford, UK: Clarendon, 1975.

Daleski, H. M., and Murray Baumgarten, eds. *Homes and Homelessness in the Victorian Imagination*. New York: AMS Press, 1998.

Darley, Gillian. *Octavia Hill: A Life*. London: Constable, 1990.

Daunton, Martin, ed. *Charity, Self-Interest and Welfare in the English Past*. London: University College, 1996.

———. *House and Home in the Victorian City: Working-Class Housing, 1850–1914*. London: Edward Arnold, 1983.

Davies, J. L. "District Visiting." In Maurice, *Lectures to Ladies*, 117–34.

Derrida, Jacques. *Given Time: I, Counterfeit Money*. Chicago: University of Chicago Press, 1992.

Devereux, Cecily. "Canada and the Epilogue to the *Idylls*: 'The Imperial Connection' in 1873." *Victorian Poetry* 36, no. 2 (1998): 223–41.

Dickens, Charles. *Barnaby Rudge*. 1841. Oxford: Oxford University Press, 1989.

———. *Bleak House.* 1852–53. Oxford: Oxford University Press, 1989.

———. *A Christmas Carol.* 1843. In *Christmas Books,* 1–76. Oxford: Oxford University Press, 1989.

———. *David Copperfield.* 1849–50. Oxford: Oxford University Press, 1989.

———. *Dombey and Son.* 1846–48. Oxford: Oxford University Press, 1989.

———. *Great Expectations.* 1860–61. Oxford: Oxford University Press, 1989.

———. *The Haunted Man.* 1848. In *Christmas Books,* 317–98. Oxford: Oxford University Press, 1989.

———. *The Letters of Charles Dickens: The Pilgrim Edition.* Oxford, UK: Clarendon, 1965.

———. *Little Dorrit.* 1855–57. Oxford: Oxford University Press, 1989.

———. *Martin Chuzzlewit.* 1843–44. Oxford: Oxford University Press, 1989.

———. *Nicholas Nickleby.* 1838–39. Oxford: Oxford University Press, 1989.

———. "Night Walks." 1860. In *The Uncommercial Traveller and Reprinted Pieces,* 127–35. Oxford: Oxford University Press, 1989.

———. *The Old Curiosity Shop.* 1840–41. Oxford: Oxford University Press, 1989.

———. *Oliver Twist.* 1837–39. Oxford: Oxford University Press, 1991.

———. *Our Mutual Friend.* 1864–65. Oxford: Oxford University Press, 1992.

———. "Perils of Certain English Prisoners." 1857. In *Christmas Stories,* 161–208. Oxford: Oxford University Press, 1991.

———. "Pet Prisoners." 1850. In *Charles Dickens: Selected Journalism, 1850–1870,* 395–407. New York: Penguin, 1997.

———. *The Pickwick Papers.* 1836–37. Oxford: Oxford University Press, 1989.

———. *A Tale of Two Cities.* 1859. Oxford: Oxford University Press, 1989.

———. "What Christmas Is as We Grow Older." 1851. In *Christmas Stories,* 19–25. Oxford: Oxford University Press, 1991.

Edgeworth, Maria. *Patronage.* 1814. London: Pandora, 1986.

Eliot, George. *Adam Bede.* 1859. New York: Penguin, 1985.

———. *Romola.* 1862–63. New York: Penguin, 1981.

———. *Scenes of Clerical Life.* 1857. New York: Penguin, 1998.

———. *Selected Essays, Poems, and Other Writings.* New York: Penguin, 1990.

Elliott, Dorice Williams. *The Angel Out of the House: Philanthropy and Gender in Nineteenth-Century England.* Charlottesville: University Press of Virginia, 2002.

Emerson, Ralph Waldo. "Gifts." 1844. In *Emerson: Essays and Lectures,* 533–38. New York: Library of America, 1983.

Essays on the Principles of Charitable Institutions. London: Longman, Rees, Orme, Brown, Green, and Longman, 1836.

Fleishman, Avrom. "Master and Servant in *Little Dorrit.*" *SEL: Studies in English Literature, 1500–1900* 14, no. 4 (1974): 575–86.

Gaskell, Elizabeth. *Cranford.* 1851–53. New York: Penguin, 2005.

———. *Mary Barton.* 1848. New York: Penguin, 1996.

———. *North and South.* 1854–55. New York: Penguin, 1970.

———. *Wives and Daughters.* 1864–66. New York: Penguin, 1987.

General Society for Promoting District Visiting. *The District Visitor's Manual.* London: John W. Parker, 1840.

Godbout, Jacques. *The World of the Gift*. Montreal: McGill-Queen's University Press, 1998.

Godwin, George. "The Homes of the London Poor." *The Builder* (1853): 201–2.

Goode, John. "*Adam Bede*." In *Critical Essays on George Eliot*, edited by Barbara Hardy, 19–41. London: Routledge and Kegan Paul, 1970.

Goodlad, Lauren. *Victorian Literature and the Victorian State: Character and Governance in a Liberal Society*. Baltimore, MD: Johns Hopkins University Press, 2003.

Gorst, Sir John. "'Settlements' in England and America." In Knapp, *Universities*, 3–29.

Graver, Suzanne. *George Eliot and Community: A Study in Social Theory and Fictional Form*. Berkeley: University of California Press, 1984.

Gray, Erik. "Getting It Wrong in 'The Lady of Shalott.'" *Victorian Poetry* 47, no. 1 (2009): 45–59.

Gregor, Ian, and Brian Nicholas. *The Moral and the Story*. London: Faber and Faber, 1962.

Hall, Stuart. "The Problem of Ideology: Marxism without Guarantees." In *Stuart Hall: Critical Dialogues in Cultural Studies*, edited by Kuan-Hsing Chen and David Morley, 24–45. London: Routledge, 1996.

Hardy, Barbara. *The Novels of George Eliot*. London: Athlone, 1963.

Hardy, Thomas. *Far from the Madding Crowd*. 1874. New York: Norton, 1986.

Harris, Mason. "Arthur's Misuse of the Imagination: Sentimental Benevolence and Wordsworthian Realism in *Adam Bede*." *English Studies in Canada* 4 (1978): 41–59.

———. "Infanticide and Respectability: Hetty Sorrel as Abandoned Child in *Adam Bede*." *English Studies in Canada* 9, no. 2 (1983): 177–96.

Harrison, Brian. "Philanthropy and the Victorians." *Victorian Studies* 9, no. 4 (1966): 353–74.

Hempton, David. *Methodism: Empire of the Spirit*. New Haven, CT: Yale University Press, 2005.

Herbert, Christopher. "Preachers and the Schemes of Nature in *Adam Bede*." *Nineteenth-Century Fiction* 29, no. 4 (1975): 412–27.

Hill, Octavia. *Homes of the London Poor*. 2nd ed. London: Macmillan, 1883.

———. "The Importance of Aiding the Poor without Almsgiving." *Transactions of the National Association for the Promotion of Social Science* (1869): 589–93.

Himmelfarb, Gertrude. *Poverty and Compassion: The Moral Imagination of the Late Victorians*. New York: Knopf, 1991.

Hints on District Visiting Societies: A Plan for Their Formation, and Suggestions to Visitors. London: Longman, Rees, Orme, Brown, Green, and Longman, 1836.

Holoch, George. "Consciousness and Society in *Little Dorrit*." *Victorian Studies* 21, no. 3 (1978): 335–51.

Hughes, Linda K. "Victors and Victims: Tennyson's 'Enid' as Postcolonial Text." *Victorian Poetry* 31, no. 4 (1993): 419–26.

Hughes, Linda K., and Michael Lund. *The Victorian Serial*. Charlottesville: University Press of Virginia, 1991.

Humphreys, Robert. *Poor Relief and Charity, 1869–1945: The London Charity Organisation Society*. Houndmills, UK: Palgrave, 2001.

———. *Sin, Organized Charity, and the Poor Law in Victorian England*. London: St. Martin's Press, 1995.

Jaffe, Audrey. *Scenes of Sympathy: Identity and Representation in Victorian Fiction.* Ithaca, NY: Cornell University Press, 2000.

Jameson, Fredric. *The Political Unconscious: Narrative as a Socially Symbolic Act.* Ithaca, NY: Cornell University Press, 1981.

Jay, Elisabeth. *The Religion of the Heart: Anglican Evangelicalism and the Nineteenth-Century Novel.* New York: Oxford University Press, 1975.

Jones, Colin. "Some Recent Trends in the History of Charity." In Daunton, *Charity, Self-Interest,* 38–47.

Jones, Gareth Stedman. *Outcast London: A Study in the Relationship between Classes in Victorian Society.* Oxford, UK: Clarendon, 1971.

Kidd, Alan. "Philanthropy and the 'Social-History Paradigm.'" *Social History* 21, no. 2 (1996): 180–92.

———. *State, Society and the Poor in Nineteenth-Century England.* New York: St. Martin's Press, 1999.

Kingsley, Charles. "The Country Parish." In F. D. Maurice, *Lectures to Ladies,* 53–66.

———. *Yeast: A Problem.* 1849. London: Dent, 1976.

Knapp, John, ed. *The Universities and the Social Problem: An Account of the University Settlements in East London.* London: Rivington, 1895.

Koven, Seth. *Slumming.* Princeton: Princeton University Press, 2004.

Krueger, Christine L. *The Reader's Repentance: Women Preachers, Women Writers, and Nineteenth-Century Social Discourse.* Chicago: University of Chicago Press, 1992.

Lees, Lynn Hollen. *The Solidarities of Strangers: The English Poor Laws and the People, 1700–1948.* New York: Cambridge University Press, 1998.

———. "The Survival of the Unfit: Welfare Policies and Family Maintenance in Nineteenth-Century London." In Mandler, *Uses of Charity,* 68–91.

Lenard, Mary. *Preaching Pity: Dickens, Gaskell, and Sentimentalism in Victorian Culture.* New York: Peter Lang, 1999.

Levine, George, ed. *The Cambridge Companion to George Eliot.* Cambridge: Cambridge University Press, 2001.

Lévi-Strauss, Claude. *The Elementary Structures of Kinship.* Edited by Rodney Needham. Translated by James Harle Bell and Richard Von Sturmer. Boston: Beacon Press,1969.

Lewis, Jane. *Women and Social Action in Victorian and Edwardian England.* Stanford: Stanford University Press, 1991.

Lewis, M. A. "The Salvation Army." *Macmillan's* (September 1882): 403–16.

Loch, C. S. *Charity and Social Life.* London: Macmillan and Co., 1910.

———. *Charity Organisation.* 3rd ed. London: S. Sonnenschein, 1905.

Lowe, Brigid. *Victorian Fiction and the Insights of Sympathy: An Alternative to the Hermeneutics of Suspicion.* London: Anthem, 2007.

Malinowski, Bronislaw. *Argonauts of the Western Pacific.* Prospect Heights: Waveland Press, 1984.

Maltz, Diana. "Beauty at Home or Not? Octavia Hill and the Aesthetics of Tenement Reform." In Daleski and Baumgarten, *Homes and Homelessness,* 187–211.

Mandler, Peter. *Aristocratic Government in the Age of Reform: Whigs and Liberals, 1830–1852.* New York: Oxford University Press, 1990.

———, ed. *Liberty and Authority in Victorian Britain.* New York: Oxford University Press, 2006.

———. "Poverty and Charity in the Nineteenth-Century Metropolis: An Introduction." In Mandler, *Uses of Charity,* 1–38.

———, ed. *The Uses of Charity: The Poor on Relief in the Nineteenth-Century Metropolis.* Philadelphia: University of Pennsylvania Press, 1990.

Maurice, C. Edmund. *Life of Octavia Hill, as Told in Her Letters.* London: Macmillan, 1913.

Maurice, F. D., ed. *Lectures to Ladies on Practical Subjects.* Cambridge, UK: Macmillan, 1855.

Mauss, Marcel. *The Gift: Forms and Functions of Exchange in Archaic Societies.* 1923. Translated by Ian Cunnison. New York: Norton, 1967.

McCaw, Neil. *George Eliot and Victorian Historiography: Imagining the National Past.* New York: St. Martin's Press, 2000.

McDonagh, Josephine. "The Early Novels." In Levine, *Cambridge Companion,* 38–56.

McGuire, Ian. "Epistemology and Empire in *Idylls of the King.*" *Victorian Poetry* 30, no. 3/4 (1992): 387–400.

McKinley, Edward. *Marching to Glory: The History of the Salvation Army in the United States of America, 1880–1990.* San Francisco: Harper and Row, 1980.

McLaughlin, Mark Warren. "*Adam Bede:* History, Narrative, Culture." *VIJ: Victorians Institute Journal* 22 (1994): 55–83.

Meachem, Standish. *Toynbee Hall and Social Reform, 1880–1914: The Search for Community.* New Haven, CT: Yale University Press, 1987.

Mearns, Andrew. *The Bitter Cry of Outcast London: An Inquiry into the Condition of the Abject Poor.* Edited by Anthony Wohl. New York: Humanities Press, 1970.

Miller, J. Hillis. *Charles Dickens: The World of His Novels.* Cambridge, MA: Harvard University Press, 1958.

———. "Narrative and History." *ELH* 41, no. 3 (1974): 455–73.

Morris, Pam. *Dickens's Class Consciousness: A Marginal View.* London: Macmillan, 1991.

Myers, William. "The Radicalism of *Little Dorrit.*" In *Literature and Politics in the Nineteenth Century,* edited by John Lucas. London: Methuen, 1971.

Newby, Howard. "The Deferential Dialectic." *Comparative Studies in Society and History* 17 (1975): 139–63.

Nord, Deborah Epstein. *Walking the Victorian Streets: Women, Representation, and the City.* Ithaca, NY: Cornell University Press, 1995.

Nunokawa, Jeff. *The Afterlife of Property: Domestic Security and the Victorian Novel.* Princeton: Princeton University Press, 1994.

Paris, Bernard. *Experiments in Life: George Eliot's Quest for Values.* Detroit, MI: Wayne State University Press, 1965.

Pascoe, David. Introduction to *Charles Dickens: Selected Journalism 1850–1870,* ix–xxv. New York: Penguin, 1997.

Peck, John. *War, the Army and Victorian Literature.* Houndmills, UK: Macmillan, 1998.

Poovey, Mary. *Making a Social Body: British Cultural Formation, 1830–1864.* Chicago: University of Chicago Press, 1995.

Pope, Norris. *Dickens and Charity.* New York: Columbia University Press, 1978.

Prasad, Thakur. *Comtism in the Novels of George Eliot.* Lucknow: Hindustani Book Depot, 1968.

Prochaska, Frank. *Christianity and Social Service in Modern Britain: The Disinherited Spirit.* Oxford: Oxford University Press, 2006.

———. "Philanthropy." In vol. 3 of *The Cambridge Social History of Britain 1750–1950,* edited by F. M. L. Thompson, 357–93. Cambridge: Cambridge University Press, 1990.

———. *The Voluntary Impulse: Philanthropy in Modern Britain.* London: Faber and Faber, 1988.

———. *Women and Philanthropy in Nineteenth-Century England.* Oxford, UK: Clarendon, 1980.

Qualls, Barry. "George Eliot and Religion." In Levine, *Cambridge Companion,* 119–37.

Rai, Amit S. *Rule of Sympathy: Sentiment, Race and Power, 1750–1850.* Basingstoke, UK: Palgrave, 2002.

Ranum, Ingrid. "An Adventure in Modern Marriage: Domestic Development in Tennyson's *Geraint and Enid* and *The Marriage of Geraint.*" *Victorian Poetry* 47, no. 1 (2009): 241–57.

Rappoport, Jill. *Giving Women: Alliance and Exchange in Victorian Culture.* New York: Oxford University Press, forthcoming.

Reynolds, Matthew. *The Realms of Verse, 1830–1870: English Poetry in a Time of Nation-Building.* Oxford: Oxford University Press, 2001.

Richardson, Samuel. *Clarissa; or, The History of a Young Lady.* 1748. New York: Penguin, 1985.

Robbins, Bruce. "Telescopic Philanthropy: Professionalism and Responsibility in *Bleak House.*" In *Nation and Narration,* edited by Homi Bhabha, 213–30. New York: Routledge, 1990.

Roberts, M. J. D. *Making English Morals: Voluntary Association and Moral Reform in England, 1787–1886.* Cambridge: Cambridge University Press, 2004.

———. "Reshaping the Gift Relationship: The London Mendicity Society and the Suppression of Begging in England, 1818–1869." *International Review of Social History* 36, no. 2 (1991): 201–31.

Rosenberg, John. *The Fall of Camelot: A Study of Tennyson's "Idylls of the King."* Cambridge, MA: Harvard University Press, 1973.

Ross, Ellen. "Hungry Children: Housewives and London Charity, 1870–1918." In Mandler, *Uses of Charity,* 161–96.

Sadoff, Dianne. "Storytelling and the Figure of the Father in *Little Dorrit.*" *PMLA* 95, no. 2 (1980): 234–245.

Sadrin, Anny. *Parentage and Inheritance in the Novels of Charles Dickens.* Cambridge: Cambridge University Press, 1994.

Sahlins, Marshall. *Stone Age Economics.* Chicago: Aldine, 1972.

Sanders, Andrew. *Dickens and the Spirit of the Age.* Oxford, UK: Clarendon, 1999.

Scott, Sir Walter. *The Antiquary.* 1816. London: J. M. Dent, 1975.

———. *Guy Mannering.* 1815. New York: Penguin, 2003.

———. *Ivanhoe.* 1819. New York: Penguin, 1986.

Sedgwick, Eve Kosofsky. *Between Men: English Literature and Male Homosocial Desire.* New York: Columbia University Press, 1985.

Semmel, Bernard. *George Eliot and the Politics of National Inheritance.* New York: Oxford University Press, 1994.

Shaw, George Bernard. *Major Barbara.* 1907. New York: Meredith Corporation, 1971.

Shaw, Harry. *Narrating Reality: Austen, Scott, Eliot.* Ithaca, NY: Cornell University Press, 1999.

Shelley, Mary. *Frankenstein; or, The Modern Prometheus.* 1818. Chicago: University of Chicago Press, 1982.

Siegel, Daniel. "Charity through Dissociation: The Task of the Bible-Woman." In *Gender and Victorian Reform,* edited by Anita Rose, 2–11. Newcastle upon Tyne: Cambridge Scholars Publishing, 2008.

Simmel, Georg. *On Individuality and Social Forms: Selected Writings.* Edited by D. E. Levine. Chicago: University of Chicago Press, 1971.

———. *The Sociology of Georg Simmel.* Edited by Kurt Wolff. Glencoe, IL: Free Press, 1950.

Sir Nathaniel [Francis Jacox]. "Mrs. Pardiggle: Typically Considered." *New Monthly Magazine* (June 1864): 174–77.

Stephen, James Fitzjames. "Doing Good." *Saturday Review,* 17 December 1859, 733–34.

Stevenson, Robert Louis. *Dr. Jekyll and Mr. Hyde and Other Stories.* New York: Penguin, 1979.

Suchoff, David. *Critical Theory and the Novel: Mass Society and Cultural Criticism in Dickens, Melville, and Kafka.* Madison: University of Wisconsin Press, 1994.

Summers, Anne. "A Home from Home: Women's Philanthropic Work in the Nineteenth Century." In *Fit Work for Women,* edited by Sandra Burman, 33–63. London: Croom Helm, 1979.

Tennyson, Alfred. *Idylls of the King.* In *Tennyson: A Selected Edition,* 667–975. Edited by Christopher Ricks. Berkeley: University of California Press, 1989.

Tennyson, Hallam. *Alfred Lord Tennyson: A Memoir.* London: Macmillan, 1899.

Thompson, E. P. *The Making of the English Working Class.* New York: Vintage, 1963.

Trevelyan, Sir Charles. "London Pauperism." *London Times,* 2 June 1870, p. 6B; 4 June 1870, p. 7B; 6 June 1870, p. 6C.

Trilling, Lionel. "*Little Dorrit.*" In *Dickens: A Collection of Critical Essays,* edited by Martin Price, 147–57. Englewood Cliffs, NJ: Prentice-Hall, 1967.

Trollope, Anthony. *Can You Forgive Her?* 1864–65. Oxford: Oxford University Press, 1977.

———. *Orley Farm.* 1861–62. Oxford: Oxford University Press, 1991.

———. *The Warden.* 1855. Oxford: Oxford University Press, 1991.

Tucker, Herbert. *Epic: Britain's Heroic Muse, 1790–1910.* Oxford: Oxford University Press, 2008.

———. "Trials of Fiction: Novel and Epic in the Geraint and Enid Episodes from *Idylls of the King.*" *Victorian Poetry* 30, no. 3/4 (1992): 441–61.

Twining, Louisa. *Deaconesses for the Church of England.* London: Bell and Daldy, 1860.

Vicinus, Martha. *Independent Women: Work and Community for Single Women, 1850–1920.* London: Virago, 1985.

Walker, Pamela. *Pulling the Devil's Kingdom Down: The Salvation Army in Victorian Britain.* Berkeley: University of California Press, 2001.

Walkowitz, Judith. *City of Dreadful Delight: Narratives of Sexual Danger in Late-Victorian London.* Chicago: University of Chicago Press, 1992.

Waters, Catherine. *Dickens and the Politics of the Family.* Cambridge: Cambridge University Press, 1997.

Webb, Beatrice. *My Apprenticeship.* London: Longmans, Green and Co., 1926.
Williams, Raymond. *Culture and Society, 1780–1950.* New York: Harper and Row, 1966.
———. *Marxism and Literature.* Oxford: Oxford University Press, 1977.
Wohl, Anthony. *The Eternal Slum.* London: Edward Arnold, 1977.
———. "Octavia Hill and the Homes of the London Poor." *Journal of British Studies* 10 (1971): 105–31.
Woolf, Virginia. *To the Lighthouse.* 1927. Orlando, FL: Harcourt Brace, 1981.
———. *The Years.* 1937. Oxford: Oxford University Press, 1992.

Index